Safe as Houses?

Ill Health and Electro-stress in the Home

DAVID COWAN & RODNEY GIRDLESTONE

Gateway Books, Bath, UK

First published in 1996 by
GATEWAY BOOKS
The Hollies, Wellow,
Bath, BA2 8QJ, UK

Distributed in the U.S.A. by
NATIONAL BOOK NETWORK,
4720 Boston Way, Lanham MD 20706

Cover design by James J. Bale of CSS, Bath

Text set in France, 10½ on 12pt by
Oak Press of Castleton
Printed and bound by
Redwood Books of Trowbridge

British Library Cataloguing-in Publication Data:
A catalogue record for this book is
available from the British Library

ISBN 1-85860-037-5

Contents

Acknowledgements

While most pictures and illustrations are the work of the respective authors, grateful thanks are due to Georg Editeur of Geneva for permission to use the graph of electronic measurement above an underground stream;

C.W.Daniel and Co Ltd. of Saffron Walden for material from *Points of Cosmic Energy;*

Caledonia Newspapers of Glasgow for their picture of the nuclear submarine; and Mark J.G.Owens of Renfrew for his picture of "The Dragon's Window" in Hong Kong.

Special thanks to Geoffrey Allen for his contribution to the chapter on Earth Stress;   Bob Sephton of Dorset for his contribution on using the oscilloscope to measure earth energies;   Laurence Blair Oliphant for the events at Ardblair, Blairgowrie.

Also to Dr.Schneck of Bideford in Devon for information on the global grids and James Wotherspoon of Glenrothes for his account of the visible earth energies at Kinross.

AND the many others, too numerous to mention who have contributed to the creation of this book.

Foreword

by Jan de Vries

It is not only with great pleasure, but with the greatest of interest that I write the Foreword for this book.

I know the hard work and effort which has gone into this material, which discusses fields of energy neglected and ignored by science as a significant factor in one's health.

The influence of earth energies has a great impact on man's health nowadays. Science has failed to look into this on a wide field, but David has researched the subject extensively, at the cost of his own health, and repeatedly walked the length and breadth of Scotland to find out exactly how and where geopathic stress disturbances are causing ill health and disease. Rodney has brought his energy and extensive knowledge to bear on the important subject of electrostress in the first part of this book.

I support this research because I know that energy imbalance can play a great part in illness and disease. I can almost circle on the map the clusters of areas where certain illnesses and disease are more prevalent, as is the case with the 20th century disease, Chronic Fatigue Syndrome (M.E.), and I have watched these clusters grow steadily since I saw my first M.E. patient almost 20 years ago.

The questions remain: has medicine failed or has science failed? In lectures I often quote "the definition of science is to discover the secrets of nature and make these available to mankind". In this book we will find many ways that science has failed to look into these fields on our behalf.

When I think of the multitudes of patients, illness and disease, I often ask myself what life is all about. Up until the 19th century we knew very little about life, although we do know a little more today. One thing is certain, life is a constant renewal of cells and cell tissue and we need constant cell renewal in order to have enough energy to live life to the full.

The forms of energy that man lives by — food, water, air and subtle energies, have never been attacked so much as they are today. The first two we can easily do something about. We can still eat organical-

ly grown food and drink clean water, but the last two are more difficult. We can do something if we help in the battle of air pollution and
pollution caused by energy disturbances.

The time has come for medicine to go back to square one. The
orthodox system might look a perfectly logical system, but we need
to review our thinking for the world we live in today.

This excellent book will give direction in the understanding in the
invisible fields of energy which surround and penetrate us. In this
modern atomic, nuclear, space age, man has to re-think the basic principles. I am sure that this book will open many minds to look at the
society of today and start to think a little more 'naturally'.

After all, we belong to nature, we are part of nature, so should we
not follow the laws of nature?

Troon,
Ayrshire,
Scotland.

Introduction

Electricity is the wonder we have come to take for granted. Convenient to use, invisible, silent in action. It is safe and clean (at least at the point of use, although power stations are another story). Available at the touch of a switch, 24 hours a day, and amazingly flexible, it can be used to provide power for transport, heating, cooking, lighting, TV and radio, communications, computing . . . where would we be without it?

As any science student knows, every source of electricity produces invisible, radiating, electromagnetic fields. It is universally agreed that a few special types of electromagetic field, such as X-rays, can be very dangerous, but surely this is not true of the wiring and appliances in our houses? To suggest that sounds to many people like paranoia. Electricity is absolutely safe if it is used correctly, isn't it? Of course you can get shocks from unprotected wires or if you poke around inside live equipment — we realise that — and it is important to connect equipment properly, leaving it to the experts if we are at all unsure. We must ensure that microwave ovens are correctly maintained so that they do not 'leak' and we should replace worn cords or wires. These obvious hazards aside, isn't it clearly absurd to suggest that simply living in a world powered by electricity could pose a threat?

The first part of this book presents a different view of electricity; as something which we need to treat with greater care and respect. The serious conclusion of a steadily growing number of doctors, scientists and others who have made a close study of this very important phenomenon, is that electricity in many of its forms produces fields and radiations which can injure, in a number of different ways, the health of people exposed to them.

Rodney Girdlestone, the writer of the first part of this book, started out as a main-stream scientist. He was at first resistant to the idea that serious hazards could be attached to electricity if properly used. Somehow life led him towards taking a closer interest in the subject and, the more he read, looked and listened, the more he became convinced that it was a subject which deserved to be taken very seriously.

He recalls that the start for him was 'accidental'. He and his wife went to visit a German health exhibition in Stuttgart, looking for any products which might be of interest to their natural products mail order company. They had in mind new or different food supplements, cosmetics, herbal teas and certainly not the little boxes of magnets which were being promoted on the corner of a stand mainly selling bandages. In fact, Rodney paid no attention to them at all on the first day, but when they were discussing what they had seen, his wife said she thought they should have a closer look at the magnets which she had briefly discussed with the man showing them. Rodney took some persuading that they were not wasting their time, but in spite of this, they came home with a distributorship deal agreed in principle. Very shortly afterwards, they took a stand at one of the early complementary medicine shows in London.

The response amazed him. He found that what was new to him was well known to Indians, Russians, middle Europeans and to many Americans. They all accepted that the fairly weak magnetic fields from little block magnets of various shapes and designs could produce profound changes when correctly applied and the Girdlestones sold all their stock.

Shortly after this they discovered a new product, flexible rubber strips impregnated with a special magnetic alloy. Despite having weaker field strengths than the metal magnets, these strips produced impressive results (see chap.10).

Rodney's work with the magnetic strips brought him into touch with a number of practitioners. He became aware that there were all sorts of therapeutic magnetic field devices being used to very good effect. Many of them were electrically powered, although there seemed to be little consistency either in the fields they produced or the protocols for their use - indeed there was little sharing of knowledge or experiences. Rodney discussed this with an osteopath called Peter Bartlett who used some electromagnetic devices in his practice. Together, Peter and Rodney came to the conclusion that they should try to help disseminate what was known and encourage the wider uses of such devices. The result was the Institute of Magnetic Therapy which they ran for some years.

It cannot be said that they achieved all of their early ambitious aims, but they staged some very interesting lectures with speakers from the UK and other countries. Rodney learnt a lot about the subject. He also began to wonder: if electromagnetic fields could produce such clear results for good, could they not, if uncontrolled, have some potential for harm? He discovered that the Germans had got there first! Much of the literature on the subject then available was in German, although the Americans were also very active. Before long, the Institute ran its first seminar on the hazards of electromagnetism and geopathic stress - and the rest, as they say, is history. His interest switched much more to this area, although he remains firmly convinced in the value and safety of much magnetic field therapy. This is one of the topics he discusses later.

The American humorist, James Thurber, tells of his eccentric aunt who was forever screwing light bulbs into empty sockets to stop the electricity escaping. What delightful nonsense! How could electricity leak out and harm us?

Thurber's aunt may have got the wrong end of the stick, but we can now see that her concern about 'leaking' electricity was not totally misplaced. What she did not know is that electricity 'leaks' from many more places than just empty sockets and there are far more effective means of protection than screwing in bulbs! So an important part of this book shows you how to avoid the dangers of electro-stress.

For reasons which will become clearer, later, Rodney has long used the word 'electro-stress' to describe the complex effects which result from our exposure to non-ionising electromagnetic fields. (If you do not know what 'non-ionising' means, that will be explained).

Why, if the evidence is there, is the idea of electro-stress not more widely acknowledged? Inertia plays a part. New and challenging ideas often take a long time to be accepted. Those with a vested interest - such as the producers of electricity and electrical equipment (and those who work for them and even those who use the products) are only too keen to ridicule any suggestion of hazard. In addition, electromagnetic fields have no smell or taste, cannot be heard, nor can we see nor feel most of them. It is difficult for people to imagine danger which they cannot sense.

Further, there is the difference between the clinical and the scientific approaches. Clinicians, knowing the urgency of their patients' needs, will often feel that using a safe, if not fully proven idea, is worth trying. Some doctors and other healthcare workers are suggesting that it may be useful for patients with 'mystery complaints' such as Chronic fatigue (M.E.), or allergies, or a variety of chronic complaints, to mini-mise their exposure to high-level fields by using the sorts of precaution and protection discussed in Chapter 9. In many cases this proves to be a valuable part of the treatment programme; so the end justifies the means. The conventional scientific approach is that any experimental result, however apparently conclusive, has to be tested again and again, often over many years, before a treatment protocol can be approved for use. While caution is good in moderation, someone with an urgent problem may feel it can be over-done.

An interesting parallel is provided by the history of X-rays. It is hard to believe that in late Victorian times people treated X-rays as fair-ground amusement. Even when the dangers were dimly perceived, some twenty five years after the invention of the Roentgen tube, the 'safe' limit for exposure was set at 15,000 times the value accepted today. As late as the 1950s shoe shops (and the armed forces) had X-ray machines so that shoes and boots could be checked for a good fit. Today we know that there is no totally 'safe' level of x-ray! There are strict exposure limits for patients and especially radiographers, dentists and others who operate X-ray equipment. Many people may have suffered the unnecessary ill-effects of X-rays because the scientific methodology may have made researchers slow to heed the warning signs.

While giving a talk in Scotland, Rodney met David Cowan from Crieff in Perthshire (the writer of the second part of this book) and was interested to find that he was working on a different facet of the electromagnetic spectrum — geopathic or geopathogenic stress — the effects produced by what many call earth or telluric energies.

David's journey into the shadowy and almost unknown world of earth energies began in the late 'seventies'. For many years, prior to this, he had venerated what he had perceived as the scientific approach to life. Watching a favourite television programme, he was surprised to note that modern technology may be spectacular, but simple methods, such as divining rods could be equally effective.

Already a staunch hill-walker, David decided to combine his new 'discovery' with his regular exercise. He took with him two simple angle rods fashioned from metal coathangers. He was amazed at how easy it was for him to detect underground water pipes using them. He could link the line of the rods' reactions with the known direction of the pipes and so find his own proof. What surprised him particularly was that he had found something within himself — an innate ability — about which he had been hitherto unaware. However, David's new 'discovery' gave him a feeling of anti-climax with the so-called scientific approach.

There was still an element of healthy scepticism present when he came across a copy of Tom Graves' book, *The Diviner's Handbook* (see Bibliography) which discussed 'ley lines' or supposed lines of an unknown energy travelling across country in straight lines from standing stones, and stone circles, churches and burial grounds. Such an idea seemed preposterous to his logical, thinking mind. The concept of lines of energy created by our 'ignorant' ancestors was something David found extremely difficult to accept. But there was a paradox. He could not reject what he was reading because of his own discoveries with his metal rods.

He went out deliberately with his rods to see what he could find around standing stones. Feeling rather foolish on his first attempt and making sure there was nobody about, David took out his rods. In the manner advised in Graves' book, he walked around a particular row of ancient standing stones on Dunruchan Hill in Perthshire, not far from his home. He found that, once again, the rods started to react. Something else was revealed to him which again came to him as a mystery.

In the following eight years, David trudged over four thousand kilometres across Perthshire and its neighbouring counties and in the process has mapped out well defined lines of ley energy forming complex patterns connected to standing stones, cup-marked stones and many other features.

Eventually, ill-health, probably linked to this work compelled him to concentrate on another less demanding aspect — i.e. harmful energies which appeared to be linked to the ill-health of occupants of so many houses, schools and factories. One thing had led to another and his research into energies from standing stones and circles compelled him to make links between the incidence of energy lines and people with serious illnesses such as some cancers, Chronic Fatigue Syndrome (M.E.), M.S., epilepsy and, most recently, the widely publicised 'flesh-eating bug' necrotising fasciitis.

This is by no means the first book to discuss either geopathic stress or the problems posed by the use of electricity, but the authors do believe that it is the first which starts to explore the ways in which these phenomena may be linked.

Man-made energy fields are easier to measure objectively using orthodox scientific instruments, while the use of a divining rod has to be learned and could be called more accurately an art form than a scientific method. Indeed, using a special meter called a geomagnetometer it is possible to measure and even produce 3D print-outs of earth energy fields in a building. Trial results have been corroborated with the findings of skilled dowsers. However a dowser can do the job more rapidly!

The work of the two authors converges in their finding that energy lines of different types may be powerful initiating factors in many of the environmental diseases affecting our modern society. The fact that similar lists of ailments can be linked to both geopathic and electro-stress suggests that similar mechanisms may be at work in the body. Both seem to do their damage subtly and slowly, rarely causing instant symptoms, but initiating a long term build-up of stress in the body which finally spills over into obvious illness.

Both authors had, from their different perspectives, begun to suspect that earth stresses and electromagnetic fields interact in some way. Rodney had noticed, when carrying out surveys, that meter readings sometimes showed mysterious 'hot spots' when there was no obvious source such as proximity to wiring or equipment. He had wondered if there could be a link with earth fields, but had no means of measuring them himself.

The investigation into the synergism or combination of man-produced energies with those found occurring 'naturally' in the landscape is the essence of David's research into geopathic stress. As we shall see, he believes that one effect may be the creation of energy 'spirals' at microwave frequencies. It seems that these occur when major electrical producers and utilities such as power and radar stations, television or communications transmitters and electrical sub-stations attract sub-surface earth energies. These can then radiate outwards to focus into existing, natural energy spirals, above underground streams forming hot spots.

If a person is exposed for too long to such a spiral (s)he may suffer illness. Every year, these microwave sources are increasing in number and intensity. Most of the population is completely unaware not only of their existence, but more important, of their likely harmful effects.

The first part of this timely book discusses the need for an awareness of the growing impact of electro-stress and ways to combat it, while the second part looks at the more 'elusive' earth energies. Throughout, the book reviews methods of tackling the more unsavoury qualities associated with all of these known types of energy. The book does not set out to say that these energies alone are responsible for illness, because ill-health can arise from all sorts of factors such as life-style or genetically inherited disorders, other types of pollution, malnutrition and more.

You, the reader, will have to make your own judgment whether you are convinced by the many examples of illness associated with the presence of energy fields. Could electro-stress, geopathic stress, other causes emanating from the planet itself, or a mixture of all of these, be endangering your health?

We hope that this book may encourage you to commence your own detection work and maybe help you down the road to better health and a better quality of life.

CHAPTER 1

DISEASE

The history of Geopathic Stress is a long one. The unhealthy spirals which dowsers detect above subterranean water have probably always been with us and the energy leys are believed to have existed for thousands of years. By comparison, electro-stress is the merest newcomer, with a history measured in decades. In the context of the length of time that humans have inhabited the earth, that is almost insignificant. There is consequently still much to be learned about electro-stress, but especially about the ways in which geopathic and electro-stress are related. It is already clear that the two have many similar characteristics and can cause similar diseases. Where they combine, as when a sub-station or television 'earths' itself into a spiral in the home as described later, the result can be especially dangerous. This part of the book will concentrate on electro-stress, but the inter-relation should not be forgotten.

It seems very much that the pattern of disease has markedly shifted in this century. The most threatening diseases up to the 1950s were diphtheria, tuberculosis, influenza, polio, heart disease and some forms of cancer. Since then there has been a great increase in the immune deficiency diseases such as allergies, asthma, Chronic Fatigue Syndrome (M.E.), AIDS, arthritis, and cancers linked to the immune system like leukemia, lymphatic, liver and intestinal.

No conventional authority has given a satisfactory explanation for this remarkable change, or for the enormous scale and rapidity of immune system vulnerability, but it has to be a large and widespread source. Candidates such as vehicle emissions, chemicals in water supplies and food, acid rain, urban stress — though all of them might be contributory — none stands out as an obvious trigger.

One has to look for a source that was not threatening 50 years ago, but which has grown very rapidly and universally. Unnatural electro-magnetic fields fulfil all the criteria. In 50 years radio has increased ten thousandfold, TV more than a millionfold, and the uses which are part of our contemporary way of life, such as microwave communications, radar, low-frequency fields (VLF & ELF) and the many devices for trans-

1

forming and transporting electric currents have spread rapidly every-where without thought of the consequences. This has immersed us in an ever denser and more complex electromagnetic 'soup' that is quite unnatural. Because electric fields cannot be sensed and are hard to measure, ordinary people are generally unaware of their dangers.

Our bodies need centuries to start to adapt to critical environmental change. The most immediate reaction in the short term (that is dec-ades), is to cause widespread sickness and extreme psychological stress. We are so caught up in the glamour of new technologies and by the riches that have accompanied them, that we have become blind to the possible effects of this technological assault on our bodies. However, the combined weight of independent research studies and clinical experience is already enough to convince many researchers that electro-stress is a key factor in the creation of the physical and psychological stresses from which so many people suffer — and which in many cases lead on to acute and chronic disease.

SOME POINTERS

It is hard to say just when it was that members of the scientific and medical community first began to suspect that the electrical revolution may not have produced totally unqualified benefits, but there has cer-tainly been a growing number of books and papers on the subject since the 1950s. I shall not attempt a comprehensive history of the subject in this book, but if you want to research it in greater detail, the bibliography lists some sources of further information. The discussion here will be limited to a selection of some of the major landmarks and to the practical implications for everyone alive today.

As early as 1964 a Russian researcher called Kholodov found that rabbits exposed to relatively strong, but steady electromagnetic fields (100 to 200 gauss), suffered increased stress levels. Autopsies showed that cells had died in some areas of the rabbits' brains. Friedmann duplicated this experiment and found that most of the rabbits had suffered a weakening of their immune system that led to parts of their brain being destroyed by a parasite which had previously been under control[1]. Further experiments by Friedmann showed that when rab-bits and, later, monkeys were exposed to similar fields, they developed elevated levels of cortisone, an adrenal-cortical hormone, which is an accepted indicator of stress.

Scientists working in Eastern Europe in the 1970s recorded similar signs of stress when rats were exposed even briefly to both micro-wave and 50Hz fields. An American researcher, Noval, discovered in 1976 that rats exposed to very weak electromagnetic fields (at the background level found in modern offices) also exhibited a typical stress response, judged by levels of a neuro-transmitter called acetylcholine.

In fact, the U.S. Navy unintentionally proved the stress connection in the 1970s with what was known as Project Sanguine. As a small-scale trial for a new type of long-range military communications system, 28 miles (45km) of cable, powered with 76Hz current, were buried in a loop near Clam Lake, Wisconsin. Many people living in the area suffered unexpected shocks from taps, wire fences and many other metal objects. More importantly, it was discovered that workers on the project showed higher than normal levels of serum triglycerides, another indicator of stress. That this was a result of exposure to the AC fields was confirmed by separate laboratory trials with human volunteers. Fortunately for everyone, the project was eventually shelved, as was a much larger design that would have involved 6000 miles of buried cable, with the Earth itself being used as part of the circuit!

Probably the most important indication of the potential hazards to human health in the everyday world, as opposed to the laboratory, came in 1975. A researcher called Nancy Wertheimer, looking for possible causes of childhood leukaemia in Denver, accidentally discovered that children living in houses nearest to 13kV (kilo-volt) power lines had a two or three times greater chance of contracting the disease[2]. It eventually emerged that the key was to be found not in the voltage but rather in the current and the resultant magnetic fields. Although her experimental methods were criticised, later and better designed studies by Wertheimer herself and by other workers have come to similar conclusions.

For instance, in the 1980s, Tomenius surveyed 2000 houses in Sweden near 200kV power lines, and found childhood cancer rates double the norm. He measured magnetic fields of at least 3mG (milli-gauss) in affected houses. (It is worth noting, as you will read later, that field strengths of the order of 3mG are quite common, even in the normal domestic environment.)

In 1986 Savitz found that 20% of childhood cancers in North Carolina could be linked to exposure to 3mG fields. In the same year a study in Texas found thirteen times the normal level of brain cancer amongst power line workers — who would be exposed to rather higher field levels during their working hours.

In 1979 Milham published an analysis of the causes of death of 300,000 workers. He claimed that those in occupations involving exposure to high electrical or magnetic fields had double the 'normal' rate of death from leukaemia. Workers in aluminium smelters (where a very high level of electrical power is used) were particularly susceptible. Other higher risk occupations included power and telephone linesmen, power station workers and motion picture projectionists (see Table 1). Although there was again criticism of Milham's research, other studies have come to broadly similar conclusions.

Author/Date	Occupations	Relative field intensity/Frequency	Reported effects/ Increased occurence of
Milham 1979	Aluminium workers	over 100 gauss	Lung cancer Lymphatic cancer Blood cancer Benign brain tumours Emphysema
US Marine 1983	Service personnel Electronic assembly workers	weak 50-75 Hz	Increase in serum triglycerides
Milham 1982	Various electrical workers	weak to strong 60 Hz (and others)	Lung cancer Lymphatic cancer Blood cancer
Wright et al 1982	Various electrical workers	weak 60 Hz (and others)	Leukaemia Leukaemia
McDowall 1983	Electrical workers	weak 50 Hz (and others)	Leukaemia
Coleman 1983	Electrical workers	weak 50 Hz (and others)	Leukaemia
Nordstrom et al 1983	Control-room operatives	various	Abnormal pregnancies Congenital deformities
	Electronic assembly workers	50 Hz (and others)	

Table 1: Occupations with chronic exposure to electromagnetic fields and reported diseases

Dr Delgado et al[3] found that chick embryos in eggs exposed to electromagnetic fields often failed to develop or else exhibited various deformities. More recently, Dr.Jocelyn Leal has carried out trials with incubating eggs and has shown that effects can occur at low exposure levels. One of her most interesting discoveries showed that very specific active 'windows' of frequency and field strength exist, above and below which the chick embryos are apparently not affected. Such findings raise the possibility of congenital defects being caused in human babies if pregnant women are exposed to hazardous fields.

You will gather from all of this that much of the research into the possible ill-effects of exposure to electromagnetic radiations has concentrated on cancers, often leukaemia, and other fatal outcomes. This is understandable enough as epidemiological studies based on death certificates are a well-recognised research method when investigating environmental factors. However, an unfortunate result has been to limit most of the debate to the potentially life-threatening effects of chronic exposure to high-power fields.

While this is clearly important if proven, we may still be talking only of an increase in deaths from one in 10,000 to 2 or 3 in 10,000. Tragic though this is, and although we should certainly not reduce our efforts to discover the truth of the matter and what may be done to combat the dangers, we may be in danger of overlooking the lesser health problems caused to much greater numbers of people. For every person who may die of leukaemia as a result of living near a power line or working on an aluminium smelter, thousands may suffer from stress and related problems, rheumatism or allergies, because of the electrical conditions inside their homes and factories.

20TH CENTURY AILMENTS

In addition to the better documented research regarding the effects of electromagnetic fields of various types, some of which has been referred to above, a whole spectrum of different health-related factors have at some time been laid at the door of electro-stress. You will find in Table 2 a summary of some of the suggested links which have been made. This is presented not as an authoritative statement of proven effects, but rather to give the reader some idea of just how much about this topic still remains to be researched.

One question that the idea of electro-stress may help to answer is why there are today so many people who are permanently stressed and tense, who are apparently unable to relax, who do not sleep well or who wake up tired or aching (or both) morning after morning. Or why so many feel eternally run down or that they 'cannot cope', although their diets and general life-style show no obvious reason why this should be so. Eventually such people may become depressed, even suicidal.

The link with suicide was demonstrated in England in the early 1980s by Dr.Perry, a physician whose practice was in the Midlands of England. He found a significant correlation between suicides and attempted suicides in his locality and the proximity of patients' homes not only to overhead, but also to the underground high-tension power distribution lines (of whose existence they must have been as unaware as he originally was — so a psychosomatic effect seems unlikely). A later study gave similar results.

In 1988 he published a study showing a correlation between illnesses of people living in a tower block and whether they lived near to the high-voltage supply cables which rise up the side of such buildings. Those in apartments near to the supply lines accounted for 62% of the hospital admissions from the block for heart attacks and ischaemic heart disease and 71% of those admitted with depressive illness.[4] Drs.Dowson & Lewith have also showed that headaches and depression could be linked to power lines.[5]

GENERAL SYMPTOMS

Headaches	Swimming vision
Weakness	Disturbed or light superficial sleep
Fatigue	Nausea
Dizziness or Faintness	Loss of potency
Bloated feeling	

EFFECTS ON THE NERVOUS SYSTEM

Functional disturbance of the central nervous system	Symptoms of neurasthenia
Functional disturbance of the sympathetic nervous system	Tendency to perspire
Neuro-dynamic events in the cerebral cortex	Slight tremor of the fingers
Loss of concentration	Weak pulse
EEG changes	Low blood pressure
Reduction of sensitivity and function in the neuromuscular system of the hand	

HEART / CIRCULATION DISTURBANCES

Cardiovascular disturbances	Tachycardia
Hypotonia	ECG changes
Hyperotonia	

CHANGES IN THE BLOOD

Qualitative and quantitative changes in peripheral blood system
Various changes in composition of blood components

REACTION TIME

Changes in reaction time
Stimulation affect
Disturbances in temperature regulation

Table 2: Health problems which have been linked to electro-stress

Allergies have also become much more common, almost epidemic, especially amongst children. Allergy seems very much a classic twentieth century ailment. Asthma, hay fever and skin problems such as eczema have all escalated alarmingly in the last twenty years.

It is just possible that the upsurge in skin problems might be explained by the increasing use of new and aggressive chemicals in cosmetics and toilet products, cleaning materials and just about everything else. (As just one example, consider how carbon paper has been largely superseded by carbonless duplicate sets, replacing a simple substance [lamp-black] with complex encapsulated chemicals.)

However, this explanation fails to convince when we consider the growth of allergies causing respiratory problems, which abound even in infants. Various sources suggest that between one in ten and one third of school age children suffer to some extent. It is surely highly unlikely that there are more pollen granules or house dust mites in the air than there were previously, and thanks to clean air laws, levels of most industrial pollutants in the air have actually diminished. It's likely that the significant increase in air pollution from vehicle exhaust emissions is at least partly to blame, but increasing numbers of asthmatic children are found in rural areas as well as in traffic-clogged cities.

Dietary allergy is also alarmingly common and although there is no doubt that improved public awareness may have led to a higher level of diagnosis, the increase cannot be explained away by this factor alone. Children in particular are not likely to develop asthma or hives after eating particular foods, just because there has been press publicity!

Another intriguing puzzle is the typical response to treatment. There are effective techniques in both allopathic and homeopathic medicine by which the sufferer's sensitivity to an allergen can be reduced or even removed. Another approach is to design strict exclusion diets so that all traces of irritant foods are avoided. The problem is that in many cases no matter how many allergens are identified and cleared, the general level of sensitivity is apparently not diminished. The sufferer's body simply seems to move from one irritant to another, in the worst cases eventually ending up reacting to almost every substance in the environment. In other words, it is as if some other factor has made the sufferer hypersensitive and that almost everything has become a potential allergen for these unfortunate individuals. Could this sensitising factor be exposure to a variety of electromagnetic fields?

Dr.Jean Monro, together with Dr.Cyril Smith, did much work at the Breakspear Hospital in Kings Langley, England, during the 1980s to investigate the connection between allergy and electrical sensitivity. They showed that severely allergic patients can react violently to minute electrical fields. Most strikingly, they could produce reactions just like those produced by allergens by generating weak but specific radio-frequency signals near to the patient. Work like this suggests that electro-stress may well be at least a part of the story.

There are some who argue that the widespread use of vaccination is another sensitising factor. Vaccines are intended to increase the efficiency of the immune system by using a supposedly harmless form of a disease to stimulate the production of appropriate protective antibodies in the blood. Statistics seem to support the effectiveness of vaccination, but it is also true that a significant number of those treated suffer definite if apparently short-lived adverse responses to the vaccine. The suggestion is that the vaccines may also produce an unwanted long-term response, causing the body to make antibodies for anything that it does not immediately recognise. These may be not just bacteria or viruses, but also new foods, unfamiliar air-borne substances and so on. If this is so, the scope for adverse reactions has certainly increased as genetic engineering produces new forms of staple foods and the food industry processes ingredients in many new ways. It would certainly be interesting to see research into the relative levels of allergy in those who have and have not been vaccinated — or whether allergic responses are seen to increase in Third World countries where vaccination is introduced for the first time.

In parallel with allergy, many apparently unrelated illnesses have also been more prevalent, some of them seeming to appear 'out of the blue'. Tinnitus, myalgic encephalomyelitis (M.E.), multiple sclerosis (M.S.) and glandular fever are just a few of this mixed bag. Could electro-stress, with or without geopathic stress, provide a clue to some or all of these? It certainly appears highly likely that many such sufferers have in fact become sensitive to exposure to geopathic, electrical or magnetic fields.

Chronic Fatigue Syndrome (otherwise known as M.E.) is a good example. Many attempts have been made to track down the causative agent which was originally widely suspected to be of a viral nature (it was often called Post-viral Syndrome in the early days of investigation). This research has ruled out mononucleosis or Epstein-Barr virus and in fact potent anti-viral drugs generally do not work with people diagnosed as having Chronic Fatigue Syndrome. Many doctors dealing with M.E. or C.F.S. patients suspect sensitivities to electromagnetic fields and of course this ties in with one of the original large outbreaks of the disease in the computerised dealing rooms of the financial markets in the City of London. Some support for this thesis is found in the fact that many Chronic Fatigue patients feel much better if they take holidays in the country or even move there permanently away from the cities, offices or factories where they have lived and worked.

Conventional ideas on the mechanism leading to AIDS have also been questioned. Some researchers have expressed doubts as to whether the HIV virus in itself inevitably leads on to full-blown AIDS. It certainly seems likely that there must be other immune system factors that are playing a part. It is interesting that in experiments in California, Dr.Daniel B.Lyall[6] showed that if human T-cells (lymphocytes which are important in the human immune system) were exposed while in culture to a low strength electromagnetic field for 48 hours their ability to deal with invading cells was significantly reduced. If there is a similar mechanism taking place in human beings exposed to electrical fields then of course their immune systems would be much less able to cope with a serious infection such as HIV.

Roger Coghill, who has conducted a great deal of research into the effects of electromagnetic fields on people in this country has shown that 11 of 12 American cities with the highest incidence of AIDS also have the highest general level of electromagnetic 'traffic' of all kinds. He believes firmly that the huge growth in electromagnetic pollution (especially radio, TV and microwave communications traffic) is a major, if not *the*, root cause of the AIDS epidemic[7].

At the moment the mechanisms causing sensitivity to normal electromagnetic fields are unknown. However it would appear that there is a direct effect upon the nervous system and that the immune system is very probably also involved. It has been shown that electromagnetic radiations can disrupt the flow of calcium through the walls of cells in the body — and this can affect a number of important cellular functions, including cell division. If it is correct that certain electromagnetic radiations can promote the proliferation of cancerous cells, as has been suggested, then this could explain how it happens. Another theory is that the effect on calcium flow changes in some way the cell's ability to fight cancer.

Recently-published research at Bristol University has put forward the suggestion that the cancer-producing effects of mains electricity may be due to the fact that it seems to bring about a localised increase in the concentration of radon gas, which is known to be carcinogenous. Much scepticism has greeted this suggestion, but it does interestingly echo the theory which Tom Williamson advances regarding radon gas and unhealthy energy lines (see chapter 17). It also has some parallels with the observation of the German researcher Dr D Aschoff[8] that he detects higher than usual levels of slow-moving neutrons above areas of unhealthy earth energies.

People can suffer for 'conventional' reasons many of the ailments discused above, such as allergy and M.E.. Perhaps they do not sleep because they are worried or weighed down by work or family problems. They develop rheumatism because of heredity or poor living or working conditions or viruses, or one of the many other accepted causes. They may also be reacting to poor diet or polluted air and water. But the case can be made that many of these factors have become less severe in the recent past. In this country, living and working conditions have improved in some ways, reducing some physical and mental stresses. Many epidemic diseases have been virtually eliminated and yet so many immune-related health problems are increasing rather than fading away.

ADRENAL OVERLOAD

The most convincing conclusion I have come to in the face of the evidence is that no matter how much many individual sources of stress may have diminished, the total stress load has steadily increased.

To the body, the precise source of stress is not so important and you have already read how researchers have shown that exposure to quite moderate electromagnetic fields can cause typical stress responses. Any stress has a similar effect on the body. Most crucially it causes the adrenals to respond by pumping adrenaline (more correctly called epinephrine) and other hormones into the bloodstream.

Adrenaline is sometimes referred to as the 'fight or flight' hormone and its production is in fact a very primitive response. Man, like any other animal when faced with danger from a predator has two choices: turn and fight, or run. In either case the need is for a sudden burst of energy, and so the adrenal glands spring into action.

We have two adrenals, one sitting on top of each kidney. Like all glands, their role is to supply hormones to the body for particular purposes. The adrenals have two parts, an outer portion called the cortex and an inner core called the medulla. It is from the medulla that adrenaline comes, one of a total of around thirty two different hormones produced by the adrenals.

So, faced with danger, the adrenals start to pump adrenaline and other hormones into the body. The heart rate increases, sending more oxygen and nutrients to the muscles, respiratory rate goes up, blood pressure rises, and all this provides the energy needed for whichever course of action is chosen. There is one problem. The adrenal response is intended to cope with occasional crises. Once primitive man had fought and won, or had fled to safety, he could normally count on a rest period before the next crisis arrived, giving his body time to recover. Specifically, his adrenals had time to recharge themselves with the necessary hormones.

Unfortunately, the types of modern stress described above, including electro-stress and geopathic stress, are not occasional crises. They all tend to be more or less continuous and in the end the adrenals simply cannot cope. Gradually they become more and more depleted. Energy levels fall, the body responds ever less effectively to stressful situations and, perhaps most importantly of all, the body's immune response system ceases to be effective.

THE WATER-BUTT CONNECTION

A useful way of visualising how electro-stress, geopathic stress and other environmental stresses combine to provide a challenge to health is to think of a water-butt into which water flows through a number of pipes coming from different gutters. The water can be safely drained from the bottom by a tap. If the rate at which water fills the butt from all sources is less than the rate at which it discharges through the tap (or at least is no more) then the butt will not overflow. The situation remains under control. If, however, water starts to flow from one or more of the pipes at a higher and higher rate, the time will eventually come when the total inflow is greater than the total outflow. At this stage the water level in the butt will begin to rise. Even then we may not be aware of the situation, particularly if we do not often lift the butt lid to look inside. For weeks, months, or even years, the water level could be rising without us knowing. But one day the butt will finally overflow and flood the surrounding area.

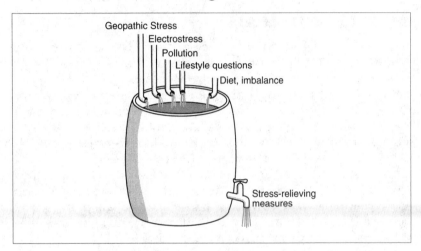

Fig 1: The water butt of life experiences

Now, substitute the body for the butt. Stresses are represented by the water flowing in and the body's various ways of coping with stress are the water flowing out. This shows how life's problems can have a steadily increasing effect over a long period without us being aware of it.

If we do not lift the lid of our personal water-butt (review our dietary and other habits, have health checks, etc.), we will never be sure whether our system is in balance or perilously near to disaster. This is why so many people delude themselves by protesting that they are never ill, that they are unaffected by a lifestyle that militates against long-term health. However, the day will arrive when the cumulative effect all becomes too much. The tragedy is that when the personal water-butt overflows it can be too late ever to return to ideal conditions.

There are only two basic ways to tackle the problem: either you can cut down the rate at which the water flows in, or you can increase the rate at which it discharges. In bodily terms, you can either try to reduce the stress overload or you can increase the body's capacity to cope with and discharge it.

You will note that it is the total amount of stress (inflow of water) which is critical. Which source provides most water does not really matter. On the other hand, if one pipe regularly produced more than the others then logically that would be the one to concentrate on. Substantially reducing that one flow could probably eliminate the likelihood of an overflow occurring. Since it is now believed that for many people in the modern world, geopathic and electro-stress account for probably more than half of all stresses, the importance of dealing with these two sources is obvious.

LOWERING STRESS LEVELS

This is not to suggest that other factors should be overlooked. You should try to identify and tackle anything that causes stress. Work pressures, travel, living conditions, relationships, diet, smoking and drinking and general lifestyle, these are all areas where changes could help to reduce the inflow. You should also think seriously about learning relaxation techniques, meditation, gentle exercises, massage, aromatherapy, etc., all of which can help reduce the stress level.

Nutritional supplements that help to boost the adrenals are valuable. Vitamins C and B are particularly helpful and including a good adrenal extract will give even better results. All of these subjects are covered in other widely available books and you will probably find local classes in meditation, yoga and similar practices which have been shown to have beneficial effects on bodily health.

For now, the objective is to help you to identify and cope with the unnecessary stress load that typically comes from the influence of electromagnetic fields on you, which is what we will discuss from now on.

NOTES

1.   Becker, R.O. & Selden, G., *The Body Electric*: Wm.Morrow, (1985) p.277.
2.   Wertheimer, N., "Electrical Wiring Configurations and Childhood Cancer": *Amer.Jour.Epidemiology*, (March 1979).
3.   Delgado, J.M.R., et al, "Biological effects of extremely low frequency electromagnetic fields": *Jour.Anat.* 134(3),   (1982) pp.533-551.
4.   Perry, S. & Pearly, L., "Power frequency magnetic fields and illness in multistorey blocks": *Public Health*, (1988); p.102, 11-8.
5.   Dowson, D, et al, "Overhead high voltage cables and recurrent headaches and depression": *Practitioner*, (April 1988), pp.435-6.
6.   Lyall, D.B. et al, *Bioelectromagnetics*, 9, (1988): p.303.
7.   Coghill, R., "All Fall Down — The Cause of AIDS": Coghill Research Labs, Pontypool (1992).
8.   Aschoff D & Aschoff J, *Neue Grundlegende Erkeninisse*, Verlag Mehr Wissen, Düsseldorf, 1986.

CHAPTER 2

VIBRATIONS

Our main concern is with vibrations and oscillations of a particular kind, the type we call electromagnetic. The difficulty is that very few of us are familiar with electromagnetic radiations, mainly because we have no direct means of sensing most of them. Because of this, it will be easier and useful to think first about some other, better known, kinds of vibration and the effects that they can have upon us.

Einstein showed us that all matter is energy and vice versa which has helped us come to understand much about the world in general and life in particular. A key outcome of Einstein's insight is the notion that nothing is still — everything is vibration. Vibrations or oscillations come in many forms and at many frequencies and are very much part of life. For instance, both sound and light are particular kinds of oscillations and there is no doubt that the human body is sensitive to them. They also have enough similarities in their nature and their effects for us to start by thinking about sound, which has the advantage of being more familiar to most of us.

SOUND EFFECTS

We all know how significant the effects of sounds can be. Sound waves are compressions of the air at frequencies which cause the ear drum to vibrate, and so we 'hear' them. Two aspects of sound can be particularly important — pitch and rhythm. Thus a high-pitched sound (a whine or screech) which goes on and on may be particularly annoying and disturbing. A persistent low rumble can be equally upsetting. People who suffer from tinnitus, a sound heard only by them and which persists day and night, can be driven to despair. (As you will read later, a specific type of electro-stress may well be the cause of many cases of tinnitus and allied problems such as 'the hum').

Now, it is also true that much more complex sounds such as music, which is a product of very many different notes and rhythms, can please or infuriate, soothe or distress. Most people will have particular pieces of music that they find soothing, relaxing or invigorating. In extreme cases music can have an almost narcotic-like effect. Indeed, there is evidence that many young people listening to rock music experience a pattern of mood swings, of 'highs' followed by depressions in a way that has striking similarities to the effects of stimulant drugs. However, for the time being we will limit our attention to simpler sounds, and two examples will illustrate the point.

Anyone who has tried to sleep in a room with a dripping tap knows just how disturbing it can be. Although the sound may not be very loud, the relentless drip, drip, drip, can be extremely distracting, making it virtually impossible to relax or concentrate. This effect has been used as the basis of water torture (adding the physical drip of water on to the head) which has driven people mad.

Before battle, many primitive cultures have used the beat of drums in regularly repeated and quite simple rhythms to stimulate the tribe into feats of heroism and daring. The rhythmic sound is commonly accompanied by dancing which serves to reinforce the effect. The end result of this preparation can be to put warriors into a semi-hypnotic state in which thoughts of fear recede and pain and even injury are scarcely recognised. The ancestry of military bands playing their more complex march tunes may be traced straight back to the tom-tom.

In both of these examples, the key factor is persistence and the repetition of a simple rhythm. Additionally, there is only a very simple frequency pattern, using one or at most a few beats. This has been a noticeable feature of some types of popular music over the last couple of decades.

LIGHT

If we turn our attention to light, we can find some similar examples. Light is a particular type of electromagnetic radiation (see later) vibrating at frequencies thousands of times higher than audible sound. It is known that epileptics and some other people can be especially sensitive to a regular 'on-off' pattern of light of particular frequencies. For instance it has been observed that driving through woodland on a sunny day, which produces a flickering effect as the car passes from patches of bright sunlight into shadow and back again, at certain speeds (i.e. frequencies or rhythms) cause an epileptic fit in a susceptible person.

Similar reactions have been observed in cinemas, where the appearance of a moving picture is achieved by changing the image on the screen many times a second, the light being effectively turned off at each change. Because the retina retains an image for a short period after the source is removed, the eye is fooled into not seeing this on-off pattern, but the brain can sense it. Apart from its effects on epileptics, such flickering has been shown to affect certain mentally disturbed people as well.

Fluorescent tubes also flicker, although at much higher rates. Many people suffer headaches and eye strain when working under fluorescent light for prolonged periods. There are many other problems with such lights, including the production of large numbers of positive ions (see glossary), poor colour rendition and so on. However, tests with alternative types of fluorescent tubes with different electrical control systems have indicated that the frequency of the flicker is indeed an important factor in the production of headaches and visual problems.

As with our examples of sound, a key factor with disturbances caused by light is that they typically involve steady (if greatly different) frequencies. For some reason in all these cases specific frequencies (or bands of frequencies) can cause a very clear reaction in the body.

SOOTHING SOUNDS

Interestingly, not all regular repetitions are negative in their effects, although their impact on the mind may be just as dramatic even if apparently benign or even beneficial.

For instance, certain sounds seem to be universally soothing. Studies have shown that the most fractious babies tend to fall asleep rapidly when they hear recorded womb music. This is the sound produced in the womb of a pregnant woman and is dominated by the regular noise of the heartbeat. Experiments have also shown that some other low frequencies can have a calming effect on people of all ages.

However, here the plot thickens, because in the womb the sound of the heartbeat is mixed with a 'watery' sound similar to 'white noise'. White noise is an artificially produced sound that is deliberately without any trace of regular form or pattern and somewhat reminiscent of gentle wind and water waves at the seaside. Could these observations be the true secret of the benefits of seaside holidays, or the instinct of many people to seek mountain streams when they need to relax? Certainly most people find sitting by a stream or fountain and listening to the sounds of moving water very soothing. White noise has been used for some time as an aid to relaxation and an experiment has shown it to have a similar effect on babies to the womb sounds.

Here we have (apparently) the direct opposite of the earlier examples. While certain persistent regular rhythms stimulate us in certain ways, totally unstructured sounds tend to relax and even sedate.

Coming back to light, we also know that specific colours can have very different psychological effects. While detailed reactions can vary from one person to another there are general ground rules. It is no coincidence, for instance, that so many fast food restaurants use red, orange and other 'warm' colours in their decor. For these colours are known not only to increase appetite, but are also generally stimulating, encouraging you to order plenty, eat it and move on rapidly, leaving space for the next hungry customer. Cooler colours such as blues and greens tend to be more relaxing.

These are only simplified examples from a complex subject but the important fact to note is that every colour has its own frequency. For instance, red has a higher frequency than blue, and so on. The observed psychological effects must surely be because of the subtle effects of these different frequencies on the brain of the observer.

ELECTROMAGNETIC FIELDS

We have less detailed knowledge about all of the effects of many other electromagnetic radiations, which is not really surprising when we often have only a few decades instead of several millennia of experience of them. However, there can be no doubt that we are sensitive to electromagnetic fields, even relatively weak ones. Just consider that almost everything in the body (the brain, nerve signals, biochemical processes, and so on) has an electrical basis. We even generate our own weak electromagnetic field, which may be what a dowser 'tunes' into. (see Chapter 14).

Work done by Davis and Rawls[1] amongst others indicates that people who have healing powers in their hands are capable of generating electro-magnetic fields which are slightly stronger than usual, and it is believed that it is these fields which have the beneficial effect on the patient. Kirlian photography also shows distinctive patterns generated by the hands of the healers.

There is no doubt that people do respond well to the techniques variously described as 'healing', 'the laying-on of hands' or 'therapeutic touch' — indeed such techniques are sometimes used nowadays by nurses in hospitals. If this effect is indeed due to the increased, but still very tiny, electro-magnetic fields from the hands of the healer, then it is a dramatic illustration of just how strong our body's response can be to tiny EMFs.

Further confirmation of our sensitivity has come from the relatively recent scientific discovery of just how dependent we are for our wellbeing on the weak magnetic fields of the Earth (terrestrial magnetism), and the low frequency Schuhmann waves (around 7.8Hz) which are found between the Earth and the ionosphere. This became apparent during investigation of the causes of the variety of symptoms suffered by early astronauts while in space for even relatively short periods. An orbiting spacecraft is of course outside the influence of all natural terrestrial magnetic fields and generating these artificially solved the astronauts' problems.

Also, we should not overlook the fact that electromagnetic fields are also successfully used therapeutically in a scientific manner. Techniques like the German Mora Therapy have been used for some decades now, and systems like Vega, EAP and others also use measurements of the body's natural electrical characteristics as the basis for diagnosis. Physiotherapists use intense low-frequency treatments to treat muscular injuries. Magnetic field therapies at various frequencies and with a variety of wave forms are increasingly used in hospitals and elsewhere for purposes which range from relieving muscular pain and repairing damaged muscles, to acceleration of wound healing and promoting knitting of broken bones. We will take a closer look at some of these beneficial applications of electrical and magnetic fields later (Chapter 10).

While these applications undoubtedly have good effects, the key question is whether there are unwanted side-effects to such therapies and, even if not, whether unintentional and uncontrolled exposure to fields at a huge range of frequencies (see Chapter 4) may have injurious effects. From the latest research, it seems clear that the danger of damage to health exists. There are pronounced frequency-dependent effects on the human brain and body. Professor Smith in his book *Electromagnetic Man* suggests that it is coherent waves (broadly, those which persist in a regular pattern for long periods, perhaps like the earth energies and energy leys discussed in Part Two) which are likely to have biological effects[2].

Specifically, we seem to be much affected by some extremely low frequencies (ELFs) in the band up to 300 cycles per second (or Hertz). Of course the most important source in this band, because it is so universal, is mains frequency (50 or 60Hz) though there are some others of interest. *It is just about impossible to escape the influence of man-made electricity anywhere in the world.*

Incidentally, some researchers suggest that we would have fewer problems if the frequency chosen for mains electricity had been higher — 200 or 300Hz rather than 50 or 60Hz. There is no technical reason why this could not have been so, as it was largely an arbitrary engineering decision. Certainly we do seem to have ended up with a very unfortunate choice. There is even a suggestion that the 50 Hz supply used in most of the world is, on balance, worse for us than the 60 Hz found in America and a few other countries. It seems possible that some of the harmonics of 50Hz resonate with the body in a particularly unfortunate way.   However, speculating on the benefits of change, with so much committed to the existing system, is not really realistic.

At the other end of the scale, extremely high frequencies of many thousands of millions of Hertz can also affect us, although in different ways. Typical examples here are microwaves, which are produced by television sets, computers, communication transmissions and radar as well as the ovens we probably think of first. Higher still, we move into the realms of ionising radiations (X-rays, gamma rays, etc.).

In between these extremes there is a huge band that includes all radio frequencies. While there is less indication of specific effects from these we do need to consider, in view of the amazing permanent smog of radio waves mentioned earlier, whether this may be contributing to the general stress overload.

The analogy with smog is appropriate. Although that sometimes choking product of general pollution of the atmosphere is probably most recalled for the number of the sickly and elderly killed by it in particularly bad winters, it was much more important as a general factor undermining public health through long-term exposure, causing chronic diseases like bronchitis. We may well discover that the situation is similar in the case of electro-stress. So far most attention has been paid to specific reactions to sources of electromagnetic fields. It is highly likely that in the long term we will come to realise that the most important consideration is the generally debilitating effect on health — the extent to which exposure contributes to our stress level long before this turns into a physical or mental disease.

QUANTITY VS EXPOSURE

When we assess the risk from anything that can affect us, whether a chemical pollutant or a dangerous radiation, we have to consider two key factors: the first is quantity, that is to say, what is the level of our exposure and at what point does a harmful factor start to pose a significant risk? We have to recognise that there is never a simple answer to this question as personal variations such as individual sensitivity, body size, age and general level of health will all have a bearing on the outcome. If the substance in question is something for which benefits are claimed, such as a drug, then we may need to balance the adverse effects against the potential gain — what is called the risk/benefit analysis.

One complication when considering dose (and one which may have great significance when dealing with electromagnetic fields) is the dilution effect, familiar to users of homeopathy. Put simply, tiny concentrations of a substance can often have even greater effects than much larger chemical doses. This can sometimes be used in a protective way; classical homeopathy is based on the fact that many highly poisonous substances, when potentised (diluted in a special way) become positive or protective in their effect on the patient, their properties having been effectively inverted.

However it is now also realised that not all substances behave in this way. For reasons that are not yet fully understood, in some cases the effect is not inverted, and high dilutions will have an even greater effect than the crude substance. The implication of this is to question the frequent assertion of those who defend the electrical industry that low field strengths must by definition pose little risk. It is possible that low field strengths may in some cases be more potent than high ones. We will consider later the question of what constitutes a 'low' field strength when we are dealing with biological systems. A similar debate is under way concerning official assurances that we need not be concerned about possible dangers from the 'insignificant' amounts of pesticide residues and additives in foods and pollutants in drinking water.

The second factor in our equation is exposure. Someone who smokes one high tar cigarette in his entire life — or even someone who regularly smokes one a month is highly unlikely to die of a smoking related disease. But someone who smokes daily ten of even the lowest tar cigarettes available is clearly at risk.

Similarly, with any environmental factor, including electromagnetic fields, we must always consider the duration and regularity of exposure. Someone who has an occasional dental X-ray has little need to fear for his long-term health, but it would not be a good idea to have this done every month. Because of this you will find that there are often references to length and frequency of exposure, as well as absolute field strengths, when the possible hazards of electro-stress are discussed. If these are not understood then unnecessary alarm may sometimes be felt about relatively harmless field sources, or serious hazards may be overlooked.

WINDOWS

An idea that arises from several research reports (including that by Dr.Leal referred to in Chapter 1) is that there may be another very important factor to bear in mind when looking at hazards. This is the concept of specific narrow bands, or windows of frequency and power, within and only within which hazards may be present. If correct, it could at least partly account for the suggestions, referred to above, that 50Hz mains are worse for us than 60Hz — or that some weak fields do more damage than stronger ones.

It could also help to explain why some apparently well-founded research findings have later been contradicted by other workers. If the researchers did not realise the crucial significance of defining the precise frequency, power and even waveform of the electromagnetic fields used then it may indeed be impossible to replicate results.

WAVEFORM

One of our key themes in examining electro-stress is the importance of both frequency and power level in determining whether a particular electromagnetic field is potentially harmful to us. The other factor which needs to be considered is that of waveform. The effect of the shape of the electromagnetic waves — the way in which the output rises and falls with time is a fairly technical subject, but it will help if you understand some basic facts.

The waves produced by electricity flowing in wires and cables or generated by electrical equipment can be examined using an oscilloscope, a device which displays on its screen a graph of the way that the waves rise and fall, as well as providing numerical information. Looking at the screen will give an idea of frequency (the higher this is — the more pulses per second — the closer the waves will be together) and how regular (coherent) or random the pattern is. As you have seen, we believe that these are both important considerations. However, the oscilloscope will also show what type of waveform we are dealing with.

Any rotating generator, such as those used in power stations, tends to produce a field which rises and falls smoothly and regularly. This will typically appear as what is called a 'sine wave' like that shown in fig.2a. It is unlikely that the wiring in our homes or offices will produce such a clean-cut trace, because the mains electricity supply, as it travels to us, tends to pick up all sorts of extra wave patterns feeding back from the apparatus which it supplies, but the general pattern will be maintained.

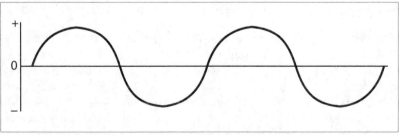

Fig.2a: Sine Wave

It is also possible to generate a square wave which rises almost instantaneously from zero to maximum, holds the peak for a period and then falls just as sharply back to zero or even to a negative value.

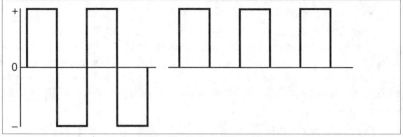

Fig.2b: Square Waves

Finally, fields will often be found similar to that shown in fig.2c. These also rise very sharply to a maximum value, but then tail off rather more gradually to zero before repeating the cycle. Because of their appearance on an oscilloscope, these are often called 'saw-tooth' waves. You will read in Chapter 10 that magnetic fields used therapeutically often have square or saw-tooth waveforms because they are found to produce the best response, perhaps because they more closely approximate the wave forms generated by the body itself. It seems a reasonable assumption that if a particular shape of wave has a stronger beneficial influence when used therapeutically, then the same shape must also have the potential to produce the most marked adverse effect when used at the 'wrong' frequency or strength. Dr Cyril Smith's work (referred to earlier) suggests that continuous exposure to a steady wave form of whatever shape is more likely to have a deleterious effect, whereas intermittent exposure to a pattern of changing frequencies and waveforms is considerably more friendly to the body. It is interesting to note that most therapeutic devices follow the latter rather than the former pattern.

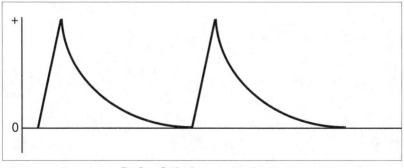

Fig.2c: Spiked or saw tooth wave

SUMMARY

You should by now realise that several different characteristics of electromagnetic fields play a part in determining whether they are likely to affect us in some way.

Frequency is certainly important. It seems that relatively low and very high frequencies are the most hazardous, with the additional thought that we may only need to concern ourselves with quite narrow bands or windows where hazard exists (once we know where these lie). It also seems likely that persistence or coherence may be as crucial as the precise frequency.

Power is another factor to take into account, though we may well need to question the automatic assumption that stronger fields are necessarily the most dangerous in all cases. The homeopathic analogy and the concept of windows of hazard both merit further investigation.

Finally, the type of wave — sine, square or saw-tooth — is also likely to prove important.

NOTES

1.   Davis & Rawls, *The Rainbow in your Hands*: Exposition Press, 1974.
2.   Smith, C.W. & Best, S., *Electromagnetic Man*: Dent (1989), p.25.

CHAPTER 3

FACTS AND FIGURES

It is important to stress how recent is the advent of man-made electricity. It was a very unfamiliar phenomenon at the start of the 20th Century. Indeed electric power was first generated commercially only a little over a century ago and it was decades before it became universally available in even the most technologically advanced and affluent countries. Yet within a few generations electricity has become a central, indispensable part of modern life.

Mains electricity was introduced in 1882. For a brief period Direct Current (DC) was the favoured source, but for technical reasons that need not concern us here, DC has severe limitations if you want to generate electricity in power stations and send it around the country to the ultimate user. So before long, Alternating Current (AC) arrived and this is now the universal power source.

Alternating Current, as its name indicates, does not flow steadily in one direction, but oscillates to and fro. In Europe and much of the world it does this fifty times every second, which is normally indicated as 50Hz, but America and some other countries use 60Hz. It is the electromagnetic fields produced by AC current that are now becoming recognised as a key contributory factor to many of our health problems.

Until the mains supply arrived, muscles rather than electricity supplied the power to wash the clothes and clean the floors. Radios, when they appeared, were powered by cumbersome accumulators that had to be taken to the shop to be re-charged at regular intervals. Even as recently as the mid 1950s many rural areas of Britain still depended on gas or paraffin for lighting and heating.

It is increasingly hard to imagine such a life. Certainly, there are today few homes in the developed world and indeed ever fewer places anywhere on Earth without mains electricity. Indeed it is almost impossible to find somewhere out of range of the oscillations of mains fields.

Because electricity provides the power source for so much of modern life, the electromagnetic picture is extremely complex. Lighting, heating, computers, domestic and electrical equipment, electrified railways, radar, television and communications, all use AC current as their power source. These work at every imaginable frequency up to several million million Hertz (10^{12}Hz) or more — and they in their turn radiate these frequencies into the environment.

THE BROADCASTING EXPLOSION

Broadcasting figures for the USA provides a graphic illustration of the explosive growth of the uses of electricity. Figures for the U.S.A. graphically illustrate the scale of growth. The first commercial radio station started transmission in 1920 and there were only a few thousand broadcast sources in 1939. This had risen to 30 million stations by 1979 and the total today is around 50 million. Radio and television waves fill the ether so that transmissions can be picked up in the most remote places on Earth. A leading U.S. expert, Dr.Robert Becker, has written that the total density of radio frequency waves penetrating every corner of the planet (and every person on it) is now 100 to 200 million times the level reaching us naturally from the Sun.[1] As we have evolved to tolerate only the natural level it is hard to imagine that we can not be affected by an increase of such gargantuan proportions over so short a time span.

Britain's first public radio station appeared less than 70 years ago, and well into the 1950s there were only three stations broadcasting in the UK (Home, Light and Third), with crackly Radio Luxembourg providing the thrills of advertisements on the air waves. Other countries had a similarly limited choice.

Today there is simply no more room in the radio frequency spectrum. If you want a new national station, you have to give up an existing one. Even low powered stations with limited operating areas are subject to strict controls to stop the transmissions of one station interfering with another. This is necessary even though a very wide range of frequencies is now in use for radio broadcasting and despite the sophistication of modern receivers which can distinguish accurately transmitters operating only a few Hertz apart.

Communications transmissions use the upper end of the radio frequency band and range from the emergency services and aircraft control to telecommunications and cell-phones. There has been rapid expansion of many such applications in the last couple of decades and the frequencies reserved for them are similarly crowded (as many cell-phone users will tell you) and ever more uses for the air-waves appear every year.

ELECTROMAGNETIC FIELDS EXPLAINED

This is an appropriate point to take a look at just what we mean by electromagnetic fields (EMF) and the different forms they can take. A simple way to picture them is to think what happens when we drop a pebble into a pond. A series of concentric ripples spreads out from the point of disturbance, weakening (becoming smaller) the further they travel.

Electrons vibrating backwards and forwards 50 times every second in a wire connected to the mains produce a similar disturbance in space, except, that in this case, the 'ripples' are the lines of force of the EMF. As with the pond, the field weakens as it moves out from the conductor. (fig.3) In the case of EMFs there are two types of 'ripples', the electrical and magnetic parts of the field and they radiate at right angles to both each other and to the conductor carrying the current. To visualise this, hold out your right hand in front of you, point forward with your index finger, then stick your thumb up vertically and your second finger at right angles to your palm. If the index finger represents the wire carrying the current, then the thumb and second finger show the direction of the electrical and magnetic parts of the radiating field.

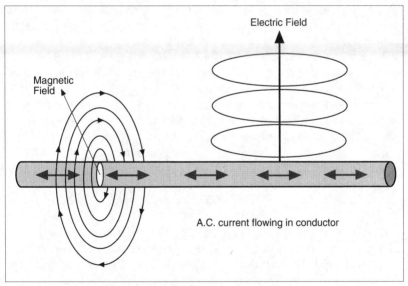

Fig 3: Electrical and magnetic fields

Electromagnetic radiations of many kinds occur in nature, although at very much lower intensities than most man-made fields. Indeed, daylight, produced by the Sun, is such a radiation. There are other sources of light in nature; glow worms and certain fish can produce dim light for instance and radioactive substances glow in the dark too.

Visible light lies within a narrow band from 4×10^{14} to 7.7×10^{14}Hz and every colour in the spectrum has its own specific frequency. I'm sorry if the notation puts you off, but you must admit that 10^{14} (which simply means '1 with 14 zeros after it') is neater and easier to read than 100,000,000,000,000. Light (which we can see) and infra-red (which is felt as warmth) are the only parts of the electromagnetic spectrum for which we have specific sense organs. This is what makes all other electromagnetic radiations both rather mysterious and, in many cases, so potentially dangerous.

Probably the most important fact about light in the context of this book is that even though it is a natural EMF we all know it can be unpleasant or even dangerous in excess. Stay out too long in strong sunlight and you will get sunburn. Do it too often, and there is a risk of skin cancer. With the much publicised 'holes' in the ozone layer increasing the amount of ultra-violet light that reaches Earth, this latter risk has significantly increased in many places. Many Australians for instance are now pale-skinned rather than the bronzed stereotype, staying indoors or wearing protective hats and clothing when outdoors, so worried have they become. Similarly, excessive exposure to infrared can be harmful, which incidentally raises questions about the long-term health prospects of supermarket check-out operators using scanning equipment on modern EPOS till systems.

The Sun produces other EMFs in the radio-frequency range — you will have heard of sun-spots and probably know that they can interfere with radio and television reception.

If we look at a chart of different electromagnetic frequencies (fig.4), we see that light is somewhere in the middle, with mains electricity at one end and ionising radiation at the other. Working up from the lowest frequencies, we have the following picture:

— certain specialised frequencies such as electric fences — 1Hz; and electric railways in some countries (not Britain) — $16^{2}/_{3}$Hz.
— mains electricity — 50Hz (or 60Hz in U.S.A. and some other countries).
— radio, television and radar — a very wide band from 3×10^{4} to 3×10^{12}Hz. At the upper end of this range are so-called microwaves, used for communications (telecommunications, military, etc.) as well as microwave ovens.
— infra-red radiation — from 3×10^{11} to 3×10^{14}Hz.
— visible light — a narrow band from 4×10^{14} to 7.7×10^{14}Hz.
— ultra-violet radiation from 7.7×10^{14} to 3×10^{17}Hz.
— ionising radiations (neutrons, alpha-, beta-, gamma- and X-rays) — up to 3×10^{22}Hz.

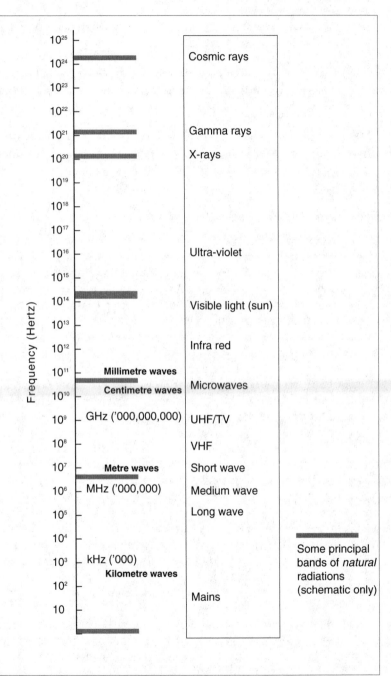

Fig.4: Electromagnetic frequency spectrum

This is a good point to clarify the matter of ionising and non-ionising radiation. (See also later in the text and the glossary.) As you can see from the outline above and from the chart, what are called ionising radiations occur at the high end of the spectrum. There is no controversy about the hazards which these represent — their name means that they will ionise or change the molecular structure of tissue exposed to them. This is what makes them so dangerous.

We are concerned here only with the lower frequency, non-ionising waves. But the fact that they do not directly affect molecular structure in the way that a gamma-ray or an X-ray will does not necessarily mean that they pose no threat to living organisms and in particular to us.

SHIELDING AND SAFE DISTANCES

There are two possible ways to avoid electromagnetic radiations: try to move far enough from the source so that the field has weakened to an acceptable level; or find some way of shielding ourselves, that is, of stopping the radiation reaching us. When talking about shielding we must distinguish between the two main types of electromagnetic radiation.

Electrical Fields are produced whenever there is a voltage in a conductor (voltage is the 'pressure' that pushes the electric current around a circuit). These fields will be present even if there is no current flowing. There is no need for anything to be connected to the circuit. (Think of a water-pipe in your house; the water in it is under pressure whether you are using it or not). Electrical fields will be absorbed by any material that conducts electricity — walls, people, trees — and so it is fairly easy to shield against them.

Magnetic Fields, on the other hand, are produced only when current flows (that is, when the circuit is switched on, just as water flows in a pipe when a tap is opened). These fields pass almost unhindered through people, the ground and many building materials, although concrete and steelwork in buildings will reduce them to some degree. Mains frequency magnetic fields are particularly persistent. Even aluminium sheeting half an inch (12mm.) thick will only be partially effective. As a result, shielding against them is extremely difficult and often, for all practical purposes, impossible. The relatively small shielding effects of common construction material is well illustrated in Table 3.

Both electrical and magnetic fields become weaker with distance. For instance, there are very strong fields immediately under a high voltage power line, but they fall away steadily as you move away. It has been suggested that the UK should follow the practice of some other countries and establish a clear zone (which can be 100 yards [91

	Permeability (%) for	
	Electrical fields	Magnetic fields
Wire mesh (1mm) - 3 cm pitch	0.5	65
Wire mesh (1mm) - 0.3 cm pitch	0.1	10
Iron sheet (2mm)	0.1	50
Copper foil (0.2mm)	0.1	90
Reinforced conrete (60 cm)	0.1	0.1

All the above are for 50 Hz fields

Table 3: Permeability by electrical & magnetic fields of common materials

metres] or more) on either side of power lines within which building houses is banned. In America or Russia the debate is whether existing zones are wide enough, whereas in the U.K. there are no regulations at all and power lines often run directly over inhabited areas.

There is no easy answer to the problem as fields from strong sources can persist over amazing distances; for instance, in Germany the characteristic $16\,^2/_3$Hz waves of the railway system have been detected in the earth 10 miles (16 km) from the nearest line (the operating voltage in this case is up to 110kV, which is far less than most power distribution lines). It is necessary to move fully $^3/_4$ of a mile (1.2km) from a 500kV overhead power line before field strengths fall off to 'background' levels, and higher voltages than this are increasingly used around the world.

However, it is not only high voltages which should concern us. Although many people worry about their house being too near a power line, few think about the wiring in their houses. A simple calculation will show that wiring in your bedroom may produce a field in your brain as strong as that from a pylon at the end of the garden. In other words, being close to a weak source can have as much effect as being further away from a strong one. In either case the effective frequency is the same, which is probably the most important characteristic. The results of exposure may be different in the two cases, but it seems likely that both can cause health problems.

SOME FACTS ABOUT FIELD STRENGTHS

To put things into perspective, it will be useful to make some comparisons between the field strengths that are found in nature, especially in the body, and those which are produced by man-made electricity. Don't worry if the actual figures do not make a lot of sense to you; it is the relationship between the strengths which matters.

Natural electrical and magnetic fields are mostly very weak. The magnetic field of the Earth in Northern Europe is around half a gauss (0.5G), and although there are small variations as you travel around the globe, it is of this order of magnitude wherever you are situated. A Gauss is a well-established measurement of magnetic field density, but nowadays scientists prefer to measure these magnetic fields in units called Tesla (T) which are 10,000 times bigger. The Earth's 0.5G becomes 0.00005T, which makes it seem even tinier.

However, even this is still massive when compared with the field produced by the human brain, which is around 0.000000000000001T. Because of the vast number of zeros, this is usually written as 10^{-15}T, but either way it is still an extremely weak field! Indeed, instruments capable of measuring it have been developed only fairly recently and in order to use them, special shielding must be used to exclude the much stronger field of the Earth.

On the other hand, when an electrical engineer talks about weak magnetic fields, he is probably referring to something less than 100G, or 0.001T, a full 100 billion times stronger than that of the brain. That is 100,000,000,000 or 10^{11} times stronger. Small wonder that biologists and engineers disagree over whether a particular field is weak or strong, as they are talking a different language.

The situation is similar with electric fields. Those generated by the body are minute compared with even the small fields in electronic circuits such as computers or radios. Of course, the latter are tiny compared to fields emitted by mains circuits used for lighting or heating. The measurement normally used for electrical fields is volts per metre (V/m).

It is important to keep these relative strengths in mind when reading the rest of the book. The key fact is that man-made fields do not have to be very strong at all to dwarf those found in the body.

Having discussed some of the background, we will now look at various sources of electromagnetic fields and consider what research has uncovered about their potential effects on humankind.

NOTE
1.   Becker, R.O. & Selden, G., *The Body Electric*: Wm.Morrow (1985) p.275.

CHAPTER 4

BEDTIME STORY

The electricity which we switch on at home has travelled through many miles of cables to reach us. From the power station it passes along high-tension overhead distribution lines at a potential of several hundred thousand volts. It then travels through sub-stations and into local distribution lines (usually overhead in rural areas or underground in towns) the voltage dropping stage by stage.

Finally, at around a modest 110 volts in the USA (or 220 volts in Europe), it comes into our houses, where a network of cables takes it from room to room and from floor to floor. The way in which power is distributed within the home varies widely from one country to another. However, there are two basic methods.

The simplest is to use a series of individual cables or 'spurs' radiating from a central distribution board. Each of these spurs will serve one or two rooms in the house and will be equipped with its own individual fuse link. It is not generally possible to supply more than one or two rooms in this way as the maximum potential load must remain within national safety levels for the cable being used. There is a further possible variation in that, whereas in many cases all electrical needs of the rooms in question will be supplied from one circuit (i.e. both power and lighting), in other countries the lighting circuits are separately supplied.

The second common type of distribution circuit is that known in the UK as the ring main, and in Australia, the USA and some other countries as the ring circuit. This is generally used for power supplies as distinct from lighting. The principle is to link all the power outlets in one area (which may be one floor of a house, or part of a floor, depending on the size of the building) in one continuous circuit, using a loop of cable which runs from the distribution board through all the power points, returning to the same point on the distribution board. A typical arrangement is to provide one ring circuit for the kitchen which is often an area with a relatively high consumption of electrical power, another for the rest of the ground floor, and another for the floor above, making three in all). The advantage from an electrical point of view is that, because each socket is in effect being supplied by two cables, one from each direction, the total number of sockets which can be placed on one circuit is greater than would be allowed on a single spur.

Matters can be complicated further as it is not uncommon for there to be short spurs off the ring supplying one or two sockets in more remote parts of the house. This is done primarily to save cable. The cabling of the ring may be run around the outer walls of the house, which is the worst possible arrangement from an electro-stress standpoint, or may run around an internal area such as a central stairwell or hallway with rather more spurs. When ring circuits are used, lighting is supplied through a separate network of cable, often run in the ceiling space above the ground floor, with spurs running up and down to supply the lights on the two floors, although a separate circuit may also be placed in the roof space to supply the upper floors.

Every centimetre of cable on this journey will radiate electrical and magnetic fields at a frequency of 50 or 60Hz. To complicate matters, most appliances and electronic equipment also produce fields, adding their own different frequencies to the electromagnetic mixture. Some of this feeds back into the mains, building up complex frequency patterns, with unpredictable peaks of power.

As a result, we literally never escape the steady 50/60Hz oscillations (mixed with many additional frequencies) from one day's end to the next. While the field strengths are generally low, as remarked before, 'low' can mean very different things in the contexts of engineering and biology.

NIGHT TIME ELECTRO-STRESS

Constant exposure to such 'extremely low frequency' (ELF) electrical fields has no history in evolutionary terms. Centuries are needed for organisms to adapt to even simple environmental changes and mains electricity is only four or five generations old. There is still a lot we do not know about its effects on basic body functions, but no-one can claim that it is natural for the body to receive continuous exposure to 50 or 60Hz.

We spend around a third of our lives in bed. Few people spend as many hours in any other place. Even jobs centred on one place, for instance, working at a desk or a work bench, generally involve moving away from time to time. In bed, by contrast, we stay in precisely the same spot for six, seven, or eight hours at a stretch.

INSOMNIA

Anyone who looks objectively at the clinical evidence has to agree that there is a strong case for concluding that the ELF fields, especially those in the bedroom, help to trigger numerous minor health disturbances, particularly those which are related to that modern bogey — stress. For instance, some abnormally high mains frequency fields are found in the bedrooms of very many insomnia sufferers. My experience has shown that when these fields are eliminated or the sleeper is shielded from them using the methods described later, normal sleep patterns almost always return.

A similar picture will be found in many cases of people who regularly suffer restless, disturbed sleep, or who always wake up tired despite seeming to sleep soundly, or the countless individuals who are used to waking with headaches, stiff muscles or 'rheumatics'. Repeatedly, above average field strengths are found where they sleep and the symptoms improve when the fields are dealt with.

I must stress that it is the *quality* of your sleep that should concern you. I find that many, if not most people, when questioned say that they sleep well. By this, apparently they mean that they are not conscious of lying awake for a long time before dropping off; they are not aware of disturbance during the night and they feel that they stay asleep for enough hours. However, if asked how they feel when they wake up, they more often than not admit that they rarely if ever feel really refreshed. If this picture fits you, then you are not sleeping well, whatever you may believe.

If people who suffer from poor quality sleep are observed during the night they will generally be found to be restless, to show signs of dreaming, to talk in their sleep. If their brainwaves were monitored with an EEG (Electro-encephalogram) then it would be found that their brain activity does not show the necessary periods of relaxation. While there can be physical causes for such a sleep pattern, it is highly likely that at least part of the reason that such people do not relax is because their brains are continuously stimulated by electromagnetic fields in their environment, especially in the bedroom. Tackling these will very often bring about dramatic improvements.

Allergies, irritability, lack of energy, inability to concentrate, hyperactivity in children are some other modern complaints that have been blamed on stress resulting from sensitivity to mains frequency radiation. Once again, reducing environmental electromagnetic field levels is very often found to be a key factor in bringing about improvements.

SOURCES

Bedrooms are a particularly common source of electro-stress problems because of the layout of the wiring in most houses. Cables for the lights in ground floor rooms run in the ceilings, which are, of course, the floors of the bedrooms above. The cables for the upstairs power supply run in the bedroom walls and wiring for the upstairs lights will be found in the ceilings above. Every appliance has its own flex, which is usually left plugged in and so is live as well. In short, most beds lie within a cocoon of mains wiring, which radiates 50Hz or 60Hz electrical fields, day and night.

In many cases, strong sources outside the dwelling can be partly to blame. Pylons or other high-tension cables may be close enough to produce a significant effect in the bedroom. A nearby factory or workshop may have electrical equipment producing strong fields. Even if the factory is closed at night, transformers that radiate powerfully are often left on around the clock. Apartment dwellers are subject to radiations from their neighbours' wiring and equipment, which is generally always left plugged in even if turned off, and so on.

As if all that were not enough, the modern bedroom tends to boast more electrical apparatus than almost any other room in the house. Bedside or bedhead lights, radio alarms, telephones, television sets (often with remote controls), electric blankets or duvets, water beds, all of these produce fields at mains and other frequencies and they all bring their own particular problems.

For instance, lights, clock radios and telephones are generally close to the bed-head. Although the fields that they produce lose power very rapidly as you move away, the brain of the sleeper is often near enough for there still to be a measurable effect. You should be particularly careful about anything containing a transformer or magnets, including telephones and many clock radios, as these will produce more powerful and persistent radiations.

Television sets give off strong fields too. Since most viewers sit ten or twelve feet away, the living room TV does not expose most people to high field levels, but they are often more of a problem in the bedroom. There are two main reasons for this. Firstly, bedroom televisions are typically placed at the end of the bed, and as the viewer is lying down or stretched out, his or her feet will be close enough to pick up a relatively high field and conduct it into the body. Secondly, the majority of bedroom televisions are, for the sake of convenience, equipped with remote controls. The trouble with remote controlled TV is that it is always 'live' and so electrical fields can remain very high all night, even though the set is apparently turned off. In these ways, sets in the bedroom can cause much electro-pollution and electro-stress.

There is no doubt that the greatest villains of the modern bedroom are often electric blankets, and especially the electric duvet or water bed, both of which are designed to be left on all night. In these cases the whole bed is criss-crossed with yards of mains cable, giving off a very dense electromagnetic field, close to the body. To make matters worse, loops of wiring produce especially high field levels, far higher than a straight cable. Measurements show that high residual electromagnetic fields can remain, even when blankets are switched off, and if they must be used, the only sensible advice is to unplug them rather than just switch off before going to bed. Of course this advice negates the whole purpose of electric duvets or water beds and sadly it is better to do without these modern luxuries!

The use of electric blankets by pregnant women has been linked by Wertheimer to an increased incidence of miscarriages.[1] Some doubts have been raised as to whether the miscarriage rate could be linked to increased body heat which would obviously be associated with use of an electric blanket. Wertheimer's later study of the use of electric heating cables in ceilings seem, however, to strengthen her case. As we shall see later, these have a uniform field as high as 10mG on a long-term basis and Wertheimer states that she has found a similar increased incidence of miscarriages amongst women whose homes are heated in this way. In this case a link with body heat cannot be argued since there is no correlation between levels of miscarriage and other forms of domestic heating giving the same temperature levels.

It is a sad fact that many of the most devoted users of electrical methods of heating the bed are people who suffer from rheumatism and hope that the extra warmth will relieve their aching joints. I have found that if asked to analyse how they felt before and after starting to use an electric blanket, many will admit scant improvement and very often will realise that they have in fact got worse. Consistently unplugging their blanket or duvet before going to bed will in such cases generally bring much relief and will avoid the need to discard it altogether. A hot water bottle will provide a sustained source of warmth during the night without unwanted side-effects.

SECRETS OF SLEEP

Even accepting that the electromagnetic environment in many bedrooms can be so unfriendly, there must be other considerations to explain why exposure to radiating fields at night should be such a uniquely important health factor. After all, many people also spend their days in highly electrically charged places. The modern office or shopping precinct can be just as bad as a factory and it is quite possible that local field strengths may be even higher than those to be found at home.

In fact, there are several additional reasons why the origins of electro-stress are so often to be found in the bedroom. As we have noted, we spend a long time in one place at night. Most people move around a lot during the day, so that even though they may encounter some high field strengths, they generally do not stay within range of them for very long. Obviously, there are exceptions linked to particular occupations and we will look later at some of these, such as electrical workers and VDU operators. However, for most of us, spending anything up to eight or nine hours out of every twenty-four in the typical bedroom provides the biggest single source of electro-stress.

Even more crucial is the role of sleep itself. Although sleep is clearly essential for everyone, its real purpose, as the time when our body repairs and regenerates itself, has only been definitely established fairly recently. Researchers were puzzled when they first examined the pattern of sleep in detail. A key question concerned what is known as 'REM' or rapid eye movement sleep. It is also sometimes called paradoxical sleep. These names derive from the observation that at the very time when sleep appeared to be at its deepest, as measured by pulse rate, breathing, etc., there was paradoxically a huge amount of brain activity. It was also observed that during this period the eyes of the sleepers moved to and fro very quickly, but with no obvious pattern or purpose. We now believe that all this is a sign that during these periods the brain is busy maintaining and repairing the body.

Every day, billions of cells in the body die and must be replaced. Some, such as skin cells, last for a few months and even the longest lived have a life span of only seven years, so that none of us has in our body a single cell left which existed seven years ago. The huge job of repair and maintenance is undertaken while we sleep. Information gathered by the brain during the day about which cells need replacement is turned into a rebuilding plan to be carried out at night.

At least some of the massive amount of information which has to be sent to and from the brain to achieve this travels along the nerve fibres. However, there is a physical limit to the speed with which such messages can pass along nerves, and hence how much 'traffic' can be carried in this way. The sheer volume of information seems just too great for the neural network to be the only route. Coghill believes[2] that it is likely that in order to get so much information around the body the brain must be acting like a radio station, sending information directly to the cells. As radio waves travel at the speed of light, this would clearly make things a lot quicker.

Whichever mechanism is in use, the messages are clearly electrical, and all electrical processes can suffer interference or jamming from external sources, just as television or radio reception can be distorted by sun-spots, atmospheric conditions, or a neighbour's electric drill. It is not really surprising that such interference, regularly experienced by the body at night, can produce stress and the stress-related illness we have described. If the situation persists for long enough the obvious risk is that the immune system becomes weakened, laying the body open to infection or even to the proliferation of 'wrong' cells that may turn out to be malignant.

In view of all this, anyone investigating possible electro-stress should always look at the electromagnetic conditions in the bedroom. (We must not forget that stressful electro-magnetic fields are amplified by any geopathically stressful lines.) In many cases, clearing up problems here will produce such significant health improvements that very little more will need to be done. Even for those people who suffer significant daytime exposure to electro-stress (for instance, VDU operators), the night time exposure will almost always still prove to be a significant factor.

There are various ways of determining whether any area may be a source of electro-stress.

INVESTIGATION

First, simply look! Any electrical apparatus is potentially suspect, although the hazard varies greatly from one device to another (see Table 4). As a general rule, it is sensible at night not to have any of the electrical items we have mentioned too near to you, particularly to your head. Nor should the flexes (cords) attached be forgotten. With modern built-in bedroom furniture, remember that wires are very likely to be hidden in the headboard.

It is impossible to predict precise 'safe' distances as even different makes of the same sort of appliance can produce very different field levels. However, as a rule, most domestic apparatuses will not disturb people if they are at least 3ft. (91cm) away from the body. This sort of guidance has to be interpreted carefully if, for instance, there are several devices connected to the mains at night, in which case the separate fields are cumulative.

Even if all the electrical equipment in the bedroom is moved or unplugged, disturbing field levels may still persist in the bed. These most often come from the mains cables which run in the walls, ceilings and floors of the room. Sometimes this will be because the cables run

SOURCE	Typical field strength in milli-Gauss (10-3G)
High-tension power lines - under the lines	220
-55m distant	1
Electric shaver -0.5" (12mm)	2-400
Vacuum cleaner - 10cm	600
Electric blanket	50-100
60 watt light bulb - 2" (5cm)	0.3
-6" (15cm)	0.05
10 watt fluorescent tube (110v) - 2" (5cm)	6
- 6" (15cm)	2
60 watt fluorescent tube (220v) - ceiling	80
Electric hotplate - 0.4" (1cm)	500
- 18" (46cm)	50
Skirting heater - 6" (15cm)	23
- 3ft (91cm)	1
Ceiling heater - entire room	10

Table 4: Some magnetic field strengths

near the head of the bed, but it may also be because the wiring layout is such that several cables are grouped in one area, resulting in a high total field level. Short of removing floorboards or plaster, you are unlikely to know where the cables run and some sort of detection meter is needed.

Simple, relatively cheap, wiring detectors, widely available in DIY shops to help you avoid putting nails through cables, will tell you where the wires are, but will not give any indication of field strength. It is still worth using one just to check where the wiring is located. More specialist meters are available to measure ELFs (fields up to 100Hz) which, of course, includes mains electricity. They give direct readings of the levels of both electrical and magnetic field components as well as an audible signal and will give clear indications of the 'hot spots' in an area. You can also get meters to measure other bands of interest, such as radio and microwave frequencies. There are even some combination meters available covering all of these bands. Some of the organisations listed in the 'Suppliers' appendix may be able to supply a suitable meter. All of these meters can be relatively expensive, however. There are one or two cheaper if less sophisticated alternatives available, but not all of these may give reliable indications. A few specialist companies offer a consultancy service and it is possible that meters may be offered for hire if you wish to do your own investigation.

You should not forget that the problem fields may be originating outside the dwelling. Overhead power-lines are clear to see, but in towns distribution is usually underground, and factories, transformer stations and other sources may be important too. So it cannot be assumed that because nothing obvious is visible from the window there is no cause for concern. If you live in anything other than a detached house you must never overlook what may be coming from the adjoining flat or house. For instance, a TV placed against the neighbour's party wall will produce strong fields in your adjoining room (as with computers, fields behind televisions are generally stronger than in front of them). Nor of course should you forget the geopathic hot spots described later in the book.

INDIVIDUAL RESPONSE

What none of the meters mentioned so far can do is to predict how an individual will react to any given electric field strength, and this can be very important, as sensitivity is highly personal. A field that is low enough to be insignificant for one person may cause a great deal of disturbance to someone else. (There is an obvious and unsurprising parallel with allergic response). Also, it seems logical that a big person will be a more effective antenna than someone petite. So although direct measurements of field strengths give important information, other tests are also advisable.

One useful test makes use of the fact that anything that can conduct electricity will have a circulating current and a voltage produced in it when it is placed in an alternating field. This is the principle used in the dynamo and alternator. The human body is a conductor, and so exposure to any mains field will provoke a response in the body. This is not in itself dangerous (we are not likely to give ourselves electrical shocks or produce sparks!), as the total amount of electricity produced is small. It does, however, mean that we will normally have a slightly higher voltage than the Earth, and any increase in that level can disturb the body. The stronger the field in which we find ourselves and the more readily we pick up such radiations, the higher the voltage that will be produced in our bodies. So if we can measure the voltage we will have an indication of both how strong the field is, and how much of it we are picking up. Why spend a lot of money on a sophisticated meter, when if you follow these simple instructions, you can use your own body to amplify a simple DIY meter, rather like a water diviner does with his rods?

In essence, all you need is a sensitive AC voltmeter (one with a 1 or 2 volts range scale is ideal and need not cost a lot) with one terminal connected to earth and the other to a probe held in the hand. (fig.5) It is important that the meter has a high enough internal resistance — look for one that has 10,000 or 20,000 ohms per volt. The most reliable and convenient earth will generally be the earth pin on a mains plug, by means of a long enough flexible wire to allow movement over a reasonable area. (NOTE: Do be sure that you connect the wire to the earth [ground] connector. If in any doubt, get an electrician or someone who knows about electricity to connect it for you.) The other wire should be connected to a piece of metal tube about half an inch or more in diameter and a few inches long (a scrap piece of copper pip-ing will do and you may be able to beg this from a friendly plumber). Do ensure that there is a good connection by cleaning the pipe with a file, sandpaper or wire wool. If you cannot solder the wire to it, then bare a good length, wind it tightly several times around the cleaned pipe and tape it firmly in place.

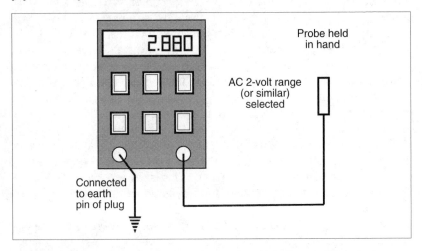

Fig. 5: Using a voltmeter to measure voltages included in the body

Equipped with such a meter, you only need to move around the room and other parts of the house holding the hand electrode and observing changes in the readings. As a test, stand over the wire connected to the mains earth (ground). The meter reading should rise - it may need a little practice and experimentation. The actual voltages recorded are not particularly significant, and will, in any case, vary from one meter to another even when used by the same subject in the same room, due to the different electrical characteristics of the meters. The deviation of the reading from the background field, not the actual reading shown, is relevant. (If you stand on a wire, it is likely to affect your reading. It just needs practice and experimentation.) If the value rises markedly in a particular position (such as when the subject is on the bed), then this indicates a place where the body is reacting to a higher radiated field level.

If the readings are fairly uniform it should not be assumed that no hazard exists until the level has been checked in an area known to be relatively undisturbed. The ground floor is generally best for this purpose (not a kitchen or utility room of course!) provided all televisions, video recorders, etc., are unplugged or well out of range. Try several different locations, to get an idea of what is 'normal' for the particular house, subject and meter. If when you have done this, you find that the bedroom readings are also normal or only slightly higher then all is probably well. If not, you will need to take protective measures.

MUSCLE TESTING (KINESIOLOGY)

An alternative to using a meter is kinesiology (often referred to as muscle testing), which can also be used to test areas of geopathic stress.

Start off in an area which is free of geopathic stress and electro-stress. The subject should stand with the right arm (if the person is right handed), held out to one side, thumb extended at right angles and facing down. Tell the subject that you are going to take the little finger of your weakest hand, normally the left hand, and curl it round the top of the subject's hand. Now tell the subject to push upwards against the pressure of your hand as hard as as possible. (S)he should usually be able to resist your pressure easily. Then try in another area, preferably one which has already been shown to have a stress problem. The difference in ability to resist pressure can be quite startling.

This is kinesiology and, provided you try not to cheat by assuming that you know the worst areas and applying extra pressure when you expect a positive response, it can be surprisingly effective and accurate if no other means of assessment is available.

DEALING WITH PROBLEMS

Whichever method you use, you will now have a better idea of how to locate 'hot spots' in a bedroom. As well as problems caused by bedroom equipment, old mains cables with porous rubber insulation behind a wall may give rise to high fields which can be transmitted along structures by wooden beams. Another source of trouble is often rising damp. Even if the wall is now dry, the mineral salts that have soaked into the plaster can still carry an electrical current.

What you do next depends on where the problems are. If the bed stands in a problem area, the first option to consider is moving it to a better spot in the room. The difficulty in most bedrooms is lack of space to move far enough to get the sleeper out of the troubled area. Very often the whole room will give high readings.

If the bed cannot be moved sufficiently, you will need to consider one or more of the protective methods which are described later. Before deciding which one to use, you must find out just where the problem fields originate. In general terms, you need to decide whether the fields come from inside the home, that is, from the wiring and appliances in the house, or if the principal source is outside, for instance a high-voltage power line, a factory, an electrified railway, or most often, neighbouring dwellings. A detached house is rarely affected by fields from the neighbours, but many semi-detached or terraced houses are. Those living in apartments are even more at risk as problems may exist above and below as well as to the side.

The quickest way to check on this is to isolate the mains supply to the house, by turning off the main supply switch at the fuse board, and then testing the problem areas again. If the situation is now acceptable, then internally-produced fields are the key consideration and demand switches, earthed conduits and protective undersheets are all worth considering. If the indications are still bad, then isolating your own wiring will not be enough, and since you can rarely do anything to remove external sources, the only alternative to moving house is shielding the bed, most easily with a protective undersheet.

If affected areas of the house are used a lot during the day, and you find that isolating the mains produces an improved but still less than ideal situation, installing demand switches and conduits may be worthwhile as this will give a generally better daytime environment. At night, you will still be wise to opt for the greater protection of an undersheet.

All of these methods of protection are discussed in more detail in Chapter 10.

NOTES
1. Wertheimer, N. and Leeper, E., *Bioelectromagnetics* 7 (1986); p.13.
2. Coghill, R., *All Fall Down*: Coghill Research Laboratories; (1992); p.6ff.

CHAPTER 5

AROUND THE HOUSE

The previous chapter concentrated on the electrical problems of the bedroom, but that does not mean you should ignore the rest of the house, particularly if you spend a lot of time at home or have young children.

As Table 3 shows p.29, while much of the apparatus we use at home does not produce very powerful fields, it is clear that many common appliances can expose us to magnetic fields of more than 1 milli-Gauss (100 nanoTesla) when we are at a normal distance from them. This field strength has become a fairly widely accepted 'safe' level for prolonged exposure; it is what we experience when at home or at work. Some equipment produces very much stronger fields (for instance electric razors or hair dryers), but as the user will not normally be exposed for more than a few minutes a day, the dose of electro-magnetic radiation is small.

Some people may still worry that regular use of an electric razor could cause a small but statistically significant increase in the chance of developing skin cancers, and similar thoughts arise with some other devices. If this is a concern, then perhaps we need to question whether there is an acceptable substitute (e.g. shaving soap and razor blade) with no risk of electro-stress. If we are honest we have to admit that a lot of electrical gadgets are not really necessary (particularly obvious examples are electric carving knives or toothbrushes) and sometimes they are not even much more convenient than the manual alternative. Not only will discarding such unnecessary items reduce our electro-stress levels, it will also reduce power consumption (good for our electricity bills and even better for the environment). If we resist electrical gimmicks that come our way in the future, we will also contain overall household expenditure.

A dramatic example is the remote control television. No-one (unless they are disabled, bed-ridden or infirm) can claim that they need one of these. It is a monument to laziness! Its potential for causing electro-stress is high, since the whole point of such a set is that it is never turned off — it is always either on standby or in use. A television gives off a strong field, but provided you watch TV in moderation, sit at a safe distance from it and turn it off when it is not in use, you should not be too strongly affected. If a remote control set is in a place where you spend much time, like the kitchen, the living room or the bedroom, and where you may often be quite close to it, the total electro-stress dose is likely to be very high.

Even worse, in many ways, it has been calculated that the remote control sets in a single country require a whole power station to be run just to provide their standby current! There is no doubt that if every-one questioned whether they bought and used electrical devices because they really needed them or just because they were fashionable, prestigious or fun, then our whole environment could be improved.

It is not even safe to assume that your ordinary television without a remote control is off when you think it is. A great many sets remain live, giving off surprisingly powerful fields even when they are switched off. Fields generated by such a set located on the ground floor can often (in my experience) still be at a high enough level in the bedroom on the floor above to cause sleep disturbance. To be on the safe side, any televisions should be unplugged, not just switched off when not in use.

LIVING WITH ELECTRICITY

Accepting all of this, few of us would want to regress to a world totally without electricity, and this is certainly not on the cards. The real need is to understand the true nature of the electrical devices in our homes (which may be hazardous and which not) so that we may be able to make sensible decisions about them.

The possible problems with televisions are similar to those of com-puter monitors, with the exception of the different distances generally involved. Someone watching television even for several hours at a time, but sitting at a sensible distance (10 or 12ft, or 3 to 4m for a typical domestic set) is not likely to suffer a very high electromagnetic dose. The situation can be very different with young children, who always seem to want to get close to anything, and the deaf, who tend to get close to avoid inconveniencing everyone else in the room. They are particularly likely to suffer from electro-stress.

Children are particularly sensitive to electromagnetic radiation, as they are to many other environmental hazards, and will react long before an adult. Wise parents will try to limit viewing even at 'correct' distances. Perhaps without realising it, most people have seen some effects of electro-stress when children become tense, over-stimulated and aggressive after a long session in front of the box, even watching something as innocuous as story-time or a soap opera!

Apart from changing the viewing position and rationing (or banning) it and always unplugging sets when not in use, there is little else one can do about television at present. Low radiation sets are promised, but are not widely available. When they are common in the High Street they will, like low-radiation computer monitors, offer at least a partial solution.

Video recorders can also emit strong fields when the power is on, which it usually will be if you regularly set yours to record programmes when you are out or asleep. As with televisions, the only practical advice is to unplug your video when it is not in use (you will need to reset the clock when you turn it back on, but there is a price for everything!).

MICROWAVE OVENS

In the kitchen, the fields from an ordinary electric oven fall off rapidly with distance and little effect will be evident from about 3ft. Food mixers, blenders and other hand-held equipment can give a high reading, but as they are normally only used for short periods, the resulting dose need not concern us too much. In general, only the person who spends most of every day cooking in an all-electric kitchen or who is particularly electrically sensitive, is likely to have anything to worry about.

There is one exception to this: the microwave oven. Normal ovens use radiant electric elements to produce heat that then passes to the food by conduction and convection, as with any other traditional fuel. A microwave oven employs a device called a magnetron which produces strong magnetic fields with very short wavelengths (high frequency). These agitate the molecules in the food at very high speed. It is this that produces enough energy in the food to cause it to heat up. The obvious hazard is that anything suitable that the microwaves can reach (including the cook) will also be heated up. This is why it is particularly important to be sure that a microwave oven is properly shielded. They are of course designed with this in mind and the walls, the door and the window with its inset metal mesh all absorb and block microwaves, so that they are almost all kept within the oven. Because it is never possible to shield anything completely, the continuing debate is exactly how much energy may 'safely' be allowed to escape.

The official view is that the emissions from ovens on the market are all below the safe level, but this begs two questions: firstly, different countries have very different ideas about what level is safe. Their standards keep on changing. Secondly, whatever the emission levels may be when the ovens leave the factory, it is impossible to control what happens to them after that. If door seals become dirty, or if the door or the hinges are distorted, microwave emissions will probably rise, but, as these are not visible there is no ready way for the user to know about this.

Some years ago a study in Germany of 101 ovens in domestic use illustrated both of these points very well. Almost all of the ovens were emitting more than the makers' design quota, but only one was over the then current German limit. However, every single oven would have failed to meet the standards in force in the U.S.S.R. at the time. The crucial, but (of course) unanswered, question was whose safety limit was correct.

Britain tends to have fairly relaxed standards. Although any supplier should be able to test an oven, very few people have such checks carried out. All in all, the situation does seem to suggest grounds for concern; the more so since microwave radiation has been linked with tumours of various types and genetic damage.

Fresh concerns have been highlighted by some recent research into the effects of exposure to microwave radiation on the DNA in rat brains[1]. After as little as two hours' exposure to microwaves *at precisely the frequency used in most microwave ovens* there was a 20% increase in breaks in the DNA strands in the animals' brains. These breaks persisted for several hours after the experiment and one question is clearly whether such damage would become permanent after repeated exposure. Worse still, these experiments were conducted at a power level which falls within the safety guidelines current in Britain and some other countries.

Quite apart from this, even a microwave oven in perfect condition will emit extremely strong low frequency magnetic fields while it is operating (well over the 1mG limit at a considerable distance). The potential electro-stress level is very high. Again, the concept of dose is important. Most households run the microwave oven only for short periods daily, particularly if it is used mainly for reheating ready meals rather than cooking from scratch. If this is so, the total dose received is probably not worth worrying about. The situation is very different for someone who works in a pub or restaurant using a microwave oven for long periods or even for someone who regularly uses their domestic microwave oven to cook meals from raw ingredients. In such cases, excessive exposure is quite a possibility.

If you feel you need to use a microwave at home, the advice must be to have it checked regularly for microwave leakage and to use it as little as possible anyway. It can produce electro-stress even when working correctly.

The difference in attitude to the use of gas for cooking and the use of microwave ovens is remarkable. When Britain changed over from town gas (produced from coal) to natural gas from the North Sea, there was great concern over the fact that natural gas had little or no odour and so leaks would not be so rapidly apparent. To overcome this, an additive with a strong smell was introduced into the supply. This was obviously a wise precaution and has doubtless saved some lives. Why then is there apparently no concern about shielding microwave ovens? No-one seriously questions the fact that regular exposure to excess microwave radiation leaking from a faulty oven will be injurious to health. It is even harder to detect than odourless gas which, at least, may make a noise as it escapes. Yet not only are ovens not fitted or supplied with detectors (which would be cheap if produced in such bulk), but the public are left in ignorance of the need for checks. These are really desirable not just once a year, but weekly or even continuously. Even if someone does know of the risks they will not find it very easy to buy a meter.

There is also the question of how microwave cooking affects the food produced. Does the process bring about electrical disturbances at the molecular level which alter the nature of the food in a permanent and potentially harmful way? Opinions vary, though the findings of the presence of higher levels of free radicals in some microwave cooked food suggest cause for concern (see Chapter 8 p.67).

Many dowsers and others claim that the food deteriorates, arguing that this is only logical if you consider that exposure of living beings to microwave radiation is known to cause tumours to develop. Some people find food cooked in this way to be less digestible than that produced by older methods. Conventionally trained nutritionists will tell you that, on the contrary, the briefer cooking time must mean that heat sensitive nutrients are less damaged, so the result must be better for us. Oldfield and Coghill describe the results of Kirlian photography which seems to show that microwave cooked food, while not the best, was better than that cooked in some conventional ways.[2] Pending a more definitive study it is a matter of weighing the pros and cons and making a personal choice. (For more about microwaves themselves, refer to Chapter 8)

ELECTRIC HEATING

Many houses still depend on electric storage heaters. These turn on at periods when electricity is cheapest and the heat generated by the electrical elements is stored in special thermal bricks contained in the case. This heat can then be released slowly during the daytime, maintaining a level of background heat in the dwelling. It is unfortunate that the main period of cheap rate electricity is during the night so the fields from these heaters (which can be quite high) are being generated at the very time when people are asleep and at their most vulnerable.

Another popular form of electric heating that is becoming popular in North America and Europe is underfloor or ceiling heating. This uses the same principle as an electric blanket with a criss-cross of wires used to generate the necessary warmth. While very efficient from a thermal point of view, these arrangements can give out significant fields (as much as 10mG from ceiling heating as shown in Table 4, p.27). Since this is generated both day and night, anyone living in a building with such heating will almost certainly suffer long-term exposure to a field level that is well above the advisable threshold limit of 3mG.

Skirting heaters are a type of electrical convection heater looking like a large skirting board. Again, their attraction lies in thermal efficiency. You will see from Table 3 (p.29) that the field levels are not particularly high once you are a few feet away from the heaters. The problem is that as they are typically fitted all around the walls the heaters and their associated wiring will produce a day long effect similar to a ring circuit for anyone spending time near them.

PHONES, HEADPHONES AND COMPUTERS

Telephones can also cause us problems because of the powerful magnets used in the ear-piece and microphone. The field strength applied to the brain when you hold a handset to your ear is several hundreds of gauss; so if you spend a lot of time on the phone you will receive a high dose of electromagnetic radiation. Indeed some people do notice that they become very stressed, tired or tense if they use the phone a lot, even if the calls themselves are pleasant and enjoyable.

For every executive or salesmen with a cell-phone there seem to be several young people plugged into the earpieces of a stereo cassette player! Quite apart from the proven risk to their hearing of the high volumes which they seem to find necessary for enjoyment of their music, they are also exposed to binaural magnetic fields for hours at a time. The field strengths are less than those of telephones, but the total electromagnetic dose received by a typical user may well be higher.

Something else found in many modern homes that can cause electrostress is the personal computer. Exactly the same considerations apply as with the commercial units, which are discussed in Chapter 7. You should pay particular attention to the comments about safe distances and fixed keyboards (much more common on home computers — especially those for games). It is particularly vital that you should consider the much higher vulnerability of children to electro-stress if they are using a personal computer a lot.

These special cases aside, it is the *total* electromagnetic environment that needs to be evaluated in the home. The location of mains cables, particularly those serving the oven, immersion heater and electric shower and any others that carry heavy currents, should be considered. The area close to the mains distribution board and consumer unit (fuse box), may also be suspect. Do not neglect the bedroom immediately above this point. In many houses the distribution board is on a wall vertically below a bedroom and it is uncanny how many times I have found that the person sleeping there has the head of their bed up against that very wall! If, as often happens, that person also has a sleep problem, then moving the bed is a high priority. In the end, if you are worried there is no substitute for an electromagnetic survey of the house. You can get a very good idea of the situation by testing it yourself using the methods described for bedrooms in Chapter 4. Alternatively you may want to find someone to carry out a professional assessment.

Because the electrical supply will be required all day, demand switches (see Chapter 9) are not likely to help and shielding is difficult, although installing earthed conduits around problem cables will help if there are severe problems in particular areas. Don't forget, however, that people do not tend to stay in areas of high radiation for long periods. But, if a survey shows that your favourite armchair is in a bad place, you should clearly move it.

LIGHTING

The way in which we light our homes can also significantly affect the overall electromagnetic environment. The type and layout of the wiring supplying the lights is clearly important, but this subject is dealt with elsewhere. What is also clear, if you look again at Table 4 (p.38), is that the type of lighting chosen can have a very significant effect.

Conventional incandescent light bulbs (simply a hot wire glowing brightly in a vacuum) are definitely the safest choice, as they produce very small fields. When you are more than a few inches from them the effect will be negligible. Incandescent bulbs are usually available with clear or 'pearl' glass and there are also some so-called 'daylight' bulbs which are the same rounded shape but which use different colours in the glass to change the light produced to something nearer to sunlight. Some sorts of strip lights (long, straight and tubular in shape, but only a foot or so long) used in such places as over bathroom mirrors and under kitchen wall units are also incandescent and the same general comments apply. If you have any doubts, an incandescent light always has two characteristics: you can usually see the brightly glowing wire inside when it is turned on and (provided it is not attached to a dimmer switch) it lights up instantly with no flickering or delay. It will also get hot very rapidly.

Fluorescent lights are most familiar to us as the tubes very widely used for factories, offices and shops, but they are quite often to be found at home, particularly in kitchens and bathrooms. They work quite differently from incandescent bulbs, using an electrical discharge to cause a special coating on the inside of the tube to glow. There is a slight delay and usually a typical flickering when these lights are switched on. Although they are usually long straight tubes several feet long you can also obtain circular ones for domestic use.

Fluorescent tubes are popular for a number of reasons that outweigh their higher initial cost. They last longer (6000 hours or more as opposed to 1000 hours for a light bulb). They consume less electricity for a given light output and finally, the type of light that they give out can be tailored for particular uses. While some of these are purely cosmetic, such as the pink types used by some butchers to make their meat look more appetising, there are also 'daylight' types producing different colour spectra that are said to be better to work under for prolonged periods.

Despite the claims which are made, many people find working under fluorescent lights to be unpleasant, leading to excessive fatigue, eye strain and headaches. Dr.John Ott, an American scientist who has studied the effects of different types of light and illumination sources on people is of the firm opinion that there is a cause and effect relationship between bad behaviour in school classrooms and illumination by fluorescent tubes.

There are reasons why this may be so. As Table 4 (p.38) shows, a fluorescent tube in the ceiling (typically 60 to 80 watts output) will have a much greater magnetic field effect on you than the 1mG limit of an ordinary light bulb.

Another factor concerns the output of positive ions (see later and the glossary). Most electrical apparatus tends to ionise the air around it with a positive charge and positive ions have a generally de-energising effect on people exposed to them. Fluorescent fittings are unfortunately very good at producing such ions.

You may have heard about so-called 'full-spectrum' lights. These are quite different from 'daylight' fluorescent tubes. Firstly, the tube (which is fatter than even the older type of conventional tube) has a unique coating which does give a light output remarkably close to full sunlight. It is so close that it can help people suffering from SAD (seasonal affective disorder). This is a severe depressive condition that badly affects some people in the winter months and has been linked to deprivation of sunlight. Sufferers have been successfully treated simply by sitting in front of a bank of these tubes for an hour or two every day. Secondly, they operate at a much higher frequency than a standard tube (because of this some need their own fittings and cannot simply be plugged in to your existing equipment). This frequency change appears to overcome the problems associated with the sub-perceptual flicker that badly affects some people. By contrast conventional daylight tubes are only normal fluorescent lights with a better colour rendition than the standard types.

Finally you should know about the latest energy-saving lights, designed to fit a standard light fitting. While they do indeed consume very little power, they are in fact miniature fluorescent tubes and so all the comments on their larger cousins also apply to them. If you have any doubts about identification, they are generally quite bulky and heavy — some are cylindrical, some are made of several thin tubes side by side. They will also flicker slightly on lighting, just like a large tube. Obviously everything said about full-size tubes applies to them as well. Since they are quite likely to be used in table lamps, reading lamps and so on, there is a higher risk of getting undesirably close to them and they may cause even more problems.

NOTES

1. Reported in *Electromagnetics & VDU News* 1995, vol.6, nos.1-2.
2. Oldfield, H. & Coghill, R., *Dark Side of the Brain*: Element Books (1988).

CHAPTER 6

POWER LINES

Powerful electromagnetic fields exist under overhead power lines. The cables carried on pylons across the countryside often have potentials of four hundred thousand volts or more. If you stand under such a line you will often be able to hear a rhythmic humming. In damp weather you can hear the crackling as some of the electricity discharges into the atmosphere.

Under the more powerful lines the fields will light up a fluorescent tube when someone stands underneath the cables holding one end of the tube. (*Warning*: This is a potentially dangerous trick, so you should **not** try it yourself!). At least one individual is on record who remembered enough school science to erect a cable strung between two poles under a power line near his home, connected the ends to his household supply and got free power until the authorities caught up with him and sued him for stealing electricity! You do not need physical connections to extract power from an electrical field.

The person with the fluorescent tube standing under the power line also had electrical currents and voltages induced in his body. This happens because the blood and other body fluids conduct electricity and, as with any conductor in a moving electric field, a current will be produced in the body. You have seen how even the much lower voltages of mains cables at home will produce this phenomenon and you can demonstrate the effect using an earthed voltmeter in the way described in the last chapter. Obviously the effect will be much bigger directly under a pylon.

You can alarmingly demonstrate this induction effect by parking a vehicle (the larger the better) under a power line. High static charges will build up in the metal body and because of the rubber tyres will only slowly be discharged to earth. A large spark will be produced if you reach out to touch the van.

Despite these obvious and measurable effects, the official position of the electric power companies has always been that, party tricks excepted, there is no possibility that even long-term exposure to high strength 50 or 60Hz electromagnetic fields can have injurious effects on health.

However, too many people who live in houses under or near power lines complain of a variety of symptoms without apparent cause for such assurances to be accepted without question. Some feel perpetually lacking in energy. In worse cases, they may feel nauseous or dizzy. The long-term effects remain to be assessed, but when we remember the findings of Nancy Wertheimer there appears to be at least a possibility of a link with cancer and there is current litigation in both Britain and the USA against power transmission companies which, if successful, will result in enormous damages being paid to affected families.

LIVING BENEATH POWER LINES

Probably the most famous mass example of illness caused by fields from power lines is that of the English (Gloucestershire) village of Fishpond, where many of the residents suffered from similar symptoms over a long period. The village had the misfortune to be effectively surrounded by several high-tension power lines, but a clear connection with the villagers' health was not made until the power line voltages were greatly increased. No-one in the village knew of this, but the incidence and severity of the symptoms increased dramatically with some people even blacking out. Measurements were taken in the village of the magnetic field strengths in the homes of those affected. While some of the houses had quite high field levels, the houses of other people living further away from the lines, but still showing symptoms had magnetic fields of as little as 1mG.

Another case has been reported from the village of Dalmally in Argyll, Scotland, where 275kV power cables pass over a council house estate, the police station, post office and within 100 metres of the school. In the estate of thirty-six houses, eight people died from cancer over a five year period, and a further three residents of the tiny village died from motor neurone disease. The council built the houses around the existing pylons and so close to them that engineers had to cut back small trees and shrubs in one garden to avoid current earthing through them. Thunderstorms caused especial havoc in that same garden, with sparks flashing to earth, terrifying dogs and the owner, who at the time of writing is confined to a wheelchair, suffering from a severe unspecified myalgic illness.

When the houses were built in 1977 no-one realised the connection between high-tension cables and illness, but even so, the buzzing and crackling from the cables, even on a dry day, is disconcerting. The incongruity of such a massive high-tension pylon in a crowded road is

Living in electrical fields in Dalmally, Scotland.

further highlighted when you look around at the wild Highland scenery, as the nearest hamlet is 18 kilometres away! It may be that the power lines are only partly to blame in this case, as David Cowan found when he investigated a case of M.E. about 150 metres from the lines. A stream runs down the back of the village and at least one line of geopathic energy passes under the affected house, causing unhealthy spirals (see Chapter 15).

Many people exposed to high voltage fields from power lines suffer the types of stress-related complaints we have discussed earlier. Some develop even more severe symptoms of stress, leading to depression or even a suicidal frame of mind, as was shown by the research of Dr.Perry and Dr.Dowson referred to in Chapter 1. There are those whose asthma and other allergic reactions can be linked to proximity to power lines. Doctors specialising in clinical ecology often find that exposure to electromagnetic fields provides a crucial trigger factor in the onset of attacks.

Animals can also suffer from adverse reactions to high-tension lines and their response helps to scotch any suggestion that what we are seeing in cases like those described is merely psychosomatic. A three part television series shown originally on British Channel 4 in 1984 and repeated since: "The Good, the Bad, and the Indefensible", illustrated the plight of an American farmer across whose land a massive power line was erected. Shortly after its installation, his hens started to lay 'scrambled' eggs, his cattle aborted and their milk production fell drastically. These results echoed laboratory experiments (referred to elsewhere) in which eggs and mice suffered ill effects when exposed to various types and strengths of magnetic and electrical fields.

THE CANCER CONNECTION

Mention was made in Chapter 1 of how the American researcher Nancy Wertheimer, during her research into childhood leukaemia 20 years ago, first identified the possibility of a link between power lines and cancer. It has to be said that when she started she had no thought of power supplies being involved. She was investigating the hypothesis that the answer lay in conventional environmental or infectious factors.

However, examination of her data eventually led her to the puzzling finding that children living in two houses nearest to the power poles that carried transformers (where the voltage was stepped down from 13kV to the American domestic 120 volts) showed the highest incidence of the disease. Further investigation showed that the crucial factor was not the proximity to the transformers and the fields that they radiated, but the current carried in the distribution lines. This in turn directly determined the strength of the magnetic field generated by them. Because of the configuration of the distribution system, the field strength fell off sharply immediately beyond the second house from the transformer.

Wertheimer, together with another researcher called Ed Leeper, carried out further detailed analysis of the results as well as some more epidemiological studies, all of which supported the idea of a link with magnetic field strengths. The results were finally published in 1979.

Several later investigations including work by Becker, Marino and Savitz in the U.S.A. and Tomenius in Sweden, have supported Wertheimer's findings. Until recently, the medical profession and the electric power companies have stubbornly refused to admit that electromagnetic fields could produce carcinogenic conditions and have generally rejected the research. There have, however, been some notable court cases in America that have, for example, led to the very expensive re-routing of a power line built near a school and to several claims for damages.

While it is clear that American researchers have led the way, notably with the New York State power lines project headed by Savitz, UK power companies have undertaken a number of research projects and it appears that some more serious investigation is now under way, even though this is still being done very discreetly and with, as yet, little evidence of a changed attitude. The official position remains stuck somewhere between scepticism and hostility, but there are signs that policies are quietly changing. Lofty dismissals of any suggestion that there may be a link are beginning to give way to more cautious reactions. New lines are being routed further away from dwellings than would previously have been the case, and enquiries from concerned members of the public are often treated with much more understanding and tolerance. Some recent planning decisions in the UK have gone against building near or under power lines.

None of this should lead anyone to conclude that the case is officially conceded. Nevertheless, over the last few years there has certainly been a marked change of attitude. A court case underway at the time of writing illustrates the increased level of public awareness which has doubtless contributed to such changes. The Studholmes, a family in the Manchester area in England, have finally been awarded Legal Aid to sue the local electricity company over the death of their 13-year old son Simon from leukaemia. The family home was near to 660kV power lines. He had slept with his head near to the electricity meter. An electricity sub-station was outside the room and two cables from it ran under the drive of the house. The same power lines run directly over a nearby pub, called 'The Sparking Clog' (producing fields 24 times the recommended Swedish limits) and the landlady complained of headaches and other illness which disappeared when she spent time away from the pub.[1]

Conversely, someone living 100 or 150ft from a high-tension power distribution line may not experience very strong fields. At these distances, the fields may often be only a few milli-gauss and thus much weaker than those from a hand-held domestic appliance, but it is again the question of length of exposure that is crucial. A hair dryer will commonly generate a 300-400mG magnetic field in the brain, but only for 5 minutes a few times a week. A power line (at 100 feet away, or more) may produce a more or less uniform field of barely 3mG in a house, but this will result in a magnetic 'dose' several times higher than that from the hair dryer for someone spending most of their time at home. Even more important, this level of background exposure will continue throughout the crucial sleeping hours.

Of course, a great many people live much closer to power lines than that. Indeed, if the line is a 400-600kV one carrying high currents, the fields produced by it will be many times higher than in our example.

AVOIDING THE PROBLEM

The only sensible advice for someone living close enough to a power line to be affected is to move, particularly if there are young children at home. Whether the symptoms felt are those that have been attributed to electro-stress or the much more worrying possibility of carcinogenic effects, even if they have not been officially 'proven', it is still wise to move.

Only constant public challenging of the electricity companies and the government will bring about a change of attitude. We may then see regulations compelling the siting of power lines routed away from existing residential areas and builders no longer able to put houses within high risk zones. Planning blight and legal action are both possible consequences of a change of policy, not to mention severe effects on the market value of houses already situated unfavourably. On the other hand, it seems to be increasingly clear that lives are at risk in the meantime.

A further concern is that electricity companies are known to be keen to develop super-conducting cables. The attraction is obvious as the resistance of any normal cable leads to significant loss of power. This is greater the higher the voltage carried and the further the distance the electricity travels. Not only would super-conductor cables cut these losses, they would also make it possible to carry even higher voltages. Unfortunately, this would mean yet more powerful fields surrounding the transmission lines, increasing the width of the blighted corridor along each line of pylons.

Safe corridors around lines in many countries are still a hope rather than fact. With so many dwellings and other buildings already far too close to lines anyway, the potential for many hundreds of Fishponds-like incidents (but of a much greater magnitude) is clear. Legislation of the type discussed later is a matter of extreme urgency.

NOTE

1. Foster, J., *The Independent* (22 January 1994); p.9.

Microwave transmission tower off the motorway in Wiltshire

CHAPTER 7

COMPUTERS

Today we have reached the point where we have computers small enough to be carried around and used on one's lap while travelling. They are many times more powerful than those which only two or three decades ago needed an entire air-conditioned room to house them. The use of computers at work and in the home has grown explosively. The extent of that growth would have seemed fanciful if predicted — even in 1970, when the electronic typewriter was just becoming standard equipment. Today, most small businesses and every large one would grind to a halt without the aid of these ubiquitous machines.

One consequence of such a short history and rapid change is that, although it is beyond question that computers produce a variety of strong electrical and magnetic fields, there is still much room for debate as to the precise effects on health of all the various emissions. On top of that, the speed of changes taking place in equipment specifications means that conclusions of epidemiological studies are likely to be out of date almost before the ink is dry on the paper.

Certain facts are undeniable. For instance, it is still the visual display unit (VDU) which produces most of the disturbing fields that radiate from a conventional office computer or work station with a conventional cathode ray tube monitor (a TV-like screen). Even that must be qualified because over the last few years there have been tremendous changes in monitors. In the late 1980s low-emission types were still a comparative rarity in the UK. Those available were made mainly by Scandinavian companies. The Swedes led the way in imposing very strict limits on the legally permissible levels of electrical, magnetic and static fields that monitors could produce. If you wanted a low radiation monitor in 1980 it took quite some finding, and you would certainly expect to pay a premium price.

The Swedish regulations were introduced following a number of studies of animals exposed to radiation from computers. For instance, in one set of experiments mice thus exposed had five times as many malformed offspring as those in control groups. As so often has been the case, the studies were generally dismissed for one reason or another, although they were duplicated later. However a subsequent survey (see also "Research" below) of a group of 1500 pregnant women in California showed that those using computers for more than twenty hours a week miscarried twice as frequently as did women in similar but non computer-based work. While the total number of birth defects was small enough to allow the statistical validity of the analysis to be questioned, the risk did seem to be of too high a significance to be ignored altogether.

Today low-emission monitors are tending to become standard equipment on all but the very cheapest makes of computer. That said, there is still no agreed international standard on what constitutes a 'safe' level of the various electromagnetic fields produced by VDUs; indeed there is still what looks like official indifference. For example, the recent EU (European Union) directive on use of computers in the workplace concentrates entirely on ergonomics and the effects of possible eyestrain and makes no mention at all of EMFs. It is therefore still worth looking at the hazards that have been ascribed to computers.

A normal screen produces high levels of both electrical and magnetic radiations at many frequencies (fig.6). First there are extremely low frequency (ELF) fields from around 15 to 50Hz. These are produced by the mains transformer and associated circuitry that controls the screen display, and are very powerfully 'spiked', which is to say there are very sharp peaks of power. There is also a wide range of radio-frequency fields and there are strong electrostatic fields, as high as 12 to 20kV. The potential hazards of all of these are on p.6. While these fields account for the bulk of the emissions from monitors, there is usually some microwave radiation. Most screens also emit some 'soft' X-rays and a small amount of gamma-radiation. However it has to be said that modern tubes produce what are probably negligible levels of these last three types of radiation.

One very important consideration is that much electromagnetic radiation emanates from the sides and rear of a VDU, so it is not only the operator who is at risk. In fact field levels can be much higher behind the computer than in front. This is important to remember when planning the layout of an office, and when considering protection.

RESEARCH

It is perhaps not surprising that a whole host of minor and major health problems have been ascribed to spending long hours in front of VDUs. The first questions were raised in the 1970s and '80s when Zaret's research suggested a causal link between working on VDUs and the

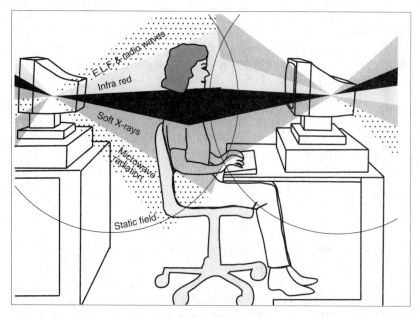

Fig 6: Radiations produced by a computer monitor are often stronger from the back (so don't sit behind one!)

incidence of eye tumours and cataracts.[1] Then, over the period from 1979 to 1982 a number of studies in Canada and the U.S.A. seemed to show that pregnant women working on computer terminals suffered an alarmingly high incidence of miscarriages and congenital deformities (Table 5). These conclusions were based on the health histories of relatively small groups of workers, and so have been criticised as alarmist, but they led in Toronto at least, to strict laws banning pregnant women from such work and severely restricting the number of hours per day which anyone could spend at a VDU. Not long afterwards the Swedish authorities also concluded that there was cause for concern and (as mentioned earlier) they introduced stringent legal limits on the levels of electrical, magnetic and static fields that any VDU manufactured or used in the country could emit.

It has to be said that the quality of VDUs has improved enormously since the date of these studies and electromagnetic emissions are far lower today. However, we still do not know what level, if any, may be considered safe. Whatever the truth eventually turns out to be, it does seem prudent for pregnant women to think carefully about whether any risk, even if not conclusively proven, is worth taking at such an important time of life. Since most thinking mothers-to-be are (understandably) almost obsessively careful about diet, use of drugs, exertion and general life-style factors it would seem reasonable to suggest cau-

Abnormality	No.
Deformities	10
Miscariages	38
Premature births	3
Respiratory Illness	2
Stillbirths	1
Total abnormalities	54
As % of total pregnancies	62.8%

Table 5: Abnormalities in 86 pregnancies of women working on VDUs (Canada & USA 1979-82)

tion about possible electromagnetic hazards such as this.

A major difficulty in researching this area has been that the introduction of computers tends to lead to many changes in working practices. It is not always clear whether it is these or the electromagnetic emissions that are to blame for some of the undoubted health problems suffered by many workers in modern offices. For instance, computer-based work is often very intensive, so that long hours can be spent without much movement away from the keyboard. Problems due to poor ergonomic design of chairs, desks and keyboards are thus highlighted. Modern keyboards needing only a very light touch make high typing speeds possible. With 'word wrap' on word processors (the machine automatically moving on to the next line when the current one is filled), there is not even the pause in rhythm and variation of movement that a mechanical typewriter required to push the carriage back to the start. Again, a complete document of several pages will often be prepared on screen before there is a break while a copy is printed.

REPETITIVE STRAIN INJURY (RSI)

A plausible case can thus be made that mental stresses, or neck, back and shoulder pains, or repetitive strain injury (RSI) an increasingly common affliction of the wrists and hands, or even some eye problems, may simply be due to considerations of a mechanical nature, or of working practices.

However, it seems unlikely that this is the whole story. Even the best designed office equipment does not appear to resolve the aches and pains associated with keyboard work. Nor are there records of typing pool workers showing signs of RSI when in the recent past they used electronic typewriters. These offered very similar 'touch' and potential for speed — and similarly intense workload.

Those who worked in the highly electromagnetic environment of the London stockbrokers' dealing rooms of the City of London, surrounded by banks of VDUs, were reputedly the first to develop M.E. (whence the derogatory name of 'yuppie flu'). The high stress levels in that environment are well documented. Many VDU operators complain of sore, dry eyes. There appears to be more to this than the simple glare from the screen, as anti-glare filters can improve the situation, but fail to cure the problem. It seems more likely that the cause is static electrical charges building up on the skin and eyes, transferred from the field surrounding the screen and resulting in charged dust particles adhering to the eyeballs. Certainly, installation of an earthed conductive screen produces noticeably better results than a simple nylon mesh.

There have also been reports of an abnormally high incidence of cataracts developing at around the age of thirty, not just in young women working with VDUs, but also in young male radar operators who use similar screens. The possibility of the electromagnetic emissions being to blame for this is supported by recent experiments which have shown that the radiations from a VDU will cause minute holes to develop in soft contact lenses, whether they are in the eye or not.

Mention has been made of the growing use of portable machines, both the so-called lap-top (which can still be fairly bulky) and also the smaller notebook devices. All of these use alternatives to cathode ray tubes (CRT) screens. There are various types of liquid crystal display (LCD) units which use a principle similar to the pocket calculator, but are much more sophisticated and can be monochrome or colour. The thin film transistor (TFT) gives a display quality equivalent to a good CRT, but these are even more expensive than the LCD models. While it would be a brave person who would claim any of these to be hazard free, they do produce less radiation and certainly not the powerful spiked fields from the transformers in the CRT monitors.

However, even the cheapest are significantly more expensive, so most offices continue to use conventional monitors and doubtless will do so for some time to come. It is also important to mention the obvious hazard of the lap-top model: if you do use one in your lap you will be likely to come into much closer contact with its electric fields than you would with a desk-top computer.

Of the remainder of the computer, the only part likely to emit noticeable fields is the hard disk drive which usually runs continuously while the computer is switched on and which will be part of almost all desk-top and portable machines. The electric motor that drives it will certainly produce measurable fields, but these are of a much lower intensity than from CRT monitors and will fall off rapidly even a foot or two away. They do not seem to have been the subject of any published studies.

PROTECTION

There are, on the market, one or two partially effective filters that can be mounted in front of a VDU to reduce some field levels to more acceptable values, cutting down glare at the same time. There are many cases recorded of good response to such protection, particularly in reduced operator stress and fatigue, as well as the virtual elimination of sore eyes.

However, you will recall how difficult it is to shield against magnetic fields and so no filter is going to offer much realistic protection against these. The electrical field component and the static field will be very greatly reduced and this is what must account for improved operator comfort. Whether any pregnant woman should consider that such a screen would offer adequate protection is a matter for individual decision. The question has to be whether any avoidable risk, however slight, is worth taking at such an important time of life.

Short of scrapping existing equipment and installing new low radiation monitors, screen filters appear to offer the best solution currently available. It must be stressed that simple nylon mesh screens will not offer significant protection. Many other types promising great improvements fail to live up to the claims made for them. While a suitable filter will give a measure of benefit to the operator, we should not forget the way that radiation is emitted in all directions. Computers should be located so that other people using the room will be at least 3-4ft. (1-1.25m) away from any part of the unit. It is also prudent to look at screening for the back of the unit, reducing the powerful spiked ELF fields. Again, there are one or two products on the market which seem helpful in this connection.

However good our precautions, until we know more about the risks, it is prudent to limit the number of hours per day an operator spends at a VDU. The latest EU legislation sets an upper limit of five hours daily at a stretch. It demands regular eye tests, although the concern is with the effects of optical glare and prolonged staring at the screen, rather than with electro-stress.

One final piece of advice is simple, but can make a lot of difference: it is to move the keyboard two or three feet from the screen. It is also sensible to avoid computers with keyboards attached to the monitor (though these are not so common nowadays). This one precaution can reduce the field levels for the operator by 30% or more.

While you will have gathered there are no entirely 'safe' distances, many researchers agree that sitting a minimum of three feet (1 metre) from the screen provides reasonable conditions for all but the most sensitive individuals. The typical magnetic field strength at this distance will be around 1mG and, together with the use of an effective screen filter of the type described (which tackles electrical and static fields), the operator will be reasonably well protected.

You may wish to refer to the list of suppliers at the end of this book if you want to know more about the availability of the products mentioned above.

NOTE
1.   Zaret, M., *Cataracts and Visual Display Units — Health Hazards of VDTs*, Pearce, R.G.(ed): Wiley, (1984).

CHAPTER 8

MICROWAVES

To most people, microwaves are associated with a quick and convenient form of cooking (and we took a brief look at microwave ovens on
p.45), but there is a lot more to them than that.

Microwave frequencies are high up in the electromagnetic spectrum, just below infra-red and visible light. There is a small amount of
natural microwave radiation, originating in the Sun, which normally
does not cause us any problems. In a way which must be becoming
familiar to you by now, it is not the naturally occuring variety, but the
massive intensity of man-made microwaves that poses the perceived
threats to our wellbeing.

With frequencies of between ten and a hundred thousand million
(10^{10} and 10^{11})Hz (which means that their wavelengths are measured
in centimetres or millimetres), microwaves have some rather special
properties. Provided there are no physical obstructions, such as buildings, a narrow, focused microwave beam can be transmitted over tens
of kilometres with relatively little loss of strength and without 'scatter-
ing' in the way which lower frequencies do. So a microwave beam
can be sent out from one tower and be accurately received on a dish
on a distant tower. This makes microwaves very useful as carriers of
information, and they are used for inland transmission of telecommunications, radio programmes and so on. They are also widely used for
air traffic control, and other civilian and military applications, including
surveillance (Early Warning) systems.

Amongst the earliest commercial microwave installations was a radio transmitter on the roof of the Empire State Building in New York in
the 1950s. The workers looking after the installation there discovered
some of the less pleasant properties of microwaves. They found that if
they put a hot-dog sausage on a stick in front of the transmitter dishes
it was rapidly heated. This is of course the principle behind microwave
ovens, which work because the high frequency oscillations agitate the
water molecules in the food very rapidly and the resultant friction produces heat. Unfortunately the workers went on to use the heating
effect in another way — to warm themselves on cold nights by stand-

ing in front of the dishes. At the time it no doubt seemed fun and a bit of a party trick. However, it all turned sour when, years later, most of the workers started to develop and (in many cases die from) a variety of cancers. It is now recognised that exposure to microwave radiation is potentially very dangerous and has to be carefully monitored and limited.

We have looked at the safety of microwave ovens as far as their electromagnetic emissions are concerned in Chapter 6, but what about the food? Most people would probably be surprised at any suggestion that food cooked in such an oven is not perfectly safe, except that it can go on 'cooking' for some minutes after leaving the oven with a consequent risk of burns to the mouth. However, people working in this area have long felt uneasy about the effect of subjecting our food to strong magnetic forces and have wondered whether there could be some permanent and potentially injurious changes to its very nature. Now there is research which has shown that food cooked in a microwave oven can have a significantly higher proportion of compounds called free radicals, compared to food cooked in the conventional way with radiant or convected heat — and free radicals are acknowledged to be potentially cancer causing.[1]

EAR PROBLEMS

It is quite a leap from cooking food to problems with the ears, but it appears that microwaves may have some other unwelcome effects. Tinnitus is a most unpleasant affliction, commonly called 'ringing in the ears' since the classic form is said by sufferers to be like eternally listening to a clanging bell. However the noise that the sufferer hears, often every waking hour of the day, can take an almost infinite variety of forms, from bells to buzzers and beyond. Classical tinnitus can be caused by many things, from physical damage to poor blood supply and most forms are considered to be effectively incurable.

Tinnitus is nothing new, mainly afflicting the middle-aged and elderly, but in recent years there have been increasingly numerous reports of a particular variant of the complaint, christened 'the hum' by many of its victims. It is always difficult to produce hard and fast proof of the origin of this phenomenon and there is as yet no certain explanation of the cause. However, many sufferers believe that its roots lie in the microwave radiations used for some types of communications and in particular by military installations designed for aircraft guidance and early warning systems.

This was originally suggested when it was noticed that the hum seemed to be reported more often in those parts of the UK with the greatest concentration of military airfields and defence installations and was also more common near civilian airports. There have also been anecdotal reports of a sudden upsurge in both the number of reported cases and the intensity of the noise experienced by sufferers during the late 1980s when, it is believed, the power of the UK's early warning system was stepped up. This is difficult if not impossible to prove as defence matters are all subject to the Official Secrets Act.

Menières Disease, which severely affects the sense of balance, also seems to be on the increase. We usually keep our balance thanks to the vestibular apparatus in the inner ear and in particular the cochlea (snail-like, fluid-filled coils). The tubes are lined with tiny hairs — the cilia — which move in the fluid and effectively amplify the effects of any movement. Quite why this mechanism should cease to function has yet to be adequately explained by medical science and there is no reliable treatment.

RESONANCE

A persuasive explanation of the way in which both of these afflictions could be caused has been put forward by a German researcher Volkrodt. He believes that the growing intensity of microwave radiations will cause the cilia in the cochlea to resonate. The cilia are short, only a few millimetres long, and this size is close to the wavelength of some microwaves commonly used for communications, especially by the military and emergency services.

To understand Volkrodt's theory, you will need to know a little about two basic principles of physics: resonance and harmonics. A steady musical note will tend to cause a wire or fibre of the appropriate length to vibrate in sympathy with it. This is termed resonance, which is exemplified by the middle C string on a piano vibrating when a tuning fork of the same note is struck and held near to it. However, if you try this yourself, you will find that the other C strings on the piano will also vibrate, although they will do so less strongly the further they are above or below middle C.

The reaction of these other notes is an illustration of the second principle: harmonics. The wavelength of the C above middle C is half that of middle C. Every C has a wavelength half that of the C below it and twice that of the C above. The same applies to all other notes, of course. When a tuning fork sounds middle C it will also produce harmonics which are notes with wavelengths twice, four times, etc, as well as one-half, one-quarter, and so on, of the main note. The harmonics are weaker the further they are from the main note but they will still have a similar effect, which is why more than one C string responds.

Finally, the frequencies at which two strings made of the same material resonate is related to their length; a string half the length will vibrate naturally at twice the frequency (half the wavelength) and so on.

Frequencies higher than those of audible sound can have similar effects; the tuning of a radio receiver or TV relies on similar principles of resonance and harmonics although achieved electrically.

Considering these facts, Volkrodt postulates that the cilia in the cochlea will tend to resonate with waves of the same length or a harmonic of that length. Because of their mass, small as it is, it is not physically possible for cilia to vibrate at microwave frequencies. There will also be the 'damping' effect of the fluid surrounding them. However they could vibrate at much lower harmonics, which could feasibly give rise to a low frequency hum. While there is, as yet, no experimental support for Volkrodt's theory no-one has so far produced anything else which gives a convincing explanation of the hum.

DYING FORESTS

Volkrodt also believes that microwaves provide a major clue to the dying of the conifer forests of Germany and other parts of central Europe as well as Scandinavia.[2] This serious problem (called Waldsterben in German) has generally been blamed on acid rain resulting from the sulphurous emissions from power stations and other industrial users of large amounts of fossil fuels. It is suggested that the acid pollution acts mainly as a result of concentrations building up in lakes and water-courses, although direct fall-out in rain will also have an effect.

Although the acid rain theory has been widely accepted it does not really explain all the facts. For instance, some of the worst affected areas are furthest from the industrial complexes said to be responsible for acid fumes. A particular case is that of the forests in central Germany along the line of the old East-West border. These are very badly affected, even though Germany has had a strict policy to control harmful emissions from both industrial and domestic sources for many years. While pollution carried on air currents from countries (such as the UK) with less rigorous controls could be part of the cause of the dying forests of Scandinavia, the pattern of prevailing winds suggests that this is less likely to be the case in Germany. Even more significantly, wind-borne effects would scarcely be likely to show up as a narrow band as along the border.

Volkrodt himself lives in Germany on a ridge in the mountains not far from the old East-West border. He has observed that trees he planted on the side of the ridge facing the east have always failed to grow well, whereas those on the western slope have flourished. Climatic factors, exposure to acid rain and other such variables are clearly not going to change much over a small area such as this.

However, a feature for many years of the German forests and those in Sweden and Finland was (and to a large extent is still) a high volume of microwave traffic since these areas were in the front line of the defence and surveillance systems of the Eastern and Western blocs. Volkrodt's land looked down into a valley which bristled with military equipment emitting microwave radiation. While his sickly trees received the full force of this radiation, the healthy ones were protected by the ridge. Volkrodt asserts that all of the worst affected forests are victims of microwaves and that this is the major factor causing their destruction.

His explanation of how this comes about again relies on the idea of resonance. The worst affected conifers are all of the type with relatively short needles, around 10mm long on average. As with the cilia in the ears, this corresponds closely with the typical wavelength of microwave broadcasts from military installations. The illustration (fig.7) shows there is a disquieting similarity between the appearance of a conifer twig and a typical aerial used to receive very short wave transmissions. This would make the twigs very efficient receivers of the defence transmissions.

The effect of resonance would, Volkrodt suggests, be similar to that used in a microwave oven. That is to say, the water molecules will tend to vibrate at high speed causing a heating or cooking effect. This certainly accords well with the scorched, dried appearance of branches on affected trees. Another fact that supports this theory is that it is usually the tops of the trees which are worst affected and the microwaves (which travel in straight, pencil-like beams) are transmitted just above the line of trees and other obstructions.

The microwave theory also explains better than acid rain why it is that deciduous trees in the forests are not so badly affected as conifers even though they are exposed to the same air, water and ground conditions. While it is true that these trees do not have needles, the tracery of veins which carry water to the leaves, once again resembles some types of aerial, so a similar 'receiver' mechanism could apply. Because broad-leaved trees do not grow as fast or as high as pines they will usually be well below the line of the microwave transmissions and of course they lose their leaves and so will be unable to receive the microwaves for half of every year. Taken together these facts could explain why deciduous trees are not suffering to anything like the same extent as conifers.

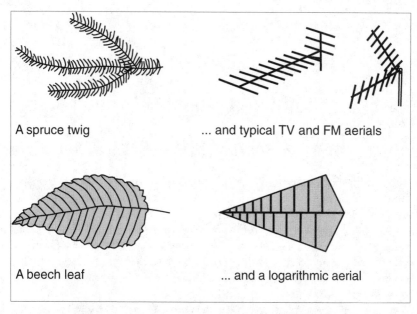

A spruce twig

... and typical TV and FM aerials

A beech leaf

... and a logarithmic aerial

Fig. 7: Tree leaves and needles as microwave receivers?

Finally, we are likely to hear more of the possible danger of micro-waves in relation to 'secret' defence installations. As this book went to press microwave radiations from the missile firing range and tracking installation on the Hebridean island of Benbecula were being consid-ered as the cause of a ten-fold increase in cancers, rather than the politically more acceptable scapegoat of caesium fallout from the 1986 Chernobyl nuclear disaster.

NOTES

1. Yashida, H. et al, "Effects of microwave cooking on the molecules of seeds of a species of pumpkin": *Nutri.Rep.Int.* 37 (1988), pp.259-268.
2. Volkrodt, Wetter, Boden, Mensch, 1988, vol 24, p.2453ff.

CHAPTER 9

SOME SOLUTIONS

Having looked at evidence of the potential perils of our electromagnetic world, we will now summarise some of the main methods of coping with many of the problems.

We will start by examining in more detail some precautions you can take and devices that you can use to reduce the level of unwanted electromagnetic fields which occur in your environment. You will find some suggestions for the sources of suitable equipment or services in the *'Suppliers'* section at the end of this book.

We will discuss some of the ways in which you can try to reduce the effect which unavoidable exposure may have on your body. Finally we will look at some of the ways in which power generators and other producers of large-volume electromagnetic radiations, such as telephone companies and the military could help (or be made to help) the situation.

SELF HELP

A theme which runs through this book is avoidance. There is still much debate about exactly what a 'safe' level of exposure to any given wavelength or waveform might be. Since we are still far from certain which frequencies may be the most hazardous, it seems logical to avoid tempting fate (without becoming paranoid). It makes sense to avoid using electrical equipment that, while sometimes helpful or novel, is not by any stretch of the imagination essential: for example the 'electrical gimmicks' you see advertised in newspapers and by mail order companies. We should also try to minimise use of the types of apparatus that give off strong fields or those to which we are likely to be exposed for long periods. We have to recognise that the convenience and efficiency of much electrical equipment is such that there will be considerable reluctance to do without it.

Where continued exposure is likely because of personal choice or conversely, lack of choice (perhaps because of your occupation), there are several possible ways of minimising the effects, some more complex than others. There is certainly quite a lot that can be done with some careful thinking about the problems and with little expenditure.

Firstly, you can do your best to keep as far as possible from the source. Remember that electromagnetic fields roughly obey the 'inverse square law'. This means that if you move twice as far away from the source, the effect on you will be reduced not to one half but to a quarter. As a result you can often achieve a real improvement by working, sitting or sleeping in a more favourable position, or by moving the source of the problem if this is possible. Increasing the distance is particularly important in the bedroom or any other place where you spend long periods. If your problems come from a power line in the garden, a factory down the road, or even the three computers in your neighbour's flat, there may be little alternative to moving house!

Secondly, you should try to select equipment producing low emissions. Though matters have improved, making an informed choice is not always easy as manufacturers are often reluctant or unable to disclose the information you need. For instance it is possible in theory to find lower radiation television sets, but they are still hard to identify and obtain. In contrast, low emission VDUs have become widespread in the last few years and are virtually standard equipment with leading computer makers although there is still no absolute definition of what qualifies as low emission. If possible, check whether the VDU conforms to the more stringent Swedish standards. The current standard (known as MPR2) came into force in 1991, replacing MPR1 which was introduced in 1987. However, any statement such as 'meets the Swedish standard' should be acceptable. Who knows, now that Sweden has joined the European Union, Europe may at last get an EU standard for VDU emissions to go with rules about ergonomics, working hours and so on.

The screens on lap-top and notebook computers employ quite different technology and can be counted as virtually emission free for all practical purposes provided they are used on a desk or table rather than on the lap. However, portable computers are significantly more expensive, especially those with high quality (TFT) colour screens. Domestic equipment can be more of a problem; the maker of a microwave oven will have a lot to tell you about turntables and power settings, but little to say about magnetic field emissions to the surrounding area (it has possibly never even been measured).

Thirdly, you should try to use equipment producing high emissions as sparingly as possible. Some of the main types to be wary of have been identified for you in this book. You may feel that you must use an electric hair dryer or razor, but you should keep the length of use and number of times it is used to a minimum. Generally, try to limit the length and degree of your exposure to high fields which you know exist. For instance, you do not need to stand right next to a microwave oven or many other appliances at home or at work while they are working.

Fourthly, ensure that equipment is kept in good working condition, and that known potential hazards like microwave ovens are regularly checked and serviced.

Finally, it is a good idea to unplug (not just switch off) apparatus not in use. Not only will all flexes give off electric fields night and day if this is not done, but in particular, electric blankets, televisions and some other equipment will often produce strong fields even when apparently turned off.

It should, by now, be obvious that it is possible to take all of these sensible precautions and still be left with significant problems, particularly at work where people generally have less control over their environment. The extent to which you are able to do anything about it other than change your job, may depend on the attitude of your employer. It is to be hoped that eventually awareness of these hazards will increase to the point at which Health and Safety regulations are as concerned with electromagnetic hazards as they are with toxic chemicals and falling objects.

DEMAND SWITCHES

Demand switches are ingenious devices that originated from Germany (where they are called Netzfreischalter) and can be installed next to or in the consumer unit (fuse box) on any domestic circuit. About the width of two mains fuses or miniature circuit breakers, a demand switch is simply wired in as shown in fig.8, a job that takes an electrician only a few minutes. It incorporates special electronics that continuously produce around 4 volts DC (direct current), and this is applied to the mains circuit. As DC is biologically friendly at low voltages it produces none of the fields which have been concerning us.

The purpose of this small voltage is to tell the switch as soon as anything connected to the circuit is turned on, as this will allow the DC current to flow. Until this happens, the demand switch remains in the 'off' position and so the whole circuit is disconnected from the mains and none of the usual disturbing AC fields will be generated from any of the mains cables, flexes, etc. However, as soon as any switch is turned on, the DC current is able to flow. This in turn causes a solenoid in the demand switch to operate, restoring mains electricity to the circuit in a fraction of a second. Conversely, a second or two after the last appliance on the circuit is turned off, the demand switch discon-

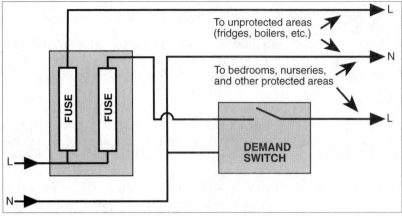

Fig.8: Demand switch

nects the mains at source, and the AC electromagnetic radiation ceases.

Such a device is obviously ideal at night, when it is possible to turn off all lights and other apparatus connected to the circuits supplying the bedroom area. The advantage over simply removing the fuses (apart from convenience!) is that should you awake while it is still dark, switching on any light will immediately restore normal power for as long as you need it.

In a typical house with a ring main or ring circuit, two demand switches are needed, one to control the ring mains serving the bedroom area, and one to control the lighting circuit. This assumes that all the lights are on one circuit, their cables passing below and above the bed to supply both floors. Occasionally, the lighting may be split into two circuits, in which case an extra demand switch may be necessary.

The situation is simpler in houses supplied by the spur system, as all that is then necessary is to insert a demand switch into the spur serving the sleeping area in question. This will generally isolate both power and lighting circuits. It is much easier in this case to identify and monitor the total supply to any given location.

Of course, such a system does mean that anything consuming power will need to be turned off at night (so no more mains clock radio!). There can be a problem if you have anything that has to be left switched on at night (for instance, boilers, immersion heaters, freezers — or home office equipment such as computers and fax machines etc.). Provided these are far enough away from the bedroom, are on a separate circuit and you can ensure that no cables connected to such circuits pass near to the bedroom — a minimum of 6-10ft (2-3m) should be sufficient (remember the inverse square law — you will probably be all right). Otherwise demand switches will be of no use to you. But it must also be noted that if a significant amount of the problem originates outside the building, a demand switch will be, at best, a partial solution.

Every case is different, and there is no space to go into all the possibilities here. However, demand switches can certainly offer a simple and effective answer in many cases where the night time environment is of concern.

There are one or two limitations to the use of these switches. For instance they are not triggered by fluorescent lights unless a simple adaptation to the light is carried out. Remember that this includes the new low-energy bulbs (which are effectively small fluorescent tubes). Nor can demand switches be used on circuits with dimmer controls. (Since dimmers and fluorescent tubes produce their own electromagnetic hazards, they are best avoided in any case as you have seen.)

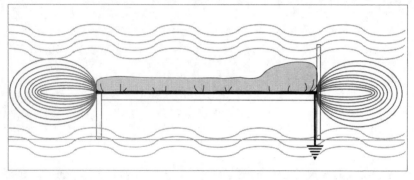

Fig 9: A protective undersheet grounds electromagnetic fields.

PROTECTIVE UNDERSHEETS

Another way to tackle the problem of the electrically polluted bedroom is to place an earthed protective undersheet under the mattress. Such a sheet is of particular value because it helps to shield the sleeper from all electromagnetic fields wherever they come from — indoors or out. A bed with a sheet is illustrated in fig.9 and you will see that radiations coming from above the bed are dealt with just as effectively as those which originate below. This is because the sheet provides an excellent earth, fields are attracted to it preferentially and are then discharged harmlessly to earth.

The action is demonstrated simply and convincingly using the earthed voltmeter method described earlier. A high induced voltage previously found when lying on the bed will be reduced to background level or less once a protective undersheet is in place. As the diagram indicates, the protected zone is in the form of a tunnel over the mattress. This can be demonstrated if the 'sleeper' sits up, when the reading will rise as the head and upper body leave the 'tunnel', increasing still further if the subject stands on the bed and returning to normal when standing beside the bed.

A typical undersheet is made from a thin aluminium film (anodised to prevent oxidation) bonded to a strong non-woven fabric sheet. A flexible wire bonded to the metallic sheet is connected to the earth pin of a suitable plug that is then placed in a convenient socket. The mains earth can normally be used for convenience and reliability, but other earths such as a pipe buried in the ground can be employed. There are circumstances where this is necessary for full effectiveness as discussed below. Adequate earthing of an undersheet is essential if it is to be effective. Simply placing a piece of foil under the bed will not provide reliable protection, nor is it easy to connect a wire effectively to ordinary aluminium foil.

Where electrical pollution from outside is a significant part of the problem, a protective undersheet under each bed may be an alternative to moving house. Of course, if the external source is a power line above the roof, you may not consider this an adequate safeguard.

Installing a protective undersheet provides a good example of just how aware we need to be today about the complications of even a simple task like arranging an earth connection. Not so long ago you could simply attach a wire to a bare water pipe or to the earth pin of a plug and be sure it would do the required job. However, that was in the days of old-fashioned earthing systems which typically consisted of a copper wire run from the house and connected to a piece of copper pipe that was buried a foot or two in the ground. From this comes the name 'earth' or in America 'ground' for the connection. These were not always too efficient, for instance if the ground the pipe was buried in dried out, or the wire was broken when someone dug the garden, a dangerous situation could arise.

Now most houses have an earth provided by the electricity company which runs along a return cable to a central earthing point. The only problem is that for technical reasons this cable typically carries unbalanced return currents and apparatus earthed to it will tend to radiate energies at mains and other frequencies. This is not usually a problem for small domestic equipment, but a large metallised sheet above which you sleep could easily produce in these circumstances, more disturbance than it removes.

This sort of earthing arrangement is becoming very common and checks show that the level of emissions from any large metal object (including such things as metal sink units or other kitchen equipment) can reach significant levels. So if you cannot have your installation professionally checked, the safest recommendation is that such sheets are earthed in the old-fashioned 'inefficient' way with a buried pipe to ensure a quiet night's sleep. Not so easy, but far safer.

SHIELDED CABLES

In parts of mainland Europe special shielded mains cables to reduce electrostress have been produced for some time. These have a metallic layer wound around the conductors underneath the insulation. You will by now realise that if this layer is earthed, all radiating mains electrical fields will be eliminated, as will a proportion of the magnetic fields.

Wiring regulations do vary widely from one country to another, so it is not generally possible simply to import cable for installation in your own home. However, similarly shielded cable (often made for installation in circuits serving fire alarms and other protective devices) is available in most countries, and it should be possible to identify a local supplier by contacting an electrical wholesaler or a professional electrician.

The alternative is to run the mains supply in conduits (metal tubes screwed together) which are earthed at intervals and this will achieve much the same effect, if not quite so conveniently. It is certainly worth thinking about if you are building a new house, but would not be as easy to install in an existing building.

GENERAL SHIELDING

In really bad cases of electromagnetic radiations coming from outside a building, a possible (though radical) protective measure is to line the walls facing the hazard with some sort of earthed conductive mesh. If the concern is with mains frequencies (for instance if there is a nearby pylon) then any normal mesh size will be effective as the wavelengths are extremely long. As you have learned earlier, screening will be effective mainly against the electrical component of the field so the measure is at best partial, but it may be the best that can be done. You will find in Table 3 (see page 29) the degree to which a number of common materials will shield against electrical and magnetic fields. You will see that while all of them will effectively block almost all of the electrical field, only 60cm (2 feet) of concrete will provide the similar protection against magnetic fields. These figures (by the way) are only for 50Hz (mains) fields. Radio and higher frequencies, having much shorter wavelengths, are even more difficult to deal with.

If a troublesome source is a radio transmitter then a very fine mesh will be needed and this will work only if any windows facing the transmitter are also shielded, which is not generally possible. Some time ago I saw a sample of a non-woven synthetic fibre randomly interspersed with metallic strands. This looked very promising, although I have not had the chance to test it in use for protection. It was originally developed to stop one form of industrial espionage, the reading of sensitive information on computers by picking up the radio-frequency broadcasts from their screens on receivers located nearby. Because of the random nature it was said to be effective over a wide frequency spectrum and because it was very thin, could be pasted to walls under normal wall coverings.

Another method which I have not tested — lining walls with the type of plasterboard that is backed with an aluminium foil layer (designed to minimise heat losses through walls) — should theoretically give a measure of protection from mains frequencies if properly earthed. However, earthing these boards effectively is difficult and it is known that if they are not earthed the foil can radiate large amounts of electropollution into the rooms. So on balance such wall lining is better avoided altogether.

If the source of concern is a local microwave transmitter (such as is used for communications links) then there really is little you can do. Because the wavelengths are so short, simply covering the walls and windows with a very fine mesh with a pitch of a millimetre or less would have little effect and that would be at best partial. Nothing short of lining the house with solid steel a centimetre or two thick or living in a deep cellar could be considered truly effective.

You can buy devices designed to be placed in affected areas of your house or office which are said either to disperse or block the intrusive radiations or else to enable those in the fields to resist their effects. In my experience you cannot test the effect with a meter or other mainstream scientific method, but those using muscle testing or dowsing claim that the results can be demonstrated.

PROTECTING YOUR BODY

Because there is no practical way in which you can exclude totally all hazardous electromagnetic fields from your environment. In any case, we still do not know for certain exactly which fields are dangerous — so it is only prudent to do what you can to protect yourselves from any ill effects resulting from unavoidable exposure.

I discussed earlier (Chapter 1) why the general level of stress which we experience is important in determining how we react to electrostress. As you may recall, I suggested a number of measures to help.

One of the key processes which leads on to cancerous conditions and other types of degeneration is the production of potentially dangerous molecules called 'free radicals' in the body. In Chapter 8 we saw that microwave cooking can produces higher levels of these in some foods and it may well be that other types of electromagnetic fields directly stimulate their production in the body. A result of this heightened awareness is the growing popularity of anti-oxidant mixtures of vitamins, herbs and other ingredients with properties known to help reverse the effects. These are certainly worth considering and as a bonus they are said to slow down the ageing process.

It is a medical truth that a healthy immune system is central to our bodies' fight against disease. It is only common sense that anything which can boost our immune system must help to protect us. As with anti-oxidants, a healthy diet rich in fresh fruit and vegetables is an important starting point, but there are various specialised food supplements and natural remedies which can also help. A nutritional consultant, naturopath or even a good health food shop should be able to give you advice in this connection.

There are also several of devices designed to be worn or carried with you which are claimed to increase the body's ability to resist the stressful effects of external fields, whether man-made or natural. Examples are Harmonisers, the Charged Card and Electronic Field Generators. It has to be said that there is little scientific evidence of their efficacy, but it is claimed that users' experience backs up the claims made for them. As most of them are not particularly expensive you may feel that they are worth trying, at least as a way of reducing stress levels.

CORPORATE AND GOVERNMENT ACTION

A question that is natural to ask is why government and science do not act to stem the increase in microwave towers, warn of the dangers of portable telephones, allow people to live under power lines or next to transforming stations?

It should be apparent to most that government is hardly impartial. Inevitably and increasingly it responds to the pressure of powerful special interests, like the electricity industry, the farming lobby, the pharmaceutical industry, and big business generally. Increasingly, universities are dependent on industry to fund research, and the poor consumer is left to discover the truth for him/herself, and to take appropriate action.

There are various steps, some of which we have touched on earlier, that could be taken to decrease electromagnetic hazards, but which are beyond the scope of individual action. They could only be achieved by voluntary codes of practice adhered to by power producers and equipment manufacturers, or by legislation. Realistically, only the latter means is likely to be successful at an international level.

Dealing with power distribution first, if the establishment of corridors along power lines within which the building of houses, factories or offices was banned, this would avoid a lot of future problems.

Another change that could bring benefits is the replacement of pylons by underground lines in built-up areas. While this does not eliminate all hazards (as you have read in Chapter 6), it could reduce levels of exposure by a useful amount. Against this must be set the fact that, since it is generally not obvious where such cables run, they are harder to avoid than pylons — and we do have the evidence of links with mental illness, even from underground cables. There is also the question whether such a move might unintentionally bring about unpredictable clashes or interactions with earth energy fields.

The number of broadcast communications transmissions (another major source of trouble) could be greatly reduced if wider use were made of fibre optic cables, sending the messages harmlessly underground instead of beaming them from mast to mast across the country. In Germany a programme to do just this has been under way for some years, but it is relatively little used in the USA and the UK, at least for long-range connections. This method is useless for police or other emergency broadcasts that need to be picked up by mobile receivers in vehicles, but a high proportion of microwave broadcasts is between fixed points.

Turning to domestic and commercial equipment, you have already read of some of the potential areas for improvement, such as the production of low-emission television sets and computer monitors or the provision of some easy, preferably automatic way of detecting microwave leakages. The consumer can do much to speed these improvements by creating a demand for them. Ask manufacturers and suppliers what is available and if nothing is, ask why not. Ask them about the field levels produced by their equipment — and if they cannot or will not — ask why not. Ask your MP or Congressman as well, and press for legislation to be framed. Do not be put off by being told that there is no demand or that the cost is prohibitive. You can create the demand and costs have a way of shrinking when there is no alternative, but to provide something!

THE FUTURE

Slowly but surely, public and other authorities are beginning to show more interest in this important subject. We need more research —

and that means funding — especially into the possible serious, even fatal, effects of chronic exposure to different types of electric field. There is a very urgent need for the results of exposure to microwave radiation, whether from ovens, from computers, radar or from communications to be investigated and for clear and responsible exposure limits to be set.

If you are convinced that a case has been made for the existence of less serious, but still distressing effects of ELF exposure such as sleep disturbance and rheumatism, then in the short term the protective measures discussed are available to you. In the longer term there is no substitute for the fundamental changes needed. We must all play our part if change is to be achieved speedily.

Truly the discovery of the means of production and transmission of electricity and our ingenuity in exploiting it has led to undreamed of complications. We must wake up to the perils before we may have done terrible damage to ourselves, to our environment and to future generations. The situation has never been more urgent.

CHAPTER 10

THE POSITIVE SIDE?

Until now, we have concentrated on the ways in which a wide variety of man-made energy fields may be harmful to us. Now let us look at some of the ways in which carefully chosen electromagnetic fields and electrical impulses are used with the intention of benefitting people.

In both orthodox and complementary medicine such electrical effects are used widely in diagnosis as well as treatment. While it is important to be aware of possible adverse side effects when using electrical interventions on the body, the general opinion is that in most cases the risk/benefit equation comes down firmly in favour of the benefits. It is very interesting to observe these positive uses of electromagnetic radiations if only because they provide yet more support for our proposition that the body is sensitive to the influence of even very weak fields.

DIRECTLY APPLIED CURRENT

Some relatively well known uses of directly applied electricity which benefit patients are:

TENS devices, in which a directly applied pulsed current is passed through an area of the body. These are used regularly in physiotherapy and by many dentists. The right sort of pulse will block pain signals from the nerves in the area of application. It is an effective and useful technique for the relief of pain, especially while the patient is recovering from an acute injury, although it is also used to control some chronic pains.

A similar device may be used to send a current through muscles causing them to contract and relax. This improves muscle tone without the need for exercise and has been used commercially for so-called slimming machines. It is unlikely to cause any weight loss but can improve the appearance by taking up the slack in surface muscles. A similar device was developed several years ago to help control involuntary urination in women. It can aid muscle tone in the pelvic floor.

A more violent, but very valuable use of the direct application of an electrical stimulus, is in defibrillators, used in hospitals and by the emergency services to restart the arrested heartbeat of a patient. At the other end of the scale, some acupuncturists use needle stimulators to heighten and accelerate the effects of their treatment, passing small pulsed currents between pairs of acupuncture needles that have been inserted into the patient.

MAGNETIC FIELDS

All the techniques mentioned so far are deemed on balance to benefit patients. However, some of the apparently healthy methods used in health care contain a hidden menace. We have already considered X-rays. Many people wonder whether a similar pattern is likely to develop in the case of MRI (magnetic resonance imaging). This highly sophisticated, if expensive, diagnostic tool has become widespread in hospitals over the last few years. It involves passing the patient through a very high intensity magnetic field of a particular type, so designed to change temporarily the alignment of the nuclei of the cells. When they return to their normal state the consequent energy release enables an image of the whole of the internal structure of the body to be obtained. This technique has considerable diagnostic advantages. Unlike X-rays, it makes it easy for the physician to examine soft tissue and in particular the brain and spinal column in detail.

The fields used are massive, indeed metal objects in near-by rooms can move when the machine is turned on. Although the length of exposure is relatively short, one has to wonder about the long term effects of so radical a disruption of the body's normal electromagnetic state. Of course we are assured that there are no possible harmful effects or, at worst, that any slight risk of disruption is greatly outweighed by the benefits of an accurate diagnosis. All this sounds reminiscent of what was said about X-rays 50 or more years ago and it is undoubtedly an area that needs to be watched with some care. There are certainly some doubts even in conventional medical circles about the possible ill effects of using MRI, the more so because patients are likely to be already unwell and in a weakened state when such scans are undertaken.

However, the potential risks of MRI are probably minor compared to those posed by CAT scans. This newer technique produces impressively detailed pictures of the interior of the body, but only by using X-ray doses some 30 times higher than a typical conventional X-ray. As even the latter (generally accepted as 'safe') are calculated by radiological experts to give rise in the long-term to around 1000 cases of cancer a year, the implications of CAT scans are of great concern.

Staying with the idea of relatively strong magnetic fields (though considerably weaker than in MRI) we come to the many forms of magnetic field therapy that are used, particularly by osteopaths, chiropractors and physiotherapists. The technical details of these devices vary greatly with little apparent agreement of the ideal frequency, strength and pulse pattern to be used. Nevertheless there is much clinical evidence that pulsed or alternating magnetic fields can have beneficial effects, including relaxation of tense muscles, stimulation of blood flow in affected parts of the body, reduction of inflammation and swelling, acceleration of wound healing and dispersal of bruises. Fields have been used with reported success to accelerate knitting of broken bones. Some even claim they stimulate underactive internal organs.

The size and cost of these units vary as widely as the fields they produce, ranging from large, clinic based machines to small hand held units designed for home use. On balance they seem to be safe, particularly when magnetic field therapy is used only over short periods for acute injury or pain. However, because of the wide variety of field patterns and strengths employed it is impossible to generalise with any certainty and this is undoubtedly an area that would benefit from further investigation.

For some reason the Scandinavian countries seem to have been particularly active in the development of a variety of rather more sophisticated magnetic therapy devices and Germany has also been involved. In these countries the beneficial effects of magnetic field therapies are claimed for a huge range of ailments, covering almost every aspect of human disease. There has been particular, if controversial, interest in the use of magnetic fields to treat a variety of different forms of cancer. In some cases dramatic cures are claimed, but although the anecdotal evidence sounds convincing, I can find no trace of any controlled studies.

In particular, devices using pulsed DC fields developed by Ivan Tröeng of Sweden were claimed to have produced positive results in many cases and the evidence certainly sounded convincing. However, I know of at least one doctor in England who acquired some of Tröeng's treatment coils and confessed to obtaining no consistent or particularly encouraging results with any of the patients he attempted to treat with them. In view of the epidemiological evidence linking some magnetic fields with tumours (discussed earlier) it would seem that this is an area to be approached with extreme caution. It would be prudent for anyone to avoid treating known cancer patients with any electromagnetic field therapies, at least without a full medical consultation and very rigorous monitoring.

STATIC FIELDS

Although a little outside the remit of this book it is worth adding a note about the specialised use of static magnetic fields, if only to support the idea that the body is indeed sensitive to very small magnetic influences. One particular form of acupuncture developed in Japan uses small magnets attached to the ends of the acupuncture needles or else applied separately to acupuncture points on the skin. I have seen this demonstrated and have no doubt that at the muscular level one or more tiny magnets with a field strength of only a few gauss can, when applied to the correct locations on the body, produce quite remarkable and instantaneous realignments of the skeletal system. I have seen a pelvis (tilted so that one leg appeared shorter than the other) immediately realigned once the magnets were applied. It is claimed by practitioners using this technique that the results can persist over a long period, even after the magnets have been removed.

Similarly, a colleague and I carried out some experiments several years ago in which we applied a rubber based magnetic strip with a field strength averaging only around 15 gauss to the necks of patients and used thermography to monitor the temperature distribution of their hands and feet. In every case circulation and temperatures improved within 10 to 15 minutes of application of the magnetic strip. Although the temperature would soon return to the starting value if the strip was then removed, there were indications that after the magnetic collar had been worn for a week or two the effect would persist for some time after removal. This suggested the possibility of achieving a more permanent physiological change. Clearly the remoteness of the point of application (the neck) to the point of measurement (hands and feet) ruled out any effect due simply to local insulation.

In what was probably our most spectacular case a patient with a severe congestive heart condition experienced a temperature rise in his toes of around $10°C$ within 15 minutes of the magnetic strip being applied to his neck. When he was checked again some two weeks later he reported not only much more comfortable extremities, but also that he had noticed an ability to take more exercise without breathlessness and discomfort, indicating a general improvement in his circulation. These examples, being concerned with static magnets rather than electromagnetic fields are somewhat of a side issue, but they do give an excellent example of just how sensitive we are to what we would normally consider to be insignificant magnetic field effects. However, if we remember Einstein's discovery that all matter is in constant vibration, then perhaps even to talk of the concept of a static field is inaccurate.

BIO-ENERGETIC DIAGNOSIS AND TREATMENT

There are many diagnostic and therapeutic devices used today which in one way or another owe their existence to the research and inventiveness of Dr.Reinhard Voll working in Germany in the 1940s and '50s. He took as his starting point acupuncture diagnosis which has been used for several thousand years in China, but which is now practised in most countries. In this technique the trained acupuncturist reads the pulse in the various acupuncture meridians. (This is not a pulse in the conventional Western sense). The meridians are energetic pathways through the body whose nature and purpose is as yet imperfectly understood and Dr.Voll reasoned that they must have electrical characteristics.

With the newly emerging electronic technology, one of the positive outcomes of the Second World War, he was able to develop measuring devices which could for the first time give some indication of the more subtle electrical fields of the body. There is not space here to go into the full development of the technique now commonly known as EAV (Electro-Acupuncture according to Voll). Suffice to say that he developed protocols which enabled someone trained in his techniques to determine the state of health of internal organs by taking electrical readings at the acupuncture points located at intervals along the acupuncture meridians.

This was impressive enough, but his second and perhaps most important breakthrough was the concept of remedy testing. When a homeopathic remedy appropriate to the patient's condition is brought near to the patient (without the patient actually taking it), a response can be measured in the form of altered readings on the relevant acupuncture points. Remarkable though this seems, it has been used clinically with great success for around 40 years now and has indeed been extended to testing a patient's sensitivity to allergens and other irritants.

The stock response from those who reject the technique has been to suggest that all readings must be the result of conscious or subconscious manipulation of the probe used by the doctor. This objection now appears to be overturned by some recent, but as yet unpublished experimental work. Means have been found of applying the probe to the acupuncture points in a totally standard way and also of avoiding any local damage of the skin at the acupuncture point. Trials have shown that not only is a consistent reading produced on any one point, but that a reproducible response to the same remedy is also obtained.

The only plausible explanation of this effect is that the body must indeed be responding to some extremely minute electromagnetic fields, far smaller than anything we have previously been considering in the book. These fields must result from some characteristic of the vibration of the molecules in the homeopathic preparation and are certainly well below the level at which any conventional scientific apparatus would be able to detect them.   Experiments conducted by Dr.Jean Monro with severely allergic patients are described in the book *Electromagnetic Man*.[1] In the most extreme cases nothing more than the introduction of a vial containing a homeopathic-like preparation into the same room as the patient was needed for the production of a clear reaction. To rule out psychosomatic effects Monro experimented with randomly bringing in vials of remedy and vials of pure water. The latter produced no reaction. In this area it appears we are truly working at the boundaries of scientific knowledge.

Homeopathy itself is a subject that still arouses strong feelings and the mechanism of which has still not been conclusively proven. However a report in *The Lancet* a few years ago surveyed over 200 experimental studies reported in the literature and concluded that on balance the case for the validity of homoeopathy was made.

ELECTROMAGNETIC TREATMENT

Amongst the many devices that have followed on from Voll's work is the 'Mora'. In addition to using Voll-like techniques to diagnose the patient's condition, the Mora has a specialised form of biofeedback device. This reads energetic information from the patient's body through electrodes and then analyses it electronically. Those parts of the signal that are considered to be beneficial are amplified and those parts that are harmful and produced by disease processes in the body are electronically inverted. This modified signal is then broadcast back into the patient through a special electrode. The theory is that the net effect will be to amplify the healthy processes in the patient's body and to counteract the disease processes. Hundreds of these devices are in daily use in Germany and elsewhere and the results certainly seem to indicate an effect. We are again dealing with quite small fields, well below those produced by domestic and industrial equipment.

Remedy testing is used in a number of devices including the Vega and Mora and has now been developed to the point where the remedy need not even be brought close to the patient. A vial containing the preparation is simply inserted into a hole in a metal block connected into the lead for the probe that is applied to the patient's acupuncture points. Despite the remoteness of the remedy from the patient the effect is similar and the technique is (as with Dr.Voll's work) successful.

This principle has been taken even further in a number of systems developed mainly in America, such as the Eclosion, the Listen, the Interro, the Discovery and the Quantamed. In these, the energetic 'signatures' (read electronically from samples or even actual specimens of hundreds or thousands of substances) are held within the apparatus. During testing the devices are apparently able to access the unique information for each separate sample and test the patient's response to it, as judged by galvanic skin resistance or other electrical characteristics of the body such as capacitance, inductance, current and voltage. All of these systems are computer based and can record and mathematically process the information gathered to give a detailed analysis of the patient's health. One or two of them also have an automated test procedure using fixed electrodes and so are apparently not subject to physical manipulation by the practitioner.

All of these diagnostic techniques have been used successfully to determine whether the patient is suffering an adverse response to geopathic or electro-stress.

EMPULSE

A remarkable system originating in England and based on a principle quite different from EAV is 'the Empulse'. Developed originally as a way of giving relief from migraine attacks, the Empulse has proved to have a far wider range of applications and indeed has apparent potential for tackling a great many symptoms.

In brief, the process starts with scanning the brainwave pattern of the patient using a novel electrode-less system. The purpose is to measure the strength of output from the patient's brain over a range of brainwave frequencies up to approximately 25Hz, at intervals of 0.1Hz, producing what is called a power spectrum analysis. Clinical work has shown that patients suffering from a given ailment tend to have a pattern of under powered brainwaves in particular, very specific areas of the frequency spectrum. These are not standard from patient to patient but do tend to occur in broadly similar areas for a particular ailment.

It has long been known, for instance, that someone in a relaxed state will produce far more Alpha waves (7-12Hz) than someone who is tense. By means of biofeedback, hypnosis, meditation or other forms of training it is possible for a patient to learn how to produce more Alpha waves and hence suffer less stress. The other major bands known as Delta, Theta and Beta have their own specific roles.

The Empulse analysis takes this concept further, recognising that individual frequencies or narrow bands of frequencies within each of the broader bands will have very specific effects on the body. They may, for instance, affect the output of certain hormones, stimulate the body's natural pain response, influence how relaxed the individual's muscles tend to be and so on.

Through computer analysis, the weaker parts of the patient's brainwave spectrum are identified and selected 'low' frequencies are programmed into a computer chip in the battery powered Empulse device. This then broadcasts the necessary fields to the patient in turn for a few seconds each, the cycle being repeated 24 hours a day. Depending on the patient's progress some resetting may be necessary as the body responds to the treatment. Results with the Empulse are very impressive with success rates (as judged by total relief from or significant relief of symptoms) rising to as high as 80% or more of those treated.

The message that emerges from consideration of the sorts of apparatus described above is simple, but seems fundamental. Namely, if the body responds demonstrably to such a variety of 'good' electromagnetic signals, many of which are relatively weak and spread over a fairly large frequency band, it lends considerable support to the thesis of this book, that the body is indeed sensitive to external electrical and magnetic influences. It must also surely underline the need to be aware of and concerned about the potential for uncontrolled and unwarranted effects on the body when it is exposed to fields of particular strengths, wave forms and intensities.

It has to be admitted that over large parts of the electromagnetic spectrum we are unsure of exactly what potential for harm exists. As you have learned, there is a body of evidence concerning extra low frequency fields in and around the mains frequency band and also for very high frequencies such as microwaves, but there is rather less certainty when considering much of the radio frequency spectrum.

However, I hope that what you have read in the preceding pages will at the very least have convinced you that the potential for hazard is something that we simply cannot afford to ignore. On the one hand, we should take such precautions ourselves as seem sensible and possible, while at the same time pressing for necessary safeguards to be developed by power providers, equipment manufacturers and indeed government. On the other hand, we should be doing everything we can to encourage that the necessary research is funded, not by those with a vested interest, but by neutral and scientifically credible bodies to discover the real truth about the implications of our modern electromagnetic world.

NOTE

1.   Smith, C.W. & Best, S., *Electromagnetic Man*: Dent (1989); 87.

CHAPTER 11

EARTH STRESS

So far, this book has looked primarily at electricity and the effects it can have on us. This second part now deals with what David calls the 'shadowy world of earth energies'.

Nowadays, there is a tendency for people to talk of 'energies', 'fields', 'ley lines', 'telluric energy', 'subtle energies' and so on. Very often these names are interchangeable. But there is little agreement about what the words mean. Usually an electromagnetic quality which can be sensed intuitively, is acknowledged. No wonder that traditional science, which can only accept the existence of something they can 'prove' is slow to embrace this world of uncertainty. Proof gives control. In this world of earth energies we do not have control.

The reader will now need to put the desire for proof on hold. Trust has to become a major element; above all, trust in one's own perceptions. Awareness has to be another. As we said in the introduction, David prefers to call dowsing an art form rather than a science. Many have achieved great things with this art, but, like all arts, it is subjective. Five dowsers examining the same subject, a standing stone, for instance, can give five different results, simply because there may be five or more patterns of energy associated with it. This obviously does not mean to say that they are all wrong. What it does show is that we have to be prepared to examine our perceptions, be able to accept different approaches. Here, we are all pioneers working on the edge of the unknown, where there are no pre-set ground rules.

David was highly sceptical of the whole business of dowsing. After many years of experience with the artform, he has to admit there is something that cannot be ignored, even if science has not yet caught up. This is not mere superstition. It is not magic, although there is the thrilling aspect of that word in all of this discovery. As electricity has its electro-stress, so these earth energies have their effect, which we will call either 'earth stress' or 'geopathic stress'. These collective terms embrace the feelings and symptoms that people experience in different ways and at different levels. The one thing common through-out is that these are the result of phenomena emanating from planet

Earth itself, for it is alive and has its own electromagnetic grid.

This chapter traces the effects on people of such different features as geological fault lines, earthquakes, volcanic eruptions and subterranean watercourses.

We have learned to put our implicit trust in the machines which we have created to make our lives less laborious and the instruments we use to measure the smallest effects. The price of doing this is that we, in our western society have lost the ability to trust the very simple abilities we all have and which, with a little dedication and rather more devotion to awareness can be reawakened. Some people do this already. Some have the ability thrust upon them without realising it.

Sensitivity to the subtle energies of the planet can be sometimes both a pleasant and an uncomfortable experience, as the tale of Geoffrey Allen will show. Here, a man discovered, albeit painfully, that his body was giving him ample indication of planetary phenomena. His body was, in essence, a detection device, a seismometer. He was picking up what are, to some, everyday occurrences, and to others, subtle energies. Perhaps a suitable definition for 'subtle energy' is something for which science has not caught up with yet, and found a suitable definition!

Geoffrey, an architect from near Dumfries in south-west Scotland, took quite a long time to relate his symptoms to the energies to which they are linked. Planetary tensions capable of causing earthquakes below 6.2 on the Richter scale seem not to affect him, but if the energies rise above this figure they cause symptoms.

For example: immediately upon waking in the morning, Geoffrey can tell if the earth energies are beginning to rise by the impression of a slight electrical charge around his body. Then a pain occurs in the left shoulder blade and later, another in the lower back, about 7cms. to the left of the spine. When the pain spreads across his back, he knows that somewhere in the world there will be an earthquake within 24 hours.

Other symptoms manifest to Geoffrey as difficulty in focusing his eyes, and an inability to wear a quartz digital watch which causes a pain in the upper muscle of his arm. Pains down the lower arm, rheumatic feelings in the hands; tingling and burning skin; upset digestive system, and a metallic taste in his mouth are other occasional irritations.

When he was studying architecture at college in Edinburgh he found that he could not work in that particular building, as he suffered from severe dizzy spells. Eventually he got permission to study at home. Having established, many years later, that natural energy fields affected his health, he investigated, and discovered several geological fau terminated under the College. Moreover, when he had been on vacation he had found that other places where he had felt equally unwell, were also at the ends of fault lines.

Another recent case reported was of an American who had similar sensitivities. In his case the intensity of his discomfort depended on which way he faced. Turning until he feels the effects are the strongest, he can then travel to another location and repeat the exercise. This gives him a triangulation, enabling him to judge roughly where the focal point of an earthquake will be.

INCOMERS SUFFER MOST

One thing common to all those who are sensitive in this way is that they are new to the area they live in. None of them suffered from these pains before they settled there and seldom suffer from them when they go away from the area, although they may find some places that do bother them. Many of the sufferers are female, Geoffrey believes, and it is possible that they are at a higher risk because they tend to spend more time in their home.

Interestingly, he does find certain locations where he can get relief, and that is in the centre of any one of the stone circles in his area. When on holiday in Wiltshire, he visited the giant stone circle at Avebury and felt that there was a great deal of natural energy in that area, causing his whole body to tingle and his head to swim. Some of the stones emitted more energy than others, some from one particular edge. They appeared also to be linked to something outside the circle.

One stone appeared to him to be much more powerful than the others, and this turned out to have been repaired, but he did notice that the constant pains from which he suffers, especially in his legs, had gone completely. It was only when he left the circle that the pains returned. The only other times he finds relief is when he walks barefoot on grass, and wearing stockings made of cotton or wool.

Mattress springs are another source of discomfort to Geoffrey, and a day or two before an impending earthquake the electric fields from television sets make him light-headed.

There are a number of similar cases to his in the area of Dumfries, which he attributes to the fact that there are no fewer than five major geological faults that terminate in the Dumfries and Galloway area. Other areas of discomfort are: Tobermory in Mull; Musselburgh, east of Edinburgh; Callander in Perthshire; and Salisbury in Wiltshire. There must be many others around the country.

Several times during the year Geoffrey also reports that he feels as if he has been engulfed by a massive electrical force which makes him feel dizzy and as if his body has been turned to jelly. These probably coincide with current storms, dramatic increases in the Earth's natural energy, which are world wide.

EARTHQUAKE PREDICTION

When he started predicting major earthquakes in 1966, Geoffrey was able to tell when they would occur some ten to fourteen days before the event. In 1988 he wrote to the Medical Department of Glasgow University to warn them ten days ahead of a major earthquake about the weekend of the 5th and 6th November. This earthquake (7.3 Richter), was on the Burma/China border on the 6th and killed 730 people, injuring a further 4,800 and affecting more than 3.2 million people in China.

When Geoffrey wrote again to the University to tell them of another major occurrence in December 1988, the devastating Armenian earthquake occurred ten days later. No other large or major earthquake occurred between these two letters and the events.

Things started to change dramatically during 1989, and by 1990 his prediction times had been reduced to just one or two days. On Friday, 19th June, Geoffrey warned Dr.Cyril Smith of Salford University, that there would be a major earthquake within the next 24 hours. At 21.00 hrs. on the 20th, Western Iran was hit by an earthquake of 7.7 which killed an estimated 40,000 to 50,000 people, injured another 60,000 and left 4,000,000 homeless.

On Friday 13th July, while at the British Geological Survey in Edinburgh, he was told that there had been an earth tremor in England during the week. Geoffrey said that it was a mere hiccup compared to what they would see at the beginning of the following week. At 07.26 on Monday morning, Luzon in the Phillippines was hit by an earthquake of 7.8 which killed 1,621 people and injured another 3,000, and on the following day by one of 6.6.

On August 17th, he told a client that he had been listening at noon to the car radio and felt that a major earthquake was imminent, and at 13.07 GMT the Solomon Islands was hit by a 'quake of 6.8.

CHANGE OF SYMPTOMS

The reason for the shortening of the prediction time seems to be that Geoffrey suffers from some of the symptoms for most of the time. This meant that he had to wait for this final extra flare-up of stinging pains all over the upper part of his back before he could make an accurate prediction. At the time of writing of these events (July, 1993), things once again seemed to be changing and the prediction time was beginning to lengthen again.

Geoffrey learned quite early in his research that sunspot activity, magnetic field changes and natural earth currents all follow the same 11.2 year cycle, from minimum to maximum and back again, although the cycle does vary, due to changes in the rotation of the Sun. The sunspots build up quickly over the first four years and then decline slowly over the next seven, but what he did not know until two years ago, was that 1986, the year he started predicting earthquakes, coincided with the apparent bottom of a cycle and 1991 the peak. To give the reader an idea of the changes that take place during one of these cycles, the following are the average daily sunspot counts since 1986, showing the major part of one cycle:

    1986 —   14;
    1987 —   29;
    1988 —   140;
    1989 —   213;
    1990 —   190;
    1991 —   207;
    1992 —   139 (provisional).

There appears to be a link between the intensity of his symptoms and these natural cycles. It will be interesting to see if they continue to change over the remainder of this present cycle, and eventually return to their 1986 levels.

Not only do his symptoms allow him to predict when a major earthquake will occur, but they also give him a good idea of how powerful it will be. Following his talk at an international seminar, The Centre of Complementary Medicine in Southampton requested more details and predictions. On the 12th October, 1989, he wrote to them, to say he was going on a week's vacation to the west coast of Scotland and would report on whether his pains, which were now building up quite quickly, would get worse or disappear. They did disappear, but not before he had gone through hell and back. On Monday 17th, he got up feeling as if he was at death's door. In the afternoon, he became so tired that he had to ask his son to drive the car. When they arrived back at their chalet he lay down on the couch and slept for several hours, a sure sign that a major earthquake was about to occur.

As soon as he awoke the following morning he switched on the television to find out where the earthquake had struck, to see all the pictures of the devastation which followed the Oakland earthquake in California at 00.04 GMT on the 18th October.

On arriving home, he wrote off immediately to the Southampton Centre to tell them that the only thing that surprised him about the earthquake was that he had expected it to be much more powerful than the 6.9 magnitude that was being quoted. When the official figures came out several months later it had been upgraded to one of 7.1, (i.e. three times more powerful).

Twice in 1992, the BBC reported that earthquakes of 7.0 on the Richter scale had occurred. His symptoms indicated that they were much less severe, which turned out to be the case.

Geoffrey believes that seismologists and volcanologists will never be able to predict an earthquake or a volcanic eruption until they accept that they can be seen as world-wide events. He recognises evidence that the area in which the earthquake or volcanic eruption will occur may appear to be dead prior to the event and that all the activity is going on elsewhere. Like the calm before the storm. Several times over the last few years, seismologists and volcanologists have predicted earthquakes and volcanic eruptions which have not occurred. For example, the U.S. Geological Survey predicted that in 1995 Los Angeles would be hit by the biggest 'quake of the century. This one did not occur, but three days later Kobe in Japan was hit by a disastrous series of violent tremors. Geoffrey has been able to predict the time, but not the location of every major earthquake since 1986.

BODY VIBRATES WHEN ENERGIES ARE VERY HIGH

On January 14th, 1993, Geoffrey could not draw a straight line and was unable to work at his drawing board. The following day it was announced that four scientists had died and ten were still missing after the Galeras volcano in southern Columbia erupted suddenly without warning. At the time the scientists were taking readings inside the crater. One of them was Professor Geoffrey Brown, one of the world's leading experts in predicting volcanic eruptions. This was a tragedy, but it seems to suggest, at least in Geoffrey's case, the human body is more sensitive than any man-made instrument which can only pick up the type of information for which they have been programmed. The bodies of humans and animals are much more sensitive.

On one occasion, however, Geoffrey's prediction did not turn out quite as he had thought. He wrote the British Geographical Survey on the 21st December, 1988 that the energies in Lockerbie had been building up and were now extremely high. On Christmas day both the Mount Tohachi volcano on Hokkaido Island and the Lonquima volcano in the Andes erupted. As far as he can find out, two volcanoes have never erupted at the same time before in recorded history.

Leading up to this event, the energies had risen even higher during the 21st December. They were so strong by the early evening that he didn't even get up from the table after his evening meal to wash the dishes, something he always does. As he sat there, he wondered if he had made a big mistake with his earthquake predictions, because suddenly the whole house shook. There was no earthquake. He could see from his home that the village of Lockerbie was ablaze following the bombing of the Pan-Am jumbo-jet which crashed there. He will always wonder if these very high energies on that fateful day had anything to do with the bomb going off prematurely.

THE GOOD, THE BAD AND THE UGLY

One of the first things he noticed after moving to Dumfries in 1977 was that whenever he crossed the border into England, he would get relief from his awful symptoms. Right on the border is a mass of overhead high tension cables. Returning northwards, however, his symptoms worsened. He has had some terrible journeys travelling back from England.

Clarencefield, a few miles south-east of Dumfries, had the same effect, where his symptoms eased after passing under the overhead power lines from the Chapelcross nuclear station. Returning home the same problems returned — dizziness as he passed the pylons — which persuaded him that some overhead power lines may have good effects as well as bad.

At Fort William, on the West coast, he felt especially bad when playing golf. Being a very methodical person, he carefully noted how he felt while playing a round, until a pattern emerged. A line of H.T. pylons bisect the course, and when he walked on the north-west side he experienced varying degrees of discomfort, from very bad to severe. On the south-east, however, he felt little or no pain. On the way home, he stopped in Callender for a break, and his symptoms returned with a vengeance. He became so dizzy walking down the street that he staggered and feared that people might think he was drunk.

He mentioned his experiences to a friend who told him that Fort William was not the place for sensitives like him, as it lies at the end of a major geological fault, the Great Glen Fault line. His friend, as it happened, had the same problems. His wife had never felt well since moving into their new home which subsequently turned out to have been built on a fault line.

Reflecting on the other problem areas, he noticed that the Dalton fault is on the side of Clarencefield where he feels discomfort, and on the A74 highway, between Annan and Carlisle, three faults end just before the mass of overhead power cables. (Carrutherstown, on the top of the Dalton fault, is, incidentally, an accident blackspot on the A74). Callander is associated with two faults, one terminating a short distance to the north, from Loch Tay, and is almost directly on top of the Highland Boundary Fault, which runs from Stonehaven in the east, just south of Aberdeen, to Helensburgh in the west, north of Glasgow. This is within sight of the Faslane nuclear submarine base.

DETECTING NATURAL EARTH CURRENTS

According to Dr.Stuart of the British Geological Survey in Edinburgh, changes in natural magnetic fields can induce currents in telephone lines and power distribution cables. It is also known that telephone lines are used to detect changes in the Earth's currents, the natural electric currents flowing just below the ground, which Geoffrey believes are released on to the surface of the planet by way of fault lines and quarries, etc. It is these to which sensitive people may be susceptible.

If the energies are picked up by overhead power cables, etc., then that would explain why there is a good and bad side to them. Cancer clusters, for instance, may occur only on the side where there were fault lines and quarries and other man-made disturbances from which the energies can flow. Geoffrey's personal experience suggests that the problem is not entirely due to the magnetic fields which surround the power lines, but from the natural energies which are drawn towards them. This will be explored further in the following chapters.

SUBTERRANEAN STREAMS ARE MOST STRESSFUL

It is interesting to note that some established methods of eliminating earth energies from houses, by using amethyst crystals, etc., actually make Geoffrey feel much worse, and holding coils of copper amplifies this effect. Areas around nuclear reactors, apparently, have no effect on him, although his body vibrates so badly when he stands above the crossing of two subterranean streams that they almost knock him off his feet. One wonders how many people are suffering from similar problems, and find difficulty in living or driving in certain areas of the country. Indeed, how many road accidents have been caused by these phenomena?

We have seen that people can react to natural phenomena without realising it. We can feel unwell and think we have a virus or we have eaten something that has not agreed with us. Perhaps we are, in fact, reacting to planetary events, underground water courses or seismic activity. What may at first sight be a symptom, to be masked with aspirin or Scotch whisky, may actually be a gift of insight into earth energies. The next chapter looks into their history.

CHAPTER 12

A HISTORY OF EARTH ENERGIES AND LEYS

In 1929, Baron Gustav Freiherr von Pohl investigated the village of Vilsbiburg, Lower Bavaria (Germany), on a tributary of the Danube, in an attempt to discover why this particular village had such a high incidence of cancer. Initially, he prepared a map of all the powerful underground water veins and streams he could find by water divining methods. He then took the completed map to the local hospital, where a map of the village and 54 cancer deaths had been drawn by the local Medical Officer of Health. When they superimposed the two maps they found that all the cancer deaths had taken place over the underground streams he had located.

Subsequently, he discovered that many cases of human illness and disease in animals, plants and trees were related to underground fissures and streams of water emitting energy vertically to the surface. He suspected that the velocity of the water was the most important factor in the strength of this disease-inducing energy. Further, he discovered that unusually high levels of natural electric currents occurred where underground water fissures crossed at different levels. These, in all probability, are very similar to the natural earth energies which cause people like Geoffrey Allen, in the previous chapter, such distress.

The earth energies were not uniform in time or season. He found them to be more powerful during the night when the earth de-magnetized itself, and also at the waxing and full Moon. Other researchers have noted differences, due possibly to the changes in the velocity of the subterranean water caused by seasonal variations in rainfall.

In an attempt to eliminate what he called an 'unhealthy' energy from an entire village, von Pohl constructed a screening station in the cellar of his home as an experiment. This was effective within a 1500 metres radius and appeared to improve the general health of the entire village. The village, mentioned only as 'D' in his book, is thought to be the village of Dachau, site of the notorious Nazi concentration camp. This unfortunate association caused other researchers, aware of the strange character of 'black streams' (see *Glossary*), to be cautious in their approach to the elimination of unhealthy earth energies.

Paradoxically, to the detriment of the health of many people throughout the world, Baron von Pohl disagreed with the policies of Adolf
Hitler. This prevented his research becoming more widely known.
Many other discoveries could have been added to his in the half century since he wrote his book on what was later to be called geopathic
or geopathogenic stress[1].

IONIZATION UNDER THE BEDS OF CANCER PATIENTS

In 1939, Pierre Cody of Le Havre used an electrometer to measure
ionization under the beds of cancer victims and discovered very high
readings vertically above the surface of the ground. To eliminate the
ionization, he used 1mm sheets of lead below the beds of a number of
patients. Strangely, the lead sheets changed colour directly beneath
the cancer victims, at the part of the body affected, to a peacock blue
or yellow-gold. Unfortunately, the lead was not a permanent protection, since it was soon irradiated, making the lead sheet itself dangerous.

Radon, the naturally occurring radioactive gas, he thought, was the
likely culprit, although he knew of no way that a free gas could rise
through a multi-storeyed building, causing 'cancer verticals' in anyone
unfortunate enough to be in its path. We shall return to that subject in
chapter 15, after explaining some of the uses of natural earth energies,
and how our ancestors understood and manipulated them.

Another researcher in more recent times, Kathe Bächler, an Austrian teacher, has worked extensively with geopathically disturbed
zones, and has listed 11,000 cases of illness which she believes were
initiated in these areas. She helped the sufferers to move their beds or
working positions to a more suitable area, with extremely beneficial
results. Her research has centred partly on the unpleasant influences
of what she called 'malign earth energies' were having on children at
school, not only with respect to their health, but also to their ability to
learn. She found that 95% of children who were unsuccessful in school,
who were slow learners, lethargic or played truant, were difficult to
handle, or hyperactive, had been in areas of geopathic stress.

Kathe believes that children in a class ought to change the position
of their desks, perhaps every three to four weeks; one row of children
alternating with the adjacent row, so that no child should suffer what
may be a stressful environment for any long period.

One interesting point she made was that Adolf Flachenegger, yet
another Austrian dowser who had worked in the area of geopathic
stress for 50 years, had noticed that 'pushing water' (that is an underground stream which flows from the feet to the head when the person
is lying in bed) causes congestion of blood in the head, nightmares

and depression, perhaps leading to suicide. She had also discovered that the opposite, 'pulling water' running from the head to the feet, can cause dizziness, blackouts, loss of balance and fainting[2].

GYPSIES ARE HEALTHIER

A recent survey by Christopher McNaney of the People's Research Centre, Alston, has revealed that gypsies and travelling people have a surprisingly low level of illness. When asked about incidences of cancer in their relatives, he found that it is less than 1%, against 25-33% mortality in the rest of the population. Heart disease and other serious illnesses so prevalent in our society are also very low. Their general lifestyle can hardly be attributed to their well-being, as they smoke, drink alcohol and ignore health foods and special diets.

He also believes that illness is primarily a disease of location, and that the travelling people's nomadic lifestyle means that they are unlikely to stay long in a highly stressed area, and if they do happen to camp in one, they are intuitive enough to leave the area after a very short time.

SCIENTIFIC MEASUREMENTS

One of the major problems of using techniques like water divining and dowsing in this field is that they are so subjective and open to misinterpretation. Despite the 56 years since Cody's experiments, there has been little scientific research to substantiate the work of earth energy researchers. Occasionally, one hears of individuals like Venceslav Palnovsky of Prague who discovered that he could detect subterranean water veins by measuring the fading of ultra short wave transmission on a radio on the 5-15 cm. wavelength. Professor Herbert Konig of Munich found that a person's blood sedimentation rate changes when he sleeps or stays in a geopathically stressed zone. He felt that this could lead eventually to heart disorders, if nothing was done.

In Switzerland, Dr.Joseph A.Kopp has claimed that scientifically measurable effects occur, such as magnetic anomalies, increase in electrical conductivity of the soil and air. Increase in the field strength of UHF waves and an intensity of infra-red radiation can also be found above subterranean water fissures. In an interesting experiment, he discovered that mice placed in wooden cages above such underground currents exhibited a variety of symptoms: restlessness, biting each other and eating their young[3].

Recently, the electrochemical potential directly above an underground stream, with sidebands (see *Glossary*) corresponding to the edges of the water has also been scientifically measured. Oscilloscopes have been used to verify the discoveries of researchers in France[4], while a few Americans are using scintillation counters to detect gamma radiation directly above aquifers. Despite this, earth energies remain as elusive as ever since they have not yet been connected with magnetism or electricity, etc.

GEOLOGICAL FAULT LINES

Paul McCartney, a geologist, has shown that all the stone circles in England and Wales occur within 1km of geological surface faults. It is thought that these circles use the piezo-electric energy, emitted from the natural movements in the faults.

Perhaps the movement of the subterranean strata intermittently feeds the energy leys from time to time in this manner, but I must admit I have never found any corroborating evidence for this theory. The energies which I have been following are energy leys and energy streams. These can be easily discovered and traced to their destination (or source) by dowsing, an ancient art similar to water divining.

EARLY RESEARCHERS

We have to go back even earlier than Baron von Pohl and Cody, in fact, to 1921 to find the origins of research into natural earth energies. This is the beginning of the rediscovery of how our ancestors used and manipulated them to make the ley system, which is so important to an understanding of both the healthy and unhealthy energies, which surround us.

Alfred Watkins, a business man and photographer from the Welsh borderlands (he invented the Watkins exposure meter and was an expert on local folk-lore and antiquities), was out in the countryside on horseback. The story goes that he pulled up his horse to survey the landscape below. It was then he became aware of "a network of lines, standing out like glowing wires across the country, intersecting the sites of churches, old stones and ancient sites".

His vision of the 'Old Straight Track' was, perhaps, not quite such an accident, however, as he had spent years of study and map-work and had a wide knowledge of classical mythology and local archaeology. Indeed, it is more likely, according to his son, that the insight occurred when he was looking at a map[5].

Alfred Watkins believed that ancient man used straight tracks for various purposes, including the transportation of flints and salt. They used staves to mark out these straight lines, constructing stone circles, standing stones, cairns, ponds, mounds, notches cut into hills, ancient tracks and other sacred sites upon which castles and churches were subsequently built. He thought that ancient homesteads should be included, but decided against this, as they were too numerous, and it was difficult to say which were old and which modern.

He summarised the work of the builders, the early surveyors, or 'dod-men' as he called them in his book *The Old Straight Track*[6], "I feel that ley-man, astronomer-priest, druid, bard, wizard, witch, palmer and hermit, were all more or less linked by one thread of ancient knowledge and power". He did not realise at the time that his 'ley lines', at least some of them, had energy flowing down them. This was to come later.

ENERGY LEYS

Before Watkins, in 1845, the Rev.E.Duke had written about an alignment from Avebury, through Silbury Hill and on to Stonehenge, passing through several other minor sites. Eventually, Alfred Watkins' idea of ley lines being lines of ancient monuments and Guy Underwood's work on subterranean energies under sacred sites were later brought together by Tom Graves. His research into energy leys (lines of ancient monuments with energy flowing down them) and his book *Needles of Stone* inspired others, including myself, to delve into the mysterious, subtle energies which surround us.

Guy Underwood, a retired solicitor, taught himself the age-old art of water divining. He took a dramatic step forward when he depicted in *Pattern of the Past*, the terrestrial energies of underground water as forming water lines, spirals and blind springs (water coming almost to the surface). He also referred to a range of secondary effects, which another author, P.Siochan, believes are mirrored as carvings on tombs such as those at Newgrange and Dowth in Ireland[7].

People who study the energies at sacred sites are nowadays called earth mystery researchers. Tom Graves described what the ancients did as "acupuncture of the earth"[8], and suggested that the ley line system was set up to help balance the Earth's natural energy system, which in the raw can cause effects disturbing to man. In that sense the ley line system can be described as man-made, though many researchers feel that it has been badly damaged by man's modern activities. Many of these sites give anomalous readings to scientific equipment.

Standing stones and circles are placed directly above flowing underground streams (and perhaps fissures or faults) which emit natural earth energies to the surface. By transmuting these, possibly through the quartz in the structure of the standing stones, streams of energy flow across the country, now above ground in a series of individual waves in an artificially controlled manner. These surface 'overgrounds' may be a straight energy ley from ordinary standing stones or a roughly circular energy stream from a cup-marked standing stone, such as the one at Kilmartin in Argyll.

The width of an energy ley between standing stones may be several hundred metres across at its widest point, although some people, possibly reacting to a central core of energy, find that it is a very narrow band a few metres wide or less.

THE DRAGON PROJECT

A zoologist passing a stone circle in the early hours one morning recorded unusually high ultrasonic readings. He made a chance remark to Paul Devereux, a leading figure in earth mystery studies, who was later to initiate the start of 'The Dragon Project' which monitored this circle for a number of years. Another 'coincidence' occurred to researcher John Barnatt. While surveying the Derbyshire henge of Arbor Low, he was approached by a stranger, who told him that the skylarks flying over the henge appeared to be attracted to the ultrasound emitted from it.

An inorganic chemist, Don Robins, in October 1978 discovered at the King's Stone, part of the Rollright circle in Oxfordshire, a very strange pulsing which occurred generally at two specific times: ten and thirty minutes before dawn. At these times his home-made ultrasonic detector would begin to fluctuate from 0 to 10 on its arbitrary scale. He discovered after some years that the readings were at their highest around the equinoxes and lowest at the solstices. He also used a geiger counter in an attempt to find if there were any radiation anomalies connected with this and other sites. Surprisingly, at a number of circles, the radioactivity inside the circles was actually lower than background level. As he put it, "There was an eerie impression of 'holes in the landscape' neatly marked by the stone circles"[9].

Since then a great deal of work has been done monitoring a number of sites in the search for radiation anomalies which may give different impressions. Some of the circles give increased measurements of radiation significantly higher, or lower, than background, sometimes by as much as 35%. Individual stones in certain circles give an even greater anomaly. At Long Meg in Cumbria, for instance, one such stone emitted three times the counts per minute to be found at most other sites[10].

Instrumental monitoring is becoming increasingly sensitive, though it may never become like a Geofrey Allen. It is becoming clear to researchers other than the most determined sceptic that stone-age man had a greater knowledge than modern orthodox archaeology has been prepared to accept. Even liquid filled compasses have been used to good effect at some megalithic sites. They show that there is a magnetic field deviation around some stones.

RESEARCH INTO MAN-MADE ENERGY SYSTEMS

Part of my long distance walking across the Scottish hills was with the intention of mapping out these strange energy streams. These are the raw energies our early ancestors used and modified, which gave rise to Stonehenge, Silbury Hill, the Callanish standing stones on the Isle of Lewis, and countless other ancient monuments scattered around the world. They were not built by ignorant cave-men. These constructions powerfully and intelligently focus, magnify and manipulate natural earth energies in a way and for a purpose we do not yet understand.

Ancient towns and cities have been laid out on geometric principles, still discernible to the present day in the way churches were placed on ancient and sacred sites. London is no exception, as discussed in *Earthstars* by C.E.Street. David Wood's inspired book *Genisis: The First Book of Revelations* also reveals the mystery of the village of Rennes-le-Château and its links with mystical knowledge and use of geometry in the placing of sacred sites.

My own little home town of Crieff, in the wilds of Perthshire, Scotland, has revealed a further key to the problem of ancient geomancy. This town has been laid out in accordance with an ancient and powerful symbol, a six-pointed star, the Star of David, or the Star of Bethlehem, with St.Michael's church at the centre. St.Michael and St.George were the dragon-slaying saints, who fixed the dragons (energy leys and energy streams) into place with their lances or swords.

Using the method of following energy leys described in the next chapter, it became clear that this symbol is more than the theoretical ground plan, which C.E.Street suggests, but that energy leys flowing between outlying standing stones are superimposed on a naturally occurring star-shaped pattern on the surface of the planet. This cannot be an isolated case, and is probably the basis of geometrical patterns already discovered by researchers, and others still to be found.

As I discovered during my practical research, another use of natural earth energy, this time from a local and powerful cup-marked stone, a standing stone with saucer-shaped depressions carved into its surface, transmits circular energy streams the same shape as the cup-marks themselves, across a huge area of Scotland and the north of England. The burial-grounds were built at the periphery of these, where the energy is at its most powerful. (Chapter 20 has more about cup-marked stones.)

Unknown to me, as I marched across the hills, Hamish Miller and Paul Broadhurst, blacksmith and author respectively, were dedicated to a similar pursuit, and were plotting the 'St.Michael Line' across the south of the country, from West Cornwall to the east coast of Norfolk. The energy streams they found were of a similar nature to those from the cup-marked stone, but meandered across the country, from one St.Michael's church to another, incorporating St.Michael's Mount, Glastonbury, Avebury, with another, the St.Mary Line, weaving across it at important sites.

ARE ENERGY LEYS ARTIFICIAL?

A hint of the artificial aspect of energy leys was provided in 1935 by two French archaeologists, Merle and Diot, who found that every standing stone and circle they investigated had been placed directly above flowing underground water. In my own research, using similar water divining techniques, I have also discovered this to be true, and it appears, as mentioned earlier, that it is the natural earth energies flowing down the subterranean streams which filter to the surface. These are captured by the standing stones and circles, and transmitted artificially across the country, now above ground, as energy leys and streams.

Unfortunately, much of the ancient knowledge has now been lost, and we are left with monoliths and stone circles, still quietly chattering away to each other in their own language. The energy system is now in decay and poisoned, radiating its own peculiar energies across entire continents, to the detriment of the health of at least some of the population of these countries.

How to locate energy leys and streams may some day be discovered, using some type of scientific equipment. For now they can, however, be investigated by invoking the ancient art of dowsing, which we turn to next.

NOTES

1. von Pohl, G.F., *Earth Currents: Causative Factor of Cancer and Other Diseases*: Fortschritt fuer alle-Verlag (1983).

2. Bachler, K., *Earth Radiation*: Wordmasters Ltd., (1989).

3. Kopp, Dr.J.A., *Imago Mundi* Journal, Austria, (1973)

4. Merz, B., *Cosmic Points of Energy*: C.W.Daniel Co.

5. Williamson, T. & Bellamy, E., *Ley Lines in Question*, Worlds Work.

6. Watkins, A., *The Old Straight Track*: Methuen, (1925).

7. Siochan, P.A.O., *Ireland: A Journey into Lost Time*: Foilsiuchain Eireann.

8. Graves, Tom, *Needles of Stone Revisited*: Gothic Image.

9. Robins, D., *Circles of Silence*: Souvenir Press, (1985).

10. Devereux, P., *The Ley Hunter*, Nos.105 & 106.

CHAPTER 13

DIVINING AND DOWSING

To explore earth energies it is essential to learn dowsing or rhabdomancy, one of the most ancient arts. For many centuries it was applied to the detection of underground water and minerals and is now used much more extensively in discovering oil reserves, tracing geological faults and the origin of unhealthy radiation from a variety of subterranean or terrestrial sources. It is also used in archaeology, to find underground remains and foundations of buildings.

In medical diagnosis, dowsing is used to pinpoint diseases and displaced vertebrae; to decide which medicine and in what amount will suit the patient, or to discover allergic substances simply and quickly and at no cost. Gardeners can use it to find plants which are sympathetic to each other and the best location for flowers and shrubs, etc. It can be adapted to anyone's individual interests, from finding blocked drains, to locating lost animals, pets and people, precisely locating hidden fractures in metals or exploring the intricate patterns of unknown energies in authentic crop circles.

Architectural surveyors find dowsing extremely useful to locate hidden services, such as: sewers, ducts, wells, cisterns, culverts, manholes, pipes containing water and gas, electric and telephone cables and methane gas in landfill sites.

RUSSIA

Russia and its neighbouring states have been using the same method, which they call biolocation, to a surprisingly sophisticated degree, even to the extent of issuing official certificates. Qualifying for one of these is said to be very difficult, such is the standard of competence. Those seeking such qualifications are often professionals in geophysics, geochemistry, ecology, hydro-electricity, etc.

One engineer, for example, found high quality water for a famous vodka factory at 122 metres depth, using water divining methods. They have also successfully discovered oil, gold, copper and deposits of other precious metals. In addition, they locate faults in electric cables, pipe lines, the electric cable network and very small cracks in hydro-electric dams which cannot be detected by conventional instruments. In one case, where serious road subsidence occurred, biolocators discovered a number of voids which, upon excavation, were found to be filled with boxes of explosives, hidden there during the Second World War[1].

Our materialistic culture, especially in the United Kingdom and America, however, has often greeted the art with scepticism, even when professional water diviners have had an almost perfect record of water detection. To observe a person following the energies from underground water with nothing more than a length of bent wire, when we are used to scientific devices of immense complexity — and price — is contrary to all we have ever learned.

A personal friend, Michael Cranfield, a water diviner and veteran bomber pilot of the Second World War, uses map dowsing to save walking. This is one of the strangest aspects of the art. Farmers, requiring him to find sources of good quality water on their land, simply fax a large scale map to his office where he will quietly explore it with a pendulum. When he has a reaction, he will mark the spot on the map, drive as near to the point as he can in his car, walk a few metres with his dowsing rods and tell the driller the precise location. He has a quite remarkable success rate using this method, about 98%.

Somehow, the trained human mind is able to project itself using even the crudest of maps of the area in question and, moreover, is able to find underground water, missing people and much more. Occasionally, after I have surveyed a house, the owner will produce a plan sent to him by a dowser who specialises in geopathic stress. Usually, our surveys show a marked similarity, although I personally find this particular branch of dowsing so strange I don't use it. No-one can begin to understand how such things work. Experts use them as powerful tools in their art much in the same way as we use electricity. No-one really knows how electricity works; we simply use it with out question.

Geopathic stress can not only be discovered, but also cleared, by using this method. My publisher who was afflicted by geopathic stress after an extension was added to his house, sent a map to a radionics practitioner which enabled him to *visualise* and dowse the problems. The dowser never went to his house, but was able to *project* into the blocked energy point and free it. The creative power of the human mind and imagination is much greater than conventional science can acknowledge because of its materialistic bias.

The human — body, brain and mind — is also a very sophisticated computer and, given some training in the receptivity of energy of whatever form is able, for instance, to detect very low levels of magnetic fields. The magnetic field of the planet is detected as a measurement on a scale from 0.2 to 0.6 gauss, depending upon location, yet it has been proven that dowsers can react to magnetic gradients of as little as 0.00000001g. The work of dowsers, in many cases, may not be scientifically proven. However, having taught a number of people how to dowse, I find the lack of scientific proof matters little. It works for almost everyone and if they have sufficient initiative, they can carry on in their own way in their own individual sphere of interest.

A HEALTH WARNING - PROTECT YOURSELF

A word of caution would not go amiss here. When you tune in to energies from any source, you may leave yourself wide open to unhealthy and unexpected effects. This happened to me, I found, when attending a lecture in Edinburgh. A lady, completely unknown to me, looked at me in amazement and asked me what on earth I had been doing. She could see the aura or electromagnetic field around my body, which contained a large, dark green 'blob', just at shoulder level. To her it looked repulsive, 'like a toad'. Just a few days before, I had been investigating the case of a girl who suffered a particularly nasty demonic possession and something had detached itself from her and on to me! She also found my throat area unusually yellow and thought I must spend a lot of time at a computer terminal, which was perfectly correct, as I had been working on this book and my next, for up to twelve hours at a stretch. I still have a healthy scepticism for many things, but after many years of research into this strange topic, I just keep an open mind. After all, we are dealing with a subject on the frontiers of traditional or orthodox scientific knowledge. I think that sometimes we forget this when we imbue science with too much authority for its presently limited view.

Some of us are more sensitive to telluric (earth) energies than others. Kathe Bächler (see p.100) became seriously ill while doing her research, and I myself chose (to my cost) to ignore the advice of several people who knew of illnesses suffered by geopathic stress researchers. Over the years, following energy leys from standing stones, and, without doubt, working with unhealthy earth energies, my feet and legs became so painful I was crippled to the extent that I thought I would become wheelchair-bound.

My water diviner friend has also had problems of this nature. So much so, in fact, that he is considering stopping the work he enjoys so much. When we compare notes, we find that the areas where he feels so depleted of energy are the same ones that I feel have unusually high levels of unhealthy energies. It is possible that he is tuning into the water which is reflecting them, making him ill in the process.

To eliminate the possibility of ill-health we therefore need to take care of ourselves when doing this work. One method of protection is to use visualisation. Imagine your body wrapped around by a beautiful white/blue or gold cloak, with your head protected by a crown or tiara encrusted with precious stones, or an egg-shaped envelope, any colour you feel appropriate, which will discourage any unhealthy energy to attach itself to you. There are many variations of this theme and a pentagram of blue fire around your feet, drawn with an imaginary sword, can be useful. Simply reciting your favourite prayer is another method, but being aware of the danger is probably the most important advice anyone can give. You would be well advised to stop working if you start to feel suddenly depleted. You are now working in an area presently beyond science, and some of the precautions which could be effective seem strange to the rational mind. When I first started this work I was at first sceptical of such methods. They smacked of 'the occult', which simply means 'beyond the range of ordinary knowledge'. We have to go beyond superstition and the fear it invokes when dealing with the unknown. We also have to learn to be careful and to protect ourselves in such circumstances.

USING A PENDULUM

The most commonly used and the simplest type of dowsing equipment is the pendulum. This is any small weighted object suspended by a thread which, through its gyrations, can show energy fields. On a different level, the pendulum can be used as an indication of answers to simple questions put to the diviner's own unconscious. A pendulum can be made from a strand of long hair tied to a gold ring, or a semi-precious stone strung on thread or fine chain. Many people prefer specially made wooden pendulums, since metals emit their own specific radiation patterns which can confuse results.

One of the simplest uses a pendulum or 'bob' can be put to is in finding to which foods and chemicals a person may be allergic. With a little practice this comes quite naturally to most people and can be extremely accurate. The answers a pendulum can give are basically 'yes,' 'no', and 'neutral'.

To find a 'yes' for example, hold the thread approximately 10cms above the pendulum. With practice you will find the best length to use, which you should then mark with a knot. First, it is necessary to find how the pendulum indicates the responses (in a sense the swing responses have to be 'programmed'). Let the pendulum swing gently to and from your body. As it swings, concentrate on the thoughts 'yes', 'positive', 'benevolent' and the pendulum normally begins to circle in a clockwise direction. Once you have accomplished this successfully a few times, try again as before, with the pendulum swinging towards you and away from you in the starting position and concentrate on 'no', 'negative', 'unhealthy'. The pendulum usually now swings in an anti-clockwise rotational movement. These two basic gyrations are your own personal 'yes' and 'no'. In some people these may be reversed; 'yes' may be anti-clockwise and 'no' clockwise, or for some people there may be a totally different regime. You might find your own personal 'yes' or 'no' requires a particular feeling and in others the basic 'yes' and 'no' can change at any time for an unknown reason. This is simply overcome by asking the pendulum for the direction of rotation for either 'yes' and 'no' prior to asking any other questions, or if at any time you use a different pendulum.

Now hold the pendulum above a food sample and ask yourself if it is fit to eat or not. The pendulum should give an accurate answer, with practice. "Is this egg/milk/cheese/margarine fresh?" "Are these apples/pears/oranges fit to eat?" It is also possible to find the vitality left in any produce after it has been picked or been in the freezer for a time. Ask the pendulum to give a countdown out of, perhaps 20 when you hold it above the specimen. Start it swinging clockwise and start counting. The bob should swing rapidly at first, then gradually decrease as you count, until the level of vitality has been reached, when it will oscillate backwards and forwards. That is the value of the energy remaining in the product. The figure of 20 is arbitrary and can be any convenient number. With practice you will learn what frame of mind allows more objective answers to your questions. A certain detachment is essential, while any desires, will or preferences will bring a subjective response.

ALLERGIES

Pendulums can be used to find out if a food or liquid causes an allergic reaction. Place one hand palm down at a right angle to your body on a table or flat surface and a substance which you wish to check (milk, cheese, meat, etc.) about 6ins (15cms) to the side of your thumb. Now hold your pendulum and start it swinging backwards and forwards between the specimen and your hand. Ask yourself if the food or chemical is compatible with yourself at this particular moment and the bob should gradually turn and swing backwards and forwards clockwise from your hand to the sample if it is in harmony with it, or to and from you if it is not compatible. You may also use this method for checking the allergic reaction of a child or another adult by substituting his hand for yours.

Beware of the amount of the specimen you are testing. The pendulum may show that a large sample of food is incompatible with you, while a smaller quantity may be neutral and a smaller amount still, benevolent. Once you have mastered these basics you can then experiment with various foods (or drinks, since alcoholism may be an allergic reaction!) to find your own personal reactions. Try using common salt or white sugar to obtain a negative response, for instance and do not be surprised if your favourite foods show a negative response. Don't forget that salt and white sugar are present as additives in most modern artificially produced foods. This is of necessity a very short introduction into allergy detecting using dowsing and you will find books in the bibliography which deal with this in detail.

Human nature being what it is, a further word of warning at this point should not go amiss. Some people become addicted to their pendulums and use them at every opportunity which may amount almost to an obsession. Others, less logical than the average citizen in the first place, may ask their pendulums questions like, "Does Mr.Smith have a dangerous disease?" and believe implicitly in what the pendulum tells them, even if the answer is obviously suspicious. Some gifted amateurs can diagnose very accurately, but they are in the minority, and, in any case, the medical profession are quite understandably furious when unqualified practitioners attempt to diagnose illness in this way. Logic and common sense are needed, especially when using the pendulum, and this facet of dowsing may best be left to the medically qualified who also have an interest in dowsing.

ANGLE RODS

Many people associate dowsing with the 'V' shaped hazel twig. In fact, there are over two hundred different types of dowsing instruments, each with its own advantages and disadvantages. For detecting earth energies, in my opinion the best dowsing implements are angle rods, two lengths of wire, about 21ins (53 cms) long, with 6ins (15 cms) bent over at right angles to form a handle. A little experience will show the length which will best suit the individual. Made from heavy fence wire or very often from metal coat hangers, they are extremely sensitive, even in the hands of a complete beginner (fig.10). For working in the open the rods should, ideally, be made of the heavier fence wire or welding rod since heavier rods are much less influenced by rough terrain and wind. This is the type of instrument we shall refer to for the rest of this book.

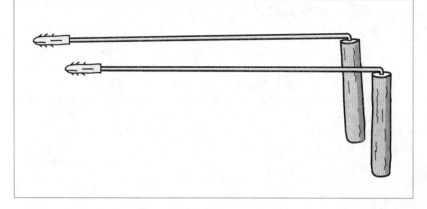

Fig.10: Dowsing rods made from fence wire, handles of wood, ballpoint cases, etc. Or bare wire may be hand-held. Protect the ends with plastic caps or tape.

Some people find it an advantage to use handles of some description, others prefer to feel the bare rods turning in their hands. For handles, ball point pen cases are perfectly good, or 1 in (2½cms) diameter dowelling rod or broom handle, bored down its length to take the short end of the instrument or even several cotton reels glued together.

For safety's sake, the bare ends of the rods may be made safe by covering with fibre wall plugs or taped over with sellotape or electrician's tape, so that they don't hurt the eye or body. On numerous occasions, climbing fences or negotiating an endless variety of obstacles, from fences to deep ravines, I have fallen on top of divining rods of this type and have been grateful that I have made them harmless in this manner.

In all cases it is essential that the rods move freely in their holders. Don't be misled by the simplicity of this instrument or any other dowsing implements. The amount of information that a person can obtain with their help is quite phenomenal.

In order to work, angle rods (like any other dowsing tools) need to be in a state of balance. Try holding the rods perfectly level in front of you, in a comfortable position, just above waist height, pointing them away from your body. Now gently raise the tips, so that the rods are slightly above the horizontal and you will quickly find that they go out of control and swing back towards you. They are at their most sensitive position when the rod tips are just a few degrees below the horizontal.

TRACING A BURIED PIPE

So let us put this into practice above a buried water pipe, preferably one whose location is precisely known to you (e.g. where your mains water pipe enters the house). This will give you a good idea of a typical wave of energy which you will find when following earth energies later, and, above all, you can relate the energy to the known location of the buried pipe until you have a little experience.

Choose a fairly calm day to begin with to avoid any chance of the wind influencing your results. To make the rods even more sensitive, give them a brisk rub lengthwise with the free hand just prior to commencing. This should give them a charge of static electricity, enabling them to work more easily. Now, holding the rods in front of you at about waist height, with the points slightly below the horizontal, walk at right angles towards the pipe, commanding the rods to turn directly above the pipe and indicate the direction of water flow. Most people will find this easily. You will also find that there are 'sidebands' on either side of the centre line of the pipe, which are called 'Underwood's parallels', although I am not sure if he realised how they were formed. Guy Underwood, an attorney, artist, sculptor, skilled water diviner and amateur archaeologist, whose book *The Pattern of the Past*, describes many forms of earth energies based upon three underground lines detectable by dowsing: water lines, track lines and aquastats, with numerous other secondary effects. He called the entire system 'geodetic'.

The distance from the centre to each of the outer sidebands is the same as the depth of the pipe. This is because a buried pipe or underground stream emits energy vertically to the surface and also at approximately $45°$ on either side. The sidebands, which are the same width as the pipe, upon reaching the surface travel vertically through the air (fig.11). The 'triad' relationships of energy waves has been recorded electronically and is reproduced in graph form in fig.12.

The plan view reveals three sets of lines running parallel to each other, each of which has three further lines of energy. Guy Underwood called these 'water lines'.

Concentrate on finding an underground stream and you should find the central wave first, directly above the flowing water. Place a marker over this. The rods will also tell you the direction of flow. Then walk on at a right angle to the stream until the rods react again at one of the outer parallels. Here place another marker. The distance between the markers is the same as the depth of the underground water.

This is a simplification of the procedure, since there are said to be other wavebands inside and outside of the parallels, also produced by

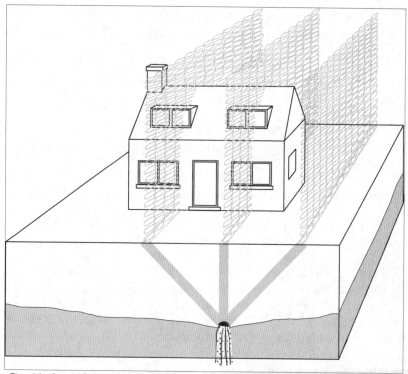

Fig. 11: An underground stream emits waves of energy vertically to the surface and as two 'sidebands' at 45° incline

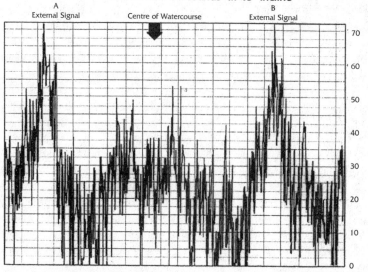

Fig. 12: Electronic measurement above an underground stream, showing main water-course and two signals at edge of stream

the running water. It is by finding these that experienced water diviners can judge how much water there might be in an underground course.

Different soil and rock types can give anomalous results; clay being notoriously awkward in this respect. Also to be considered is the Moon which can cause the angle of the sidebands to vary from $45°$ at certain phases, allowing the outer sidebands to alter their distance from the centre[2]. It is clearly the soil or rock above the pipe or underground stream which causes Underwood's parallel waves of energy, as I discovered when I followed a buried hydro-electric pipe across a moorland bog. As it emerged from the ground, the outer parallels gradually veered in towards the pipe as its depth decreased, until in the open, they converged into the pipe. As you become more proficient, you will discover that it is quite possible to use the rods with their tips pointing sharply downwards, at their most insensitive position. This is very useful in a high wind, for example. Sometimes I have used the rods with no difficulty in winds which snatched the breath out of my mouth and literally drove me to crouch down in the lee of the nearest boulder to recover my breath. Some writers state that using angle rods in a wind is difficult. When beginning, at least, it is best to practise on calm days. With perseverence you may find you can work with only one angle rod, in the hand you normally use. This can give much more accurate results.

LOCATING ENERGY LEYS

If you are fortunate enough to have a standing stone or other energy power point (sacred site) in your neighbourhood, try using the angle rods there. At a standing stone, for example, you must make your mind as detached as possible and relax the body. Now programme your mind (see p.120) to look for earth energies around the standing stone and walk across its face, silently commanding the rods to move in the direction of any energy waves which may be emitted or attracted. Note that as you intercept the energy waves the rods will detect them going towards or away from the stone. Choose which and specify clearly, as if talking to the rods. Woolly-minded dowsing gives woolly results. The rod tips should move slightly either towards the stone or away from it. Follow the rod tips in the direction they indicate, noting the sinuous, serpent-like shape of the wave. A little experience will eliminate any doubts that you are following a real wave, instead of your own thought pattern, which beginners occasionally find confusing.

Author using dowsing rods at a standing stone near Comrie in Scotland

If the standing stone happens to be of the flat-faced type with a narrow spine, then the ideal place to start is outward from the spine, since this is where a complete energy stream is focused. Whichever wave you chose, follow your divining rods carefully. As you move forward, both your rods should move smoothly in unison, following a sinuous line, similar to the illustration of the standing stone at Nether Largie, near Kilmartin in the West of Scotland (fig.13). This is only part of the structure of the wave. The full waveform is shown in fig.14, and includes another wave of much lower amplitude. These are some-times called 'overgrounds' by Tom Graves and resemble the caduceus, the emblem of the medical profession, or the winged staff of Mercury. Could there be more than coincidence in this?

Fig.13: Cup-marked standing stone at Nether Largie, Argyll, emitting a sinuous wave of energy

The sinuous effect is caused by a combination of the wavelength and amplitude of the energy emitted from the stone and can easily be measured by using just one rod close to the ground and placing peg markers along its length. A tape measure can then be used to find the wavelength, from the crest of one wave, to the crest of the following one, and the amplitude, from the centre line to the widest part of the wave as shown in fig.14.

The standing stones I have worked on have a wavelength of approximately 54ins (137cms), with an amplitude of 11ins (28cms). This corresponds to 219MHz, a VHF frequency in the range detectable on our radios. Also the wavelength can be as long as 8ft (244cms) from some sources, such as nuclear reactors or missiles. It is interesting that modern utilities emit waves of energy in similar patterns to what we call earth energies. Again, is this a meaningful coincidence, or is there a simple explanation?

Another researcher, the late Dr.J.Havelock Fidler, of Sutherland in North-west Scotland, formerly a natural scientist at Reading University, portrayed energy waves from a standing stone as being vertical rather than horizontal [longitudinal][4]. This difference may be one of instrumental interpretation".

Fig. 14: 'The Chieftain', Loch Rannoch, Scotland, showing horizontal energy wave in the shape of the caduceus, symbol of medicine (as inset). The vertical arrow is the wavelength, the horizontal the amplitude.

All the energy waves dowsed and discussed in this book have the same double sinuous wave effect, and are shown as horizontal waves, since this is the way they can be revealed with angle rods. These are shown as straight lines in the other illustrations for the sake of simplicity.

COMMON FAULTS

One common fault, when using two rods, is that one rod points in one direction and the other points at right angles to it. This happens with a failure to 'programme' your mind properly. What has usually happened in this case, is that one rod may follow the type of wave which you are looking for, and the other rod tunes into another crossing wave.

Another very common error is when the rods turn in circles. This may be due to different reflexes coming into play rather than the appropriate one. The dowser may have inadvertently tuned into other waves from the soup of energies which surround us all. The answer is to learn from one's experience or to compare another dowser's reactions at the same site.

Repeat to yourself firmly that the rod or rods must follow one individual wave from the standing stone. If nothing happens, it may be because you are too tense. Initially, responses may be very weak. After a little time you will gain confidence and the conscious mental process of searching for earth energies will be discarded as the unconscious mind takes over.

PROGRAMMING YOURSELF

We are surrounded by a confusing mixture of different energies, so you can only get results by tuning into a specific form of energy. This is very easy in practice, for we do this naturally every day in 'tuning in' while conversing with a friend or at a party, when you can listen above the surrounding noise to what one person is saying, even if that person is some little distance away. In dowsing it is the same in relation to subtle energies. A good way to tune into your target is to hold a sample of whatever you are looking for.

For instance, a water diviner might hold a bottle of water in his hand, thus 'programming' him/herself to pick up nothing else but energies radiating from water. Another approach is to use a Mager disc, which has coloured segments. Holding this in the free hand, a more experienced dowser can put one finger on a colour, blue for instance, which to that person means water and find nothing but underground water veins of drinkable water, or, by holding the black segment, polluted subterranean water — the traditional 'black stream'. The energy ley dowser can do the same, to find either healthy or unhealthy energy waves. After some experience the keen individual will find that no props of any kind are needed, as the mind/body will have become sufficiently attuned to the work to do it on its own.

Some people working in the field of earth energies use the traditional forked hazel twig, but this has disadvantages. The dowser has to reset his/her hand grip continuously. This will show the wave direction and amplitude only with great difficulty.

The pendulum is even more difficult to use, as it is impossibly slow and following a wave can be exasperating, especially in a wind. You may, however, find that pendulum or twigs, rods — single or double — any of them, may suit you better individually. There is no harm in trying all of them until you find one which gives you confidence.

It is possibly the dowser's intuition, working through the neuro-muscular area of the brain, the cerebellum, which may produce the driving force behind dowsing. The cerebellum controls the reflexes of the body, in this case the forearms and wrists, and gives tiny, almost unnoticeable involuntary reactions which are amplified by the rods or any other type of dowsing instrument to give a noticeable reaction. The uncontrolled spasm you get when you put your finger into the electric light socket by mistake is a very much exaggerated example of this!

SUPPLYING POWER TO ANCIENT SITES

Recent discoveries by Blanche Merz[3] in France have found that the cathedral of Chartres (a renowned site of intense earth energies), has no less than fourteen subterranean veins of water, arranged like a fan, below its choir, with black marble inlays in the side corridors to iden-tify their positions.

Santiago de Compostela, the famous pilgrimage site in northern Spain has a similar fan of water veins. These, however, were con-structed and reinforcements of the foundations had resulted in the drying up of the source of the water. Subsequently, there have been no more 'miracles'.

In the ancient temple of Hathor, near Denderah in Egypt, the same researcher found more corroborative evidence. One subterranean stream is split as it approaches the temple, flowing around all four sides in a rectangle, below the temple of Isis.

Many of the six-stone circles in my area of Scotland have water flowing beneath them, well below the roots of the stones. It seems that there is an underground stream below each one, with a well tapped into it. From this well, still below the surface, a vein of water exits between each standing stone, sometimes coming to the surface after a short distance. A great deal of work remains to be done to verify this. It has to be said that there are probably too many of these stone structures in Perthshire for them all to be situated above naturally oc-curring streams.

With a dowsing rod it is easy to find the subterranean water veins under a standing stone. Hold a small bottle of water in your free hand, with the top removed, the water trickling over your palm to tune your mind into the fact that you are looking for underground water and underground water only. Painting the divining rod blue can also be a visual prompt. Slowly walk across the face of the stone, and at the edge, the divining rod should gradually turn either away from, or toward the stone, depending upon the direction the water is flowing. If the rod turns away from the stone, follow it carefully, noting the sinuous, snake-like nature of the energy wave. If the rod turns toward the stone, you can follow it through the opposite corner and on its way. The course it will take will be typical of the meandering nature of an underground stream, quite different from the regimented waves of the 'overgrounds'.

TRY TO VERIFY RESULTS

I have always tried to verify my reactions when I locate patterns of telluric energy of any sort by following them back to their source, and on to distant targets. This usually gives an exciting picture of the pattern of natural energies in the landscape.

PATTERNS AROUND A MONOLITH

The number of energy waves from any one single standing stone can be quite amazing. As I approached within a half mile (1km) of one particularly powerful monolith, I could dowse the waves, even at that distance, about a metre apart. They did not feel at all healthy. At the foot of this huge stone lay the remains of a sheep, which I duly carried off and buried. I'm not sure whether the sheep's remains had made any difference or not to the energy ley. Years later this same stone was to give the locals a fright after I attempted to 'clean' the unhealthy waves from it. I succeeded in evoking a strange witch-like apparition from it which approached a family out for a walk, then dematerialised from the feet up, in front of them!

The pattern of energies around a standing stone can be complicated. Not only are energy leys transmitted across country, above ground from the flat faces of the stone, (overgrounds), but standing stones can also be surrounded by a roughly circular spiral. Apart from this, the act of hammering and carving these strange monoliths also injects a form of energy which will be discussed later. There is also a 'shape wave', a wave which spirals out from the stone. Looking at the plan view, it describes the same shape as the stone. There are also others initiated by the Sun and the Moon which are beyond the scope of this book. To some this weakens the credibility of dowsing. Dowsers can disagree among themselves about these patterns. As I said earlier — this is a subjective art.

OTHER INTERESTS

Dowsing is not just about locating earth energies. You can follow a person across country, for instance, if you have a 'witness', a strand of that person's hair, used clothing or picture for example. You can 'walk' with your dowsing rods the energy trail that person leaves behind him/her. If you would like to take this further, try following animal tracks in the snow, noting the different wavelengths and amplitudes for different animals. You can even walk some distance across the snow and follow your own footprints back, tracing your own line. Once again, note the double sinuous wave, with the edge or amplitude of the waves coinciding with the width of your body.

For the reader wishing to study the telluric energy emitted from subterranean water, wells, standing stones, stone circles and volcanic plugs, it is imperative that you don't begin to believe that most earth energies are harmful. Teach yourself to identify the different types, using rods painted with one colour for finding healthy energy, and another for unhealthy (this is explained more fully in a later chapter). If you believe your house has a high incidence of unhealthy energy, it can be partially, or even completely, negated by healthy energy. There are also ways of eliminating the unhealthy energy waves, while retaining the healthy ones, and knowing that there is a problem, you can avoid that particular part of a room.

There are a number of books which go into the subject of using divining implements of various types in much greater detail. Some of these books are listed below or in the bibliography.

NOTES

1. Dubrov, Dr.A., A Talk given to the British Society of Dowsers; (July 1993).
2. Davis, P.V., "Moon on Depthing"; *B.S.D.* Magazine, No.203.
3. Merz, B., *Points of Cosmic Energy*: C.W.Daniel Co Ltd.
4. Havelock Fidler, J., *Ley Lines - Their Nature and Properties*: Turnstone, 1982.

CHAPTER 14

UNHEALTHY ENERGIES

THE HARTMANN NET AND CURRY GRID

The Earth is an electromagnetic body, with its own electromagnetic grid pattern. The most important is called the First Global Grid, or Hartmann Grid or Net, comprised of parallel energy waves rising vertically from the ground. Dr.Hartmann, a German doctor, describes them as alternatively positive and negative, running from north to south and from east to west. He found that they are 4ins. (10cms) wide and 38yds (35m) apart in Switzerland. The distances differ from area to area.

Dr.Hartmann believes that where two of what he calls 'negative' lines cross (Hartmann knot), irritations of the nervous system and rheumatic illnesses can occur. He states that twelve hours prior to an earthquake, weak secondary rays can be found, one on each side of the main wave, gathering in strength until they are the same as the central one.

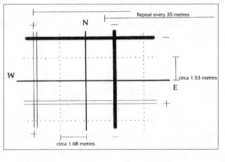

Fig. 15: First Global or Hartmann Grid.

At the time of an earthquake the Hartmann grid is distorted, taking about 30 minutes to resume its former state. In addition, at the more powerful crossing points of this system, there is a 50% increase of radioactivity. The energy leys and streams which I have investigated and which are the context of this book do not alter their character in such circumstances.

There is another much tighter grid pattern called the Second or Curry Grid, after a Swiss doctor, Dr.Manfred Curry. He identified this as travelling from south-east to north-west and south-west to north-east, with energy waves about 10ft. (3m) apart, with medically significant double lines 47yds (50m) apart. Kathe Bächler referred to them as 'lines' or 'strips', about 30in. (75cm.) wide. Again, where two 'negative' lines cross (Curry crossings), there may be sleep disturbances, depression, tendency to inflammations and diseases of the rheumatic complex. Where the positive lines cross Dr.Curry found enhanced cell enlargement and proliferation, even to the point of cancerous growth.

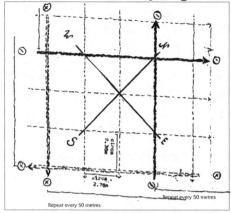

Fig. 16: The Curry Grid

Dr. Patrick MacManaway of Strathmiglo, Fife, Dr.Schneck of Bideford, Devon, and I found that the rays, lines and strips referred to are actually the same double sinuous wave, but of different amplitudes and wavelengths to those earth energy leys and streams referred to in this book. A great deal of research has been done in Continental Europe on these grids and nets and there has been much published, but very little in Britain and in the United States.

At the moment, I find that energy leys and streams are much more powerful and potentially responsible for illness, and I usually tend to ignore the Curry and Hartmann grid waves, to avoid confusion. For this reason I do not intend to write further on this topic here, but for those who would like to find out more of the work in Europe, I commend Blanche Merz's book *Points of Cosmic Energy*.

*   *   *   *   *   *   *

Underground streams of water emit energy vertically to the surface, and it is this energy which a standing stone transmits, presumably from the quartz crystals in its structure. They propagate as streams of individual waves or 'overgrounds' across country, above and through the ground. These overgrounds have already been described as straight energy leys, and the wider energy streams, and can be easily identified as they run in orderly, parallel lines. If the subterranean stream is polluted, by natural chemicals dissolved in it, by acid rain, pesticides, sheep and cattle droppings, radon gas or radioactive fallout, then the surface energy ley or stream may affect the health of anyone living in its path.

Some people refer to these waves of energy as positive or negative, as the case may be, but for most people the use of these words is misleading in this context, as the word positive, for instance, conjurs up an image of healthy energies. This is confusing, since positive ions, for instance, are unhealthy, while negative ions are essential to our well-being. Because of this, for the rest of this section of the book such energies are referred to as 'unhealthy' in their harmful character, or otherwise 'healthy'. For example: an energy ley comprised solely of waves of healthy energy, crossed by another similar energy ley at right angles, will form a grid of healthy energy. The effect of such a pattern is not harmful.

On the other hand, if the same two energy leys have passed through an area of decaying material; downstream of these areas, each wave will have changed its character to an unhealthy wave. There you will have a grid pattern which could have very unpleasant effects.

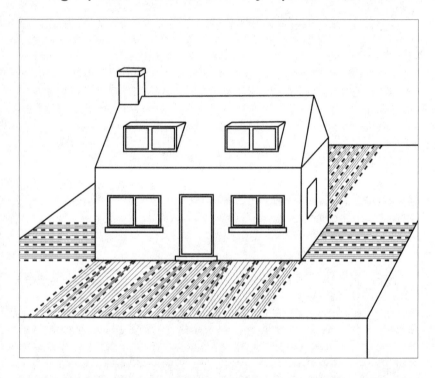

Fig. 17: A 'normal' house with a grid of healthy and unhealthy energies.
The unhealthy energies (dashed lines) won't pass through glass and seek weak points such as doors. The crossing points of these lines are more stressful.
The healthy energies (solid lines) will pass easily through glass and stonework.
The energy ley stream, here travelling from bottom to top, may initially consist of healthy waves, but after passing through decaying matter, some of the waves will change to unhealthy, forming this grid of both polarities.
(For simplicity the double sinuous aspects of the waves, their vertical polarity and the waves which do not pass through the house have been omitted.)

Energy leys and streams are comprised of various combinations of healthy and unhealthy energies. An 'average' building could have unhealthy waves one metre apart, with healthy energies every 4ins (10cms) apart, and a badly irradiated building may have the polarity reversed. They are vertically polarised (fig.13, p.118), and can irradiate even the top flats and offices of the tallest buildings.

Very roughly speaking then, a house in any area may have waves of: entirely healthy energy; entirely unhealthy energy; one unhealthy wave to, say, thirty healthy waves, or one healthy to thirty unhealthy waves, or any combination in between.

FENG-SHUI

There are some similarities in China to that which we have already discussed. Feng-Shui (feng = wind, shui = water, pronounced 'foong schway') means to live in peace and harmony with the land, with prosperity, good luck, and good health. Living and working in a good feng-shui site will ensure good fortune and a longer life.

Repeatedly during this research I have encountered a relationship between Chinese feng-shui and some aspects of telluric energy systems in the United Kingdom. China does not have an exact parallel, however, since it does not appear to have the stone age structures found in Britain. The concept, however, of 'ch'i,' or dragon and tiger lines, (two types of natural energy currents which traverse the country, one Yin, the weaker female element, and the other Yang, the stronger male aspect), is very similar to the propagation of the energy streams in the Sma' glen mentioned later.

Similarly, in Chinese literature the dragon/tiger lines follow the contours of the land and the two forces travel along rivers and watercourses, above and below ground, although the sources in this case are natural ones in the mountains. It is thought that at the point where Yin, the blue tiger, and Yang, the blue dragon meet is the best point to situate a burial ground for example, and that the ratio of energy should be three-fifths of Yang to two-fifths of Yin.

Where a landscape is predominantly yang (mountainous), a powerful place will be where there is a yin or flat plain within it. One of the most powerful places in my own mountainous area in Scotland is the Sma' Glen, which has a bowl-shaped depression with a very powerful megalithic stone in the centre. Conversely, a flat plain with a hill or rock (like Silbury Hill and Glastonbury Tor in England, or Ayers Rock in Australia) would also be powerful.

There are however, the unpleasant aspects of feng-shui to be taken into consideration. 'Sha ch'i' the noxious breath or exhalations, is the opposite of healthy 'ch'i'. It can be produced by the topography of the land. Where the ch'i passes through stagnant water, bogs, toilets, deep gullies and ravines, large cavities, there is particular need to be careful of the unpleasant influences that it will pick up en route. These unpleasant influences can be diverted in similar ways to telluric energies in Britain. These may include placing a mirror in their path, building a pond or fountain or a wall in the correct position, or by screening a site with trees.

A landscape predominantly flat, with eroded geological outcrops on the earth's surface, is bad Feng-shui, as the ch'i is unable to breathe. Straight roads and streets are also very bad feng-shui, as are railways, tramways, lines of electric pylons and telephone poles. Equally bad are straight lines of trees, rivers, canals and rooftops, which all have the unfortunate ability of running off the good 'ch'i' too quickly. It has to be slowed down and pooled to do its beneficial work. Despite the aversion to straight lines of any description, however, it is possible in feng-shui wisdom to have straight streets, as long as any harmful influences are counteracted by, for example, constructing pagodas and statues of dragons, of the correct size at the appropriate points!

MODERN 'SHA CH'I'

Today, bad Feng Shui are stagnant canals and rivers, decaying granite (which gives off deadly radon gas), burial grounds, mortuaries, plague pits, sewage farms, rubbish dumps, possibly chemical and nuclear waste dumps that pollute the energy lines. These appear to be some of the places through which energy leys and streams passing through become poisoned by the unhealthy contents, turning into 'unhealthy streams' of energy.

The subterranean rock strata have also to be taken into account. Georges Lakhovsky found that some forms of cancer are more prevalent in certain areas. Plastic clay, muddy alluvial areas, slate, limestone and beds of carboniferous sediments are unhealthy, he thought, while places based on sand, sandstone, and gypsum have a low cancer-inducing density[1]. There is an alternative theory which I shall discuss in Chapter 20.

LOCATING UNHEALTHY WAVES

Now it is time to study and find for ourselves with the aid of the divining rod the unhealthy vertical waves from an energy ley which pollute our own home. Since standing stones are powerful emitters of energies of different types, we will concentrate on these for the moment. No matter in what part of the country you live, your house will be irradiated by an energy ley or stream of some form. Most houses will have a grid pattern of healthy and unhealthy energies passing through them from distant standing stones, geological faults or other features, or major electrical devices.

To find healthy and unhealthy energy waves with a divining rod: first, (having considered your own protection as described in Chapter 13) prompt your mind with the fact that you are looking for unhealthy waves, paint your divining rod with an appropriate colour or wind coloured electrician's tape around it, or even hold something coloured in your free hand. Holding your divining rod/s loosely, tip/s slightly down, walk slowly down the length of the room you are surveying, asking the rods to turn in the direction of any unhealthy energy wave.

Unhealthy energy waves will not normally pass through glass, e.g. a window, or a mirror, but they will enter through a weak spot such as the wooden uprights in a traditional window frame or through the edge of a door. If a modern side-hinged window is partially open, the energy waves will shift along until they are once again obstructed by the glass. They can also find cracks in a building (or spaces between ceramic tiles) and penetrate these.

If you have no success, try again, remembering to hold the rods so that they turn freely in the hand, or holders, points slightly down — the lower you hold the points the more insensitive they become. Also remember to rub the rods lengthwise with the free hand prior to commencing, and to concentrate on what you are looking for. If the rods turn in circles, you have probably tuned into the aura which surrounds your own body. Lower the tips a little, focus your mind on what you are looking for, and walk at a slow pace, not too quickly or slowly. Accuracy will come with just a little practice.

When the rods do begin to turn just at the edge of the window, follow the wave carefully. It may turn perhaps at right angles to the window. Note any gently weaving effect from the rods. For accuracy, try using one divining rod and draw a diagram of the roughly parallel lines on a notepad, being particularly careful at your bedspace or area where you spend a lot of time — your favourite armchair, for instance. Repeat this at the wall at right angles to the first, and you will have a grid pattern of the unhealthy waves in the room. You can also do a survey for the healthy waves, by painting your divining rods another colour or winding coloured electrician's tape around them, if you wish.

Outside the house, if there is sufficient space, follow one wave for a short distance. Locate as accurately as you can the direction from which it comes, either by using a compass, or by fixing its bearing on a distant object and translating the line on to a map. This may give a clue as to its origin, but unless you actually walk to its source, you could be misled. There may be no standing stones in that direction, and the energy source may be a television repeater station, electrical sub-station, or generator (which emit a somewhat similar type of wave). Remember that you can command the rods to follow the energy in either direction. You can also, if you wish, follow the wave through the house, and on to its distant target, i.e. another standing stone or circle if it is part of the ancient system, or a quarry, one of the more modern attractions to certain types of earth energies.

If you make a rough drawing of the ground floor plan of your home, you should find that any rooms above will roughly comply with the same pattern, since an unhealthy wave manifests vertically as well and will only deviate slightly as it is warped to the side of any windows or glass on the upper floor. (There are houses, however, which do not conform to this general rule). The bedroom is the most important place, since telluric energies are said to be more powerful at night. We are at our most susceptible when asleep, when the body is trying to repair itself, and the brain is broadcasting messages to every cell.

It is unusual to find a room in a house which has not at least a few

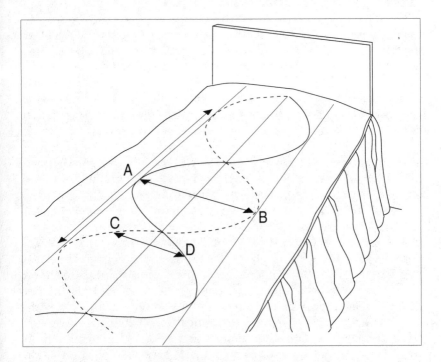

Fig. 18: One wave traversing bed top to bottom, 'A' is the wavelength and 'A'-'B' the amplitude.

unhealthy waves running through it. If you happen to have such a wave traversing the length of the bed, that could be a bad place to sleep, as the waves from standing stones and other more modern sources are about 4ft.8in.(142 cms.) to 6ft.(183cms.). The height of most humans fall into this range. Since antennae (like the human body when lying in bed), with the same length as the wave's length will receive maximum impact from the wave, there could be some risk to the person sleeping in that bed.

The single wave traversing the bed will only cause trouble to a person if it has been there for some years. If there are two unhealthy waves crossing the bed at the head or vital organs level, for instance, this could eventually initiate an illness. This will also depend on the sensitivity of the individual and the source of the wave. Few of us stay in one place long enough for any ill effects to manifest themselves. Most people move house or bedrooms from time to time, or even shift the bed if there is enough room, or mirrors and pictures whilst re-decorating. Most people unconsciously avoid such crossing points, and young children in cots, especially, can be found in the morning huddled away from such an area.

The usual way to overcome a problem of this nature is to find an area in a bedroom where there is no crossing point and shift the bed there. This is not always possible, due to the layout of a crowded bedroom or the number of crossing waves. It might help if partners change places every so often, or individuals can change their position in a double bed, for instance.

Some dowsers write about 'rays' of energy through beds, etc., and draw them as parallel lines. These rays are, I suggest, one and the same as the double wave in Chapter 13, and can be seen in fig.18. The confusion is, I believe, because many dowsers use the traditional type of forked hazel branch or pendulum which will react at any point on the sinuous wave, giving a range of widths, from the full amplitude of the wave *(A-B)* as in the illustration, to an apparently narrow wave if the operator happens to try closer to the nodal points of the wave *(C-D)*.

ELECTRICAL APPLIANCES, TRANSFORMERS AND POWER STATIONS

Another source of energy waves which can be found with divining rods in the home emanates from television sets, microwave ovens and VDUs (See Chaps 5&7). Switch on the appliance of your choice and use your divining rod to follow the emitted wave.

A microwave oven, for instance, radiates alternately positive and

negative waves similar to the much more powerful electrical generators at power stations in all directions, like the spokes of a bicycle
wheel. This effect is called a frequency window — the wavelengths
are slightly different in length — and can be found with the dowsing
rod as a gently weaving wave. The wavelength is approximately 12½ins
(32 cms.), and the amplitude 3½ins (9 cms.) at the highest setting.
My television set emits waves of 8ins (20cms.) wavelength and 2ins
(5cms.) amplitude, according to my divining rod, and a spiral of a
radius of approximately 7½yds (7m). Strangely, like power station
generators and radar stations, etc., I find the positive and negative
energy as a low energy sinuous wave.

The unhealthy waves from household appliances will transmit through
glass, unlike those from standing stones, which are deflected around
the sides of glass objects. There have been similar occurrences from
underground streams, and we shall explore them later.

Electricity sub-stations, whether buried or above surface, also emit a
similar radiating pattern of alternately positive and negative waves
with a wavelength and amplitude very similar to those of some standing stones. Their polarity can also be altered by passing through areas
of high decay, turning unhealthy in the process.

Apart from the wavelengths, the main difference between, say, a
standing stone and a power station generator is that the energy ley
from a standing stone widens out from its face, to give a wide stream,
perhaps several hundred metres across as it traverses the country.
Eventually, it narrows to focus into another standing stone, but an
electric generator or transformer emits waves which radiate out equally,
until they are captured by a telluric attractor, like a quarry, and (presumably) return to source underground to complete the circuit. I call
these 'radial leys' to differentiate between them and the Megalithic
energy leys and streams.

One transformer, stepping down from 33kV to 11kV, situated at the
edge of my home town of Crieff, was almost ideally placed for me to
follow its waves across country to find what special qualities they had,
and how they behaved. The waves radiated outwards like the spokes
of a wheel from the transformer, not from the H.T. pylons linked to it.
I followed one with a wavelength of 73in.(185 cms.) and amplitude
9in.(23cms.), across the fields, until it earthed itself in a quarry.

Every quarry produces a large telluric 'image' of itself, which spirals
out for some considerable distance, following the shape of the quarry,
until the wave collapses back to begin the cycle afresh. The wave is
actually a composite of two waves, one moving clockwise and one
anti-clockwise. I found that in the case of the quarry at Crieff incoming

waves from the transformer touching the much magnified image focused themselves into the centre of the quarry via this image. A high proportion of them focused down the road leading into the quarry, then spread out to the perimeter, where they earthed themselves. Such waves usually 'prefer' vertical cracks in rock faces.

HUMANS AND ANIMALS AS WELL?

One intriguing aspect of the concept of alternate healthy and unhealthy energies radiating out from transformers and sub-stations, etc., is that there are very similar waves from animals and humans. My own is 17in. (43cms.) wavelength, 5ins. (13cms) amplitude. I read that the wavelength of human cells has been found to be half of this: 8 ^{2}/$_3$ins. (22cms.), which is, perhaps, a surprising coincidence'[2]. With one colour-coded divining rod I can find vertically polarised waves of 'healthy' energy radiating out from a person, very similar to the radiations from standing stones, etc. By using another divining rod, I find that they are separated by 'unhealthy' waves. I also find that the waves are directional, and will not alter their vector even if the person turns around. Further, the number of waves can change as the day goes on. From seven waves early in the morning they gradually change to eight, then nine at mid-day, then back to seven at night. These emanations seem to be a product of what esotericists call the human 'aura'. The reader's attention is drawn to similar radiations mentioned in Kathe Bächler's *Earth Radiation*.

Since cats are known to sleep in the centre of unhealthy radiations of this type, I checked a number of them, which gave an unexpected twist — they emit 'unhealthy' waves, which is not to say that it is unhealthy to keep a cat!

NOTES
1. Lakhovsky, G., *The Secret of Life.*
2. Merz, B., *Points of Cosmic Energy.*

CHAPTER 15

SPIRALS, CROP CIRCLES and DEMONS

There have been earlier references to spirals. The Chinese see spirals as yang energy, the charging, centripetal, contracting force, coming from outer space to the centre of the Earth; and yin energy, the discharging centrifugal expanding force travelling from the centre of the planet into space. They observe the results of these energies in, for example, fruits like the plum or apple, where spirals entering the fruit from both top and bottom cause their distinctive shapes. The spiral of hair on the head of a young child is another example, and is believed to show the yang energy passing down into the brain, then to the vocal chords, heart, sex organs, and finally to the feet, where it is

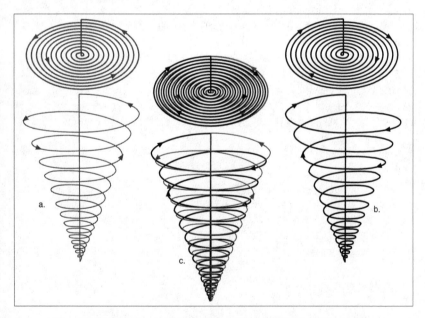

Fig. 19: (a) Healthy anti-clockwise spiral, and its plan view above.
(b) The unhealthy clockwise spiral.
(c) Both combined give an unhealthy noxious vortex.

earthed. The yin spiral from the Earth, passes up in the opposite direction, using the same channel and causes the aura and the chakras. It should come as no surprise that anyone sleeping or living in an energy spiral of the wrong polarity can suffer damage to his health.

SPIRALS

Underground streams of water produce a series of overlapping spirals which can be found directly above them, on the surface, the radius of the spirals being the same as the depth of the water.

There are basically two types. From the plan view they are:

The anti-clockwise spiral travelling upwards, from an aquifer, stream (or pipe), which gives a healthy form of energy. At the surface, this will be found as a single spiral, travelling outwards anti-clockwise from the centre. Secondly, the double spiral. This is formed by a clockwise spiral, again travelling upwards, superimposed on the basic anti-clockwise spiral (fig.19).

This is the pattern which I have found to be associated with so many different illnesses, although the directions may change in the southern

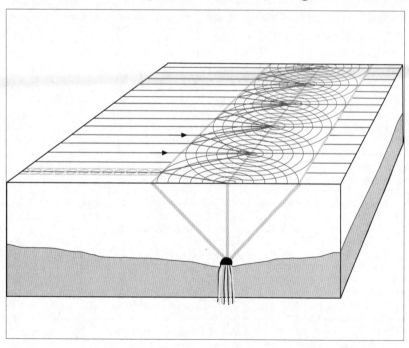

Fig. 20: The healthy energy stream from the left focuses into the beneficial anti-clockwise spirals above an underground stream, like-energies attracting like (for simplicity waves are shown as single lines).

hemisphere. Note: unhealthy spirals are depicted in the following illustrations as being formed clockwise from the centre without the anti-clockwise component, and healthy spirals as anti-clockwise.

In a typical case of a healthy spiral, you may find the basic spiral above a pipe, with the incoming energy ley, radial ley or energy stream focusing into each of the centres as in fig.20. Notice that some of the individual waves split into two, to tune into the centre of two spirals. This illustration is based on the large hydro-electric pipes found at reservoirs, which are much easier to survey than natural subterranean streams.

A dwelling built on an unhealthy spiral above a natural subterranean stream has the pattern shown in fig.21, almost like a spider's web. Here, on the ground floor, the individual unhealthy waves from a standing stone or other source, possibly some considerable distance away, each encounter the outside edge of the double spiral. The relationship of unhealthy to healthy waves will depend upon the amount of decaying material that they pass through. The unhealthy waves, if you are unlucky, may be as close as 2ins (5cms.) apart or less, and will be warped at 90° from the outer edge of the unhealthy spiral and deflected into the centre, giving a vortex of particularly unhealthy energies ascending more or less vertically.

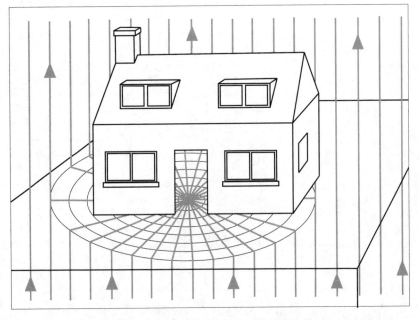

Fig. 21: A house built on an unhealthy spiral

You will always find the healthy waves from the telluric energy tuning into a healthy spiral, and the unhealthy waves into an unhealthy spiral. Unlike magnetism, where like poles repel; in this case like polarities attract.

The spiral can penetrate all the floors in a high building, and the spirals in the ground floor will be repeated, generally, in the rooms directly above. Inevitably, some houses will have the misfortune to have one or more spirals in their bedrooms. These may be the 'cancer verticals' that Cody discovered, which he thought may be initiated by radon gas (fig.22). (See Chapter 12).

Two unhealthy waves crossing each other at an angle can eventually, over a period, cause illness in a person. The vastly increased number of waves focusing into the centre, plus the spiral itself, is more likely to cause ill-health to anyone within the circumference of the spiral. In addition, if it appears through a bed, there is every chance that the occupant will be in line with one or more of the energy waves.

LINES OF SPIRALS ABOVE AQUIFERS

Often, when surveying a house, I have found what appear to be two, or sometimes three streams with associated spirals running roughly

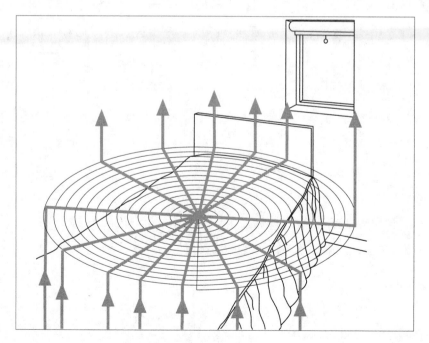

Fig. 22: An unhealthy spiral in a bed.

parallel within a short distance of each other. These occur, apparently at random, like subterranean streams. It has happened so frequently that I asked a hydrologist if these could really be natural veins of underground water. He did not think that subterranean streams behaved in this manner, and I could only surmise that they are caused by aquifers which are large, naturally occurring masses of water flowing in gravel, sand or limestone, above an impermeable layer of rock. To check this idea, I went to a valley which had a wide grassy swathe cut through the heather, with a spring at the foot. Water percolating down the pass between the two hills flowed on top of an igneous rock aquifer producing a lush growth of grass on the surface. This gave a pattern of energies similar to veins of water running roughly parallel below ground, and may be the reason why many water diviners and hydrologists disagree. The hydrologists know that much subterranean water percolates slowly through aquifers, while water diviners might detect apparently individual veins of water (fig.23).

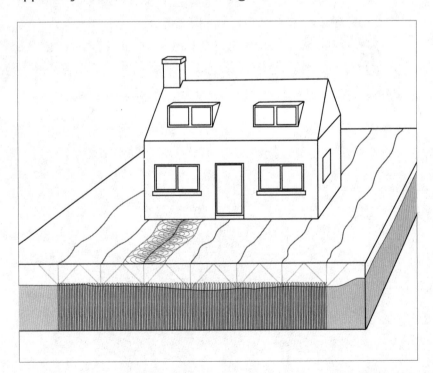

Fig. 23: Most underground water percolates through aquifers, but water trickling through gives the impression of individual veins (only one row of spirals shown for simplicity).

STAKING A WATER VEIN

If you hammer a metal stake into the ground, vertically above an underground pipe or stream, this immediately becomes the focal point of a spiral. For some time, water diviners have used a similar method, discovered by the late Major Ralph Creyke in 1930, to calculate the depth of water veins. A spiral caused by a stake positioned in this manner is contained by the outer parallels, which are the same distance from the centre of the water vein as the water vein is below the surface. All the diviner had to do was to stake the centre of the stream at any point, then walk in any direction until he found the outer edge of the spiral. Measuring from the centre to the outer edge of the spiral would give the depth. This is a simplified description of his method which could determine not only the depth of the vein, but the width.

Another interesting aspect of hammering in a metal stake above a stream is that the vertical energy from the vein will bend towards the circumference of the nearest spiral until it touches the outer parallel, then curves back further downstream.

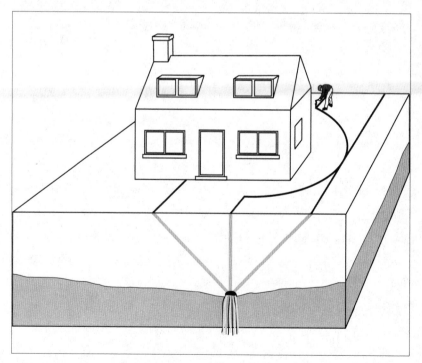

Fig. 24: Diverting an unhealthy energy line above an underground vein of water by hammering a stake into the ground directly above the vein. The diverted energy is contained by one of the outriders.

In cases where a natural subterranean stream has caused flooding, perhaps in a building, water diviners, according to folklore, have been able to divert it by using this stake method upstream of the building. The water is supposed to turn away directly below the stake, and travel down the nearest secondary channel. I must admit to being very sceptical of this, since when I stake the water flow above an underground pipe, the wave is immediately turned away to one side or another, but the water most certainly stays in the pipe! It may be that free flowing underground water in its natural environment tends to follow the diverted wave, by the nearest weak point in the subterranean strata, but this is only conjecture.

HUMANS AND ANIMALS IN SPIRALS

In the previous chapter I pointed out that humans have vertically polarized waves which are emitted from their bodies. In the natural environment, they radiate out equally on all sides, like the spokes of a bicycle wheel. If the person is within the circumference of some forms of unhealthy spiral, the waves are 'captured' by it. The unhealthy spiral seems to behave like a black hole, sucking the waves of the same polarity from the person and earthing it, with which symptoms I am

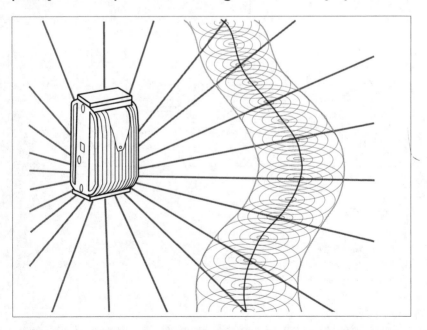

Fig. 25: Unhealthy energies from an electricity sub-station ground into the centre of unhealthy spirals above an underground water vein.

sure its victims, suffering from a debilitating illness like Chronic Fatigue Syndrome (M.E.), can readily identify. Its counterpart, the healthy spiral, seems to charge anyone within its range with healthy radiation.

Likewise, when a person is sitting in front of a television, or VDU, his/her energy (both polarities in this case) is also warped into the centre of the unit itself. This is rather bewildering. If it can be verified by others, which I am sure it will be, this could lead to some interesting theories on the effects of electro-stress on the human body, and the addiction of some people to computers, television, and amusement arcade gaming machines.

The unhealthy energies radiating from televisions and sub-stations can themselves be attracted to the unhealthy spirals above subterranean streams, before continuing on their way. Let us not forget also that the healthy energies from sub-stations and other utilities are attracted into healthy spirals.

In the previous chapter I mentioned that cats had no positive radiations. It is probably because of this that they are content to sleep in unhealthy spirals. Oddly, the unhealthy radiating lines from a cat are not captured by such a spiral. They radiate out from it. Bees also fare better in what are to us, unhealthy energies. One swarm settled in my back garden on a handy post very close to an unhealthy spiral. Ants are also reputed to favour unhealthy spirals. It does seem odd that stinging insects should favour such areas. Perhaps they help the insects to make the chemicals for their stings.

It has been noted that bacteria thrive in unhealthy spirals, which may be one of the major reasons that they are associated with so many illnesses. Even Louis Pasteur is reputed to have said on his deathbed, "It is not the microbe, it is the terrain after all" — an obvious reference to unhealthy earth energies. One person even stated that the only use for an unhealthy spiral is as a site for the garden compost heap!

Dogs, according to most practitioners, always seek sites which are favourable to humans. I must say that in many cases I have found this to be incorrect, perhaps due to pets living, as we do, in an artificial environment. This lowers our (and perhaps their) instinctive awareness to areas of stress. One dog owner, alarmed at her pet dying of cancer of the mammary glands, told me that her previous dog suffered the same fate, even though they were from different litters. She had unwittingly placed the dog's basket on an unhealthy spiral. Neither dog apparently objected to it sufficiently to show its displeasure by refusing to sleep there.

Noting the behaviour of cattle and sheep can be a good indication of the presence of telluric energy. In Germany, farmers at one time used to put sheep into an enclosure and observe their reactions. If they were restless and huddled to one side it would be a harmful place to build. If, on the other hand, the animals were content and spread themselves over the area, they could build their own home there. Russians used the same technique, but followed this practice with a variation — they would put pieces of meat down in a grid pattern. A few days later an inspection of the meat would reveal, by the decay or lack of it, what type of energies were present, and where.

Storks have been associated with childbirth for as long as mankind has settled in communities. According to Baron von Pohl, they will always choose a healthy earth energy field in which to build their nests — presumably healthy spirals. This also has the added advantage that they do not attract lightning, unlike their unhealthy counterparts. Recently I was amused to see a television programme which, to the consternation of the scientists, proved mathematically that there was a much higher incidence of childbirth in villages which had a large population of nesting storks!

A TYPICAL SPIRAL AND ITS EFFECTS

The reader may relate to the following example of an unhealthy spiral and its effects on people within its range. This was the first time that I had personally felt the effects of a powerful unhealthy spiral.

In East Retford, near Nottingham, a client asked me to check his hairdressing salon. The atmosphere inside was unpleasant. He said that one area was unnaturally cold and his wife refused to go up to the top flat on her own. The hairdressing assistants, too, felt the oppressive atmosphere and became uneasy when they entered the premises in the morning. I was sceptical, but nevertheless agreed to do a survey.

During one of the warmest days of that summer, we entered the shop. Immediately, in the inner doorway, I experienced a cold, clammy atmosphere. The feeling was even worse on the first floor. I was not surprised that the hairdresser's wife and her assistants refused to go there on their own. Fortunately, at that early stage in my research, I knew just enough about this form of spiral to eliminate it with a Lakhovsky coil (see the section in Chapter 19 on "Eliminating Spirals"). The last I heard was that the salon had a much better atmosphere, and customers had noticed the change in the feeling of the place.

Interestingly, the hairdresser also pointed out that the more people there were in the salon, the less noticeable the oppressive atmosphere. It was as if the energy was being shared out and diluted between the people present. The cold, clammy atmosphere experienced in such an area can also give damp spots in houses, sometimes vertically above one another in a multi-storey building. One lady was delighted when

I traced a spring from its outlet near her front door through her cottage, until I came to the wall. Half way up the wall, directly above the centre of an unhealthy spiral, was a damp patch which had persistently defeated all attempts at rectification by the builders.

CROP CIRCLES

Early in my research I was becoming increasingly aware that scientists would be extremely sceptical of the theory that spirals from underground water could cause illness and other effects, but fate decided to play a helping hand to bring the spirals to the attention of the general public and the world at large in a sensational manner.

This was the advent of the beautiful crop circles which over twenty years have grown in number and complexity in the south of England and elsewhere; beginning with pristine purity, but becoming later confused by hoaxers trying to discredit it as a natural phenomenon.

In 1981, Pat Delgado, a retired electro-mechanical design engineer, had his attention drawn to some mysterious circles in fields of crops at Cheesefoot Head, Hampshire. In the following years he studied the rapidly growing phenomenon with a group of colleagues, and by 1989 an international scientific effort was under way to try to find its cause.[1]

The patterns in growing crops are beautifully symmetrical, usually circular, with the stalks bent above the surface of the ground in a clockwise or anti-clockwise pattern. On occasion, a clockwise swirling pattern has been overlaid with a subsequent anti-clockwise pattern, or vice versa. The circles come in a variety of shapes and configurations, sometimes in geometric patterns, and often strongly symbolic. The edges are mostly sharp and well defined. The circles are formed at night in a variety of crops, but also sometimes in field grass or in trees.

In twenty years there have been several thousand crop circle events in many countries around the world, with the greatest number and the most complex in southern England; they are too widespread, complex and numerous to be explained away as hoaxes.

THE BLAIRGOWRIE CROP CIRCLES

There have been very few crop circles reported in Scotland. However, I was able to see one of the earliest ones which occurred on Friday night, 15th June, 1990, within 100 metres of a disused quarry.[2]

Two circles, the larger 74ft.1in. diameter, the smaller 37ft.7in., were both swirled anti-clockwise in a field of 3ft. high grass near Blairgowrie, in Perthshire. This crop does not have tramlines (tractor wheel tracks) which can encourage hoaxers. Laurence Blair Oliphant, the farmer and owner of the nearby Ardblair Castle insisted he was the first person to enter the pattern. The circles looked beautifully symmetrical and round, but they were actually slightly oval in shape, with a tightly wound bunch of grass in each of the slightly offset centres. The grass stalks were pressed hard into the ground, with each blade looking as if it had been steamed, pressed and curved into shape.

The pattern was beginning to lose its highly coherent design due to the fact that grass can recover quite quickly from damage. These particular crop circles had an anti-clockwise spiral of energy, sensed by my divining rods, and there was no sign of a clockwise spiral at all.

There were incoming waves with a wavelength of 60in. (152cms.), and an amplitude of 5in.(13cms.), which may have come from a distant standing stone. At that time I was unable to follow it back to source as I would have liked. It is obvious to me that it is by the use of divining rods that any sensitive person with experience will have a better chance of differentiating between a natural and a hoaxed circle.

Jenny Blair Oliphant, the farmer's wife, told me of several other incidents which had occurred in the space of a few years prior to this event. It is possible that they could have been caused by the same energy phenomenon.

UNIDENTIFIED AERIAL PHENOMENA AND DEAD CATTLE

Two years before the crop circles occurred, Jenny Oliphant was in the castle kitchen, when she was amazed to see a huge circular object hovering above the pine trees in the courtyard. She watched it for several minutes, then called her husband. They both went into the courtyard and watched the object which had variously coloured lights on its circumference. They said they felt powerful vibrations coming from the spinning shape. Suddenly, without warning, it disappeared, and all was still again. Only some weeks after the circles occurred, did they realise that the two mysterious occurrences might be connected.

Early one morning, the farm manager entered the same field in which the crop circles were to manifest themselves the following year. He was horrified to find two stirks (immature calves), a stot (bull calf), and a heifer, lying dead at the circular feeder. He carefully noted the positions of the animals. They were on their knees and the heads of both were twisted in the same direction. He dragged the bodies to the edge of the field and summoned the vet, who took blood samples and tested for anthrax, which is the usual practice, before cutting open the neck of one to confirm his suspicion that it had died of a broken spine. There were no other signs of damage to the calves. He suggested that they had died at around midnight, 23rd November, 1989.

The injuries had been inflicted by some powerful physical trauma.

and he conjectured how this had occurred. There had been no low flying aircraft during that period, or thunder or lightning, or hoof scrapings on the ground, and the food hopper was in its original position. Both the stot and the stirk had been feeding at the same quarter of the hopper, which suggests that both animals had died simultaneously, and there had been no struggle.

The two crop circles had an underground stream running down through their centres. It was this which seems to have been one factor which linked the two incidents. It was relatively easy to follow the track of this stream, from the large circle, through the smaller, then down to the area where the hopper had been the year before. It continued on to Ardblair Castle, into the well in the centre of the building, out to the pine trees where the aerial phenomenon occurred, then on to a stone circle nearby. This circle is unique, since it has a road running through it, which may or may not be relevant.

It is possible that the circular hopper had induced an energy field from the underground vein of water which attracted a form of aerial energy. Instead of manifesting as a crop circle, the energy had earthed itself, striking the two animals with sufficent power to break their necks. Alternatively, a powerful electric shock, like clear air lightning, for instance, may have struck the hopper and shorted through the cows, causing a powerful muscular spasm, sufficient to break their necks. Laurence Blair Oliphant assured me that the necks of cattle are immensely strong. It takes a very powerful physical blow to cause damage of this nature. He also showed me his map of the area, with three energy leys intersecting at that point from nearby standing stones and circles.

Whatever might have caused the aerial display seen by Mr. and Mrs.Oliphant, or killed the cattle, or formed the crop circles remains a mystery. Gustav Freheirr von Pohl discovered that lightning earths itself preferably into two crossing subterranean veins of water. Oak trees flourish over these zones, hence the higher than average number of times that oak trees are hit by lightning. Perhaps it is a disorganised form of ionized energy from some source which earths itself into the ground, initially forming a tubular shape whose width is determined by the width of the stream of water, causing a tightly twisted bunch of crop in the centre, then spirals outwards, culminating in highly complex designs — the same earth energy designs which are all around us. This vortex theory was initiated by Dr.Terence Meaden, and I have adjusted it somewhat to take into account the hidden spirals above aquifers.

Recently it has been impossible to say just how many of these circles are natural and how many are hoaxed, but well-informed opinion is that it is a genuine phenomenon with a history of at least 20 years which in Britain in the last six years has been largely undermined by an intensive and financially well-backed disinformation campaign by a semi-official group actively encouraging particular groups of hoaxers. The most complex and symbolically significant ones are still very much part of the genuine phenomenon. At some level it seems that government is clearly concerned that public interest in the phenomenon will lead people to become more inquisitive about the UFO phenomenon, to which the crop circles may be closely related!

It is very sad that the crop circle phenomenon has not been taken more seriously. Some aspects of 'paranormal' behaviour, and the recovery of the knowledge of the ancient megalithic culture also depend, I believe, on understanding these same energies.

DEMONS

The object which Mr. and Mrs.Oliphant saw may be similar to the huge glowing sphere of light one Edinburgh woman saw approaching her house at what she described as a fantastic speed. To her horror it struck the house, then seemed to dissipate itself in her living room, glowing orange, before gradually subsiding. The living room had a powerful unhealthy spiral near the centre which apparently attracted it. Her sister told me that she had then been attacked in her bed by a 'demonic force'. Both bedrooms had unhealthy spirals in them, one at the head of the bed, (where the sister told me she had been violated by the entity) and the other about a metre from the foot of her sister's bed. Like most cases of this kind, both women had also become ill.

Some investigators might think that the ladies were suffering from delusions, but finding spirals in these positions gave the story credibility to me. Claims of such attacks are similar to the medieval incubi stories. There have been four reported cases in one district of this city that I know of. I have investigated other stories in different parts of the country, of people being almost strangled by 'invisible hands', and suffering poltergeist effects.

There is also a surprising number of people who have been pushed violently into their beds by an 'invisible force'. All of them had unhealthy spirals in their beds and were suffering various illnesses. It is very likely that there are many more people suffering from these particularly nasty manifestations, unable to tell their stories to anyone for fear of being considered mentally unstable. Perhaps once telluric energies are understood a little better, people will be able to inform their doctors of such events in relation to their associated illnesses.

INCONSISTENCIES

In addition to my divining rod I use a small Kombi meter to register electric and magnetic fields in connection with ill-health or paranormal activity like demon attacks, poltergeists, or crop circles. This monitors electric fields from 0 to 100V/m (volts per metre) and magnetic fields from 100nT to 1nT. It is significant that the meter shows no unusual reaction whatsoever even in the centre of an unhealthy spiral of any type, despite its apparent ability to cause a range of illnesses. The particular type of energy which can be found with divining rods does not seem to come within the normal spectrum of electric or magnetic fields for which the instrument was designed.

With more specialised and sensitive equipment, however, it has been found that there are fluctuations above crossing underground streams and faults. The former gives a variation of reading from 65000nT to 53000nT, and the latter from 6500nT to 73000nT.[3]) In addition, an electro-encephalograph taken of the brain of a person on a geopathically stressed area shows gross abnormalities. This is hardly surprising, for it has long been known that the brain registers an impulse when an electric light or other appliance is switched on in the same building.

MEASURING WITH AN OSCILLOSCOPE

R.M.Sephton, of Dorset in England, has been recording energy leys with an oscilloscope for some time. He believes that if a wave from an energy ley passes through a person who has an illness, like a cancer, for example, and then passes through another person some distance away, that second person may be more prone to the same disease due to resonance. He insists that this is just food for thought at the moment. A great deal of further work is needed.

Mr.Sephton also believes that energy leys are at a different frequency or system to the Earth's electromagnetic grid, and time progresses at a different 'rate.' The energy leys, he believes, are carrier waves for other signals, and, using a special oscilloscope set-up, has picked up BBC Radio 4 at 200kHz, and submarine frequencies at about 20kHz at a standing stone. The energy leys act as aerials and subsequently conveyors of a signal or signals.

Here is some information on the circuit he uses, for which I am grateful. Firstly, no connections have to be made to earth, so if the secondary side of the mains transformer in the cathode ray oscilloscope (CRO) is earthed, it has to be disconnected. Power can be supplied via magnetic fields, i.e. the mains step-down transformer. The magnetic field seems to act as a barrier. The outside case of the CRO can still be earthed provided the circuit to be measured makes no connection to it.

In his experiments, the return circuit can be via a metal conductor, living vegetation and/or human beings. However, every part of the return circuit must be isolated from Mother Earth. If it isn't, the signal is negated. One further point is that the copper coil should be scramble wound and not magnetically wound. Fig.26 is the diagram of his experimental circuit.

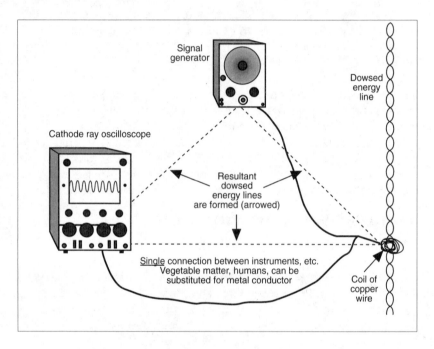

Fig. 26: A circuit used to measure telluric energy

NOTES

1.   Delgado, P. & Andrews, C., *Circular Evidence*: Bloomsbury (1989).
2.   Blair Oliphant, L., Personal Correspondence with, Blairgowrie, Scotland.
3.   Scott-Morley, A., in *The Journal of Alternative Medicine*.

CHAPTER 16

CROSSING LEYS AND THE ION EFFECT

Illness may also be initiated by exposure to crossing energy leys and streams. For example: where an energy ley widens out between two standing stones, forming a corridor, and is then crossed by other similar energy leys, radial leys and energy streams, you will find a grid pattern of individual waves.

The sources may not only be from standing stones. They could be much more modern: conventional power stations, electric sub-stations, nuclear submarines and missiles. These send out waves in all directions, instead of energy leys across country. The waves are all so similar that the source makes no difference — an energy ley from a standing stone, crossed by the waves radiating from an electric generator will also have a grid pattern of waves. Many of these crossing points initiate a different type of spiral to that of underground streams.

Castles are often situated at the crossing of energy leys. Not only were they built in a good defensive position, they were also carefully placed where telluric energies of various types met as 'power points'. I assume that the original intention of this would be to empower the occupants.

I was invited to Duchray Castle, Aberfoyle, in the Scottish Trossachs, where some rooms had three or four unhealthy spirals, but unlike any I had encountered before. There had been serious past illnesses in this castle. The previous owner had died of Alzheimer's disease. The new owner, being aware of the concept of earth energies, asked me to check her new home. Although this castle had an unpleasant telluric energy pattern, a stone-built stable just a few metres away had a normal grid pattern, devoid of spirals.

Some castles in these modern days seem to be anything but pleasant, perhaps because the incoming energy leys have turned unhealthy, or over the years they have picked up some of the unpleasant deeds almost invariably associated with them, like Garth Castle, which we will investigate in the next chapter. The energies do, however, seem to alter over the years.

SOME WAVES INDUCE SPIRALS

I became somewhat confused when I discovered that over a short period the pattern of waves in some of the houses I had visited had apparently changed to spirals and the normal grid of waves had vanished. There were two logical reasons for this, either: (a) the earth energy pattern had altered for some reason, and the waves now formed spirals, or (b) the spirals were an interference pattern formed directly above the crossing points of waves.

The answer was neither of these, and it was actually rather more complicated, as I discovered when I did a more careful survey of another house elsewhere. The spirals, both positive and negative were induced *between* the energy waves, to give a pattern of both waves and spirals. I had originally tuned into the waves, unaware of the spirals which accompanied them. Later, more aware of spirals, I had automatically focused into these and ignored the waves. The spirals captured their energies from the waves around them. Fig.27 is a simplified interpretation of this, as the spiral itself also has a double wave effect.

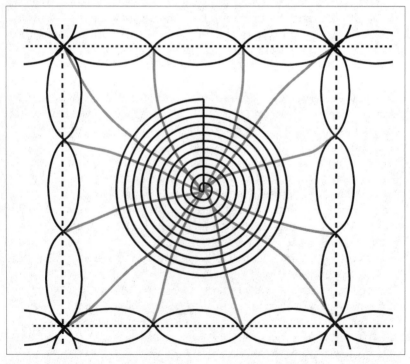

Fig. 27: Spirals may be induced between crossing waves. The unhealthy spiral feeds from waves on either side.

Spirals are not always induced inside two crossing waves in this manner. Sometimes I find only waves without their associated spirals. This applies to both healthy and unhealthy energies.

ALLERGIC TO MICROWAVE OVENS

There is another curious pattern, comprised of spirals of opposite polarities. The first time I became aware of this was when I read of a housewife in a small village near Kinross in Central Scotland, who was allergic to microwave ovens. She would become ill when she visited the houses of family and friends, if they had microwave ovens, even if they were not switched on. When she switched on her own oven, she felt as if she was burning up inside. She fell ill for at least two weeks at a time with stomach problems. This had baffled her doctors for years. From newspaper reports, I located the tiny village she lived in, to find that it had been built on an energy ley between the remains of a stone circle and a standing stone. The woman explained to me that her house had originally been a manse, with the church about fifty metres away. Another energy ley from a stone circle to a standing stone passed through the church and her house, at right angles to the first one, giving a crossing point. Her home was in the central core of both energy leys.

This woman's house was full of unhealthy spirals, the most important of which were in her kitchen, transmitted vertically into her son's bed at chest level (he had back problems), and in her own bed, which had two. This ruled out underground water as the cause, as the spirals from water streams are usually much larger and further apart.

The spiral in her kitchen attracted not only the energy ley 'overgrounds' into its centre, but also the unhealthy waves from the TV and, no doubt, the microwave oven before it had been removed, in a similar manner to the spirals absorbing the energies from humans described in the previous chapter. It may be that spirals can retain the unhealthy energy from such sources for some time, perhaps like the terrahertz generator mentioned in the Introduction, or feed it into the geological sub-strata where it may be emitted later.

It was the incoming energy ley as well as the spiral capturing the unhealthy waves from the microwave (and her own), which seem to have been the cause of her unusual allergy. Her immune system, finally unable to cope with the stress, may have broken down under all of this. She also told me that she had lived there for twenty years, which puzzled me greatly at the time, as the house seemed a very unhealthy place to live in. I would have thought illness should have been more common there, but it was only later, when I visited a 'sick road' in Dundee that I found the answer.

VISIBLE LEY POWER

The energy leys which seem to have been associated with the micro-wave allergy case are still working, sometimes quite powerfully, and can even make themselves visible on occasion.

James Wotherspoon of Glenrothes, an electronics engineer and his wife, were driving past that same stone circle at Kinross one summer evening when they noticed what looked like five semi-transparent tubular pillars, seemingly dancing together in a field nearby. The pillars were smokey grey in colour, approximately 18ft.(5m) in height and 1ft.(30cms) in diameter. As they watched, the pillars slowly alternated in and out of their vision, some finishing their cycle as others began. The pillars passed from being almost invisible to opaque in about thirty seconds. This phenomenon lasted about thirty minutes.

Adjacent to this was a row of telephone poles, with a multi-core telephone cable strung about half way up each one, waiting to be placed underground. The cables between the two poles nearest the tubular shapes were vibrating, although there was no wind[1].

SICK ROAD

The problem of the Kinross lady who lived in her house for so long before becoming ill was resolved some time later in a somewhat similar case in Dundee. There, a gentleman had diabetes; his wife suffered from depression; his mother died of lung cancer; their daughter had a large tumour removed from her abdomen and the pet dog died of lymphatic cancer. One side of the street of bungalows had problems of this nature, while the houses on the other side had very few incidents of ill health. His house was full of unhealthy spirals, very similar to the house at Kinross. The spirals were spaced about two metres apart. One was at the foot of his bed, where the dog slept, and another was near the top of the bed where his mother had died of lung cancer.

There was a similar pattern of spirals repeated in another house at the end of the road. Here, a man would often have to retire to bed early in the afternoon, exhausted and feeling unwell. I found there was an unhealthy energy spiral through his bed where his abdomen would be when he lay down. He often retired to bed in an endeavour to get some rest, but was putting himself in a position which achieved the opposite effect. Avoiding this location by moving his bed and having the energies balanced, would, I am sure, have helped this man avoid serious illness in the future.

Every case I have encountered gave me additional insight. Instigated by that houseowner who felt ill in some places in his house and healthy in others, I tried also to find healthy energies there. I found that the pattern of unhealthy spirals has a mirror image of healthy spirals, in alternating sequence, healthy/unhealthy/healthy/unhealthy, etc.

GEOLOGICAL FAULTS

The problem these men were experiencing did not appear to be from a crossing of energy leys and streams from the usual source, as in the previous allergy case. There were no megaliths or stone circles in that area. Instead, under the houses on one side of the street, there was an intrusive volcanic dyke — these give out energies similar to megaliths.

Faults and volcanic dykes are said to focus radiation from decaying radioactive elements through the earth's mantle, as well as electric fields. One local dyke in my area gives an unhealthy standing wave of 23ft.4in. (712cms) wavelength, 47in.(119 cms) in amplitude, down its length. Faults and dykes such as this can with practice, easily be traced underground.

After a little more investigation, it transpired that an energy ley or stream, crossing a volcanic dyke, can form little healthy and unhealthy spirals in an alternating sequence. These are induced, as I have said, between waves of similar polarity. This obviously is not, in the short term, quite as dangerous as a line of unhealthy spirals from underground water. Provided that a person is not aware intuitively of the presence of such energies in his home, it would be a matter of chance as to how much of the time he is exposed to the healthy or unhealthy spirals. If he moves his sleeping and sitting arrangements about, then he may be lucky enough to find that the effect of one spiral counterbalances the other, thus cancelling the effect.

EDINBURGH GRAVEYARDS ALTER ENERGY WAVES

In Edinburgh I investigated a house where a family had recurrent health problems. As I surveyed the three-storeyed building, I happened to glance out of the window and noticed a tombstone partially hidden in undergrowth at the other side of the road. When I left, I checked around the area to confirm my suspicions. It was an old decaying graveyard and incoming healthy waves passed into it on one side, every 4in. (10cms.) apart, with the occasional unhealthy ones about 3 metres apart. After passing through the cemetery they were all unhealthy — giving a decidedly unpleasant stream of closely spaced energy waves to the houses on the other side of the street.

I eliminated the unhealthy energies in the buildings effectively, using an ancient method which I had by then discovered. We shall look at this more closely in a later chapter. A postcard received later from the lady of the house happily told me that the family were recovering their health, and also that she had contacted her immediate neighbours, who had very similar health problems. There are quite a number of old graveyards in the ancient capital. The possible damage to health they cause is unknown and previously unsuspected.

An added twist to these stories was provided by yet another house in Edinburgh. A young man had been ill almost from the day he entered his new flat. When I arrived, one look at the cemetery next to the building was enough to confirm my fears. There was a powerful unhealthy energy ley passing through the building from this modern cemetery. Another equally unpleasant energy ley came from the north; not a cemetery this time, but a crematorium, just a few hundred metres away. The incoming energy ley to the crematorium was perfectly healthy, but as I expected, when it passed through the crematorium it changed character to a decidedly unhealthy energy ley.

What I certainly did not expect was that the energy ley also changed polarity to unhealthy after it passed through the adjoining church hall! The only suggestion I can make is that it picks up the unhappy feelings in the hall from the families of the bereaved.

DUNDEE GRAVEYARDS

Months after the last event a lady gave me the address of a friend in Dundee who had Chronic Fatigue Syndrome (M.E.), and asked me to try and solve her problem. The town map gave me an immediate clue, as the house was close to one of the city's old graveyards. When I arrived she invited into the house her two neighbours who were both suffering from the same illness. Yet another neighbour further along the road had the same problem. As I suspected, a survey showed that there was a stream of unhealthy energies coming through the houses from the cemetery. Surprisingly, from the north, another equally unhealthy energy stream passed through the house, forming a grid pattern. On this occasion, the waves were very closely spaced, and there were very few healthy waves. In this case, there were no spirals.

When I left I looked about to find a possible cause. I could find nothing immediately obvious to account for the unhealthy energy leys. Determined to find the source, a few days later I again consulted the town map with the intention of returning to the area to continue my search and I noticed in tiny writing the word 'Necropolis' to the north of the street. The culprit was another very large and old cemetery, fairly close to the woman's house. Living downstream of one old graveyard is bad enough, but two are decidedly unpleasant.

I hate to think what happens to an energy ley after it passes through the decay in a modern graveyard, bearing in mind that the waves travel through the substrata almost as easily as above ground. Earlier in my research I surmised that the problems had been known until perhaps quite recently, when church manses were built safely 'up-stream' of their nearby graveyards. Perhaps they were, but nowadays there are many other artificial energy leys and streams to confuse the issue.

My research into long-distance energy leys indicates that the old Pre-Reformation burial grounds were built at very precise points on interconnecting systems, using a surprisingly sophisticated knowledge of telluric energy in its various forms. Perhaps those old burial grounds 'earthed' the unhealthy energies safely away. The lack of earthing may explain why the energy ley at that crematorium in Edinburgh had picked up such an unhealthy content. It is more likely that the ancients also had a much better esoteric understanding which has been lost over the centuries.

QUARRIES

In a small village in central Scotland the spirals in two houses were so close and powerful that one woman told me she could see black shapes out of the corners of her eyes. The shapes disappeared when she looked directly at them. This is a phenomenon I occasionally hear of from people sensitive to earth energies, and includes black circles on the floor, black/blue lines and spirals on the ceiling and 'faces' spiral-ling around. They do not necessarily have to be psychic phenomena, and may simply be the mind of the victim trying to rationalise amor-phous blobs. This is analogous to results obtained in the Rorshach test (see glossary), although we must take into consideration that the eyes can play tricks.

In these two houses there were spirals of alternating polarity about half a metre apart from each other. In fact, the telluric energies were so bad that I decided to return to the area some time later to make further investigations. The pattern had changed for the worse during my absence. The spirals had apparently vanished, but I now found incoming parallel energy waves some 2½ins.(6½cms) apart; all of them unhealthy — there were no healthy waves at all. As I followed the energy ley back to its source, the culprit presented itself in the dis-tance, in this case, a huge quarry. As if to emphasise the fact that I was on the correct trail, a loud explosion rocked the area and a cloud of dust rose from the quarry face. Sometimes I feel as if I am being led by the nose in this work!

The incoming energy lines into the quarry were mainly healthy, about 2½ins.(6½cms) apart, with the unhealthy waves 36ins.(92 cms) apart. On the downstream side, all of the waves were unhealthy. Even some few kilometres away, there were closely spaced waves through the small village. Another energy ley passing through the quarry at right angles to the first had the same effect on a much larger town in the distance. One lady living in a high rise tower block on that unhealthy energy ley stream, told me that when she awoke in the morning she felt so weak, miserable and unhappy that she would bang her head on the bedroom wall in sheer frustration!

There is an even darker side to quarries, however; they can give out unhealthy earth energies which can attach themselves to the electric high tension cables of the national grid. This will be explored in the following chapter.

COAL MINES

Those who suffer from Chronic Fatigue Syndrome (M.E.) have supplied me with a great deal of information on the relationship between their illness and highly stressed areas. In Dalkeith, south of Edinburgh, one lady pleaded with me to help her find the source of her problem, although her doctor, as so often happens, had been unable to find any clinical signs of illness. She felt the atmosphere in the house was very bad. Returning from vacation, when she had, as usual, recovered her health, she very nearly asked the taxi driver to take her away again, as she could not face walking through the front door. There was a spiral in her bed which she felt sometimes engulfed her with unpleasant forces, one at the head of her father's bed (he died of cancer), and one in the living room. In addition, her asthma was particularly bad, presumably because the spiral was centred at her chest.

Neighbours were suffering from a wide variety of illnesses. The general activity of the earth energies over a wide area seemed to be unusually unpleasant. She pointed me in the direction of a nearby field, which was untilled, due to subsidence from disused coal mines.[2] There I found a high incidence of unhealthy overgrounds in an apparently haphazard fashion, completely unlike the coherent, parallel streams of waves I was used to. All of them focused into obvious depressions in the ground caused by old mine workings. I am still not sure whether they were emitted from the collapsed and waterlogged tunnels, or were attracted to them.

RIVERS AND CANALS

A dirty canal I surveyed in Nottingham, England had a pattern of un-healthy spirals down its length. Healthy rivers have an alternating pattern of spirals of both polarities on their banks. It would seem reasonable to suggest that it is the quality of water and condition of the river bed which causes the differences. This prompted me to survey a Highland stream high in the hills where there should be relatively little pollution. Here, healthy energy waves, every 6ins.(15cms) apart, ran parallel to the banks, but instead of spirals, each wave gave a curious horseshoe shape every metre or so, but only on one side of the burn. This was caused by an unhealthy energy ley crossing the water at roughly right angles. This attracted the vertical parallel waves (which are always to be found following running water) towards it.

The interference pattern on that small stream struck me as particularly interesting. Each unhealthy wave crossing the water had changed its characteristics. The only reason I could think of was that it had picked up negative ions from the tumbling water and carried them across the stream, until it encountered the parallel waves following the banks, bending them into the horseshoe shapes. This was to be an important insight into the behaviour of earth energies, although at the time I had no idea that it had already been discovered by others.

THE BENEFIT OF NEGATIVE IONS

Ionisation occurs in many situations, such as waterfalls and thunder-storms. Here, water droplets are split, and in the process, form positive and negative ions which give up their charge when they encounter solid airborne particles, like dust. It is the negative ions which can give rise to the feeling of well-being you experience after a thunder-storm, standing near a waterfall or in a domestic shower. This also applies to high altitudes, where the ions are produced by cosmic rays colliding with atmospheric air molecules.

Under such conditions burns and wounds heal more rapidly, respiratory illnesses are reduced, and a calming influence is the result of the consequent increase in alpha brain pattern. On the other hand, cities with high atmospheric pollution, workshops and stuffy offices with electronic equipment increase the number of positive ions, giving headaches, anxiety, lack of concentration, irritability and illness. Even synthetic fibres in clothes have an upsetting influence on the well-being of some people, as they surround them with positive ions, the negative ones escaping.

Can it be that the energies which I have been working with for so long are, at least partially, waves of ions? Is it possible that this is the reason why the negative ions, which have been described as zig-zagging wildly with great speed, can pass through glass so readily, while the unhealthy (positive) ions, much slower, with less energy, cannot? It would seem reasonable to assume that when a healthy energy ley (negative ions), encounters decaying material, such as refuse dumps, graveyards, stagnant water and sewers, it picks up positive ions, thus changing its character to an unhealthy energy ley.

So often I have encountered places where people feel that the 'atmosphere' is unpleasant, to find that there is a surfeit of unhealthy waves and spirals there, and its opposite, of course, light, airy, cheerful places, where healthy waves are predominant. This is very similar to what we feel in a positively or negatively ionised environment.

COMING CLOSER TO THE TRUTH

The mystery of the quarry could also be explained by ionisation. Working quarries are very noisy and dusty, and dynamiting rock faces emits huge clouds of positively and negatively charged dust particles. Since dust captures and eliminates the negative ions, only the 'unhealthy' positive ions will be left. The incoming energy ley stream, with its healthy waves very close together, must take up and transmit the positive ions across country for some considerable distance, wreaking havoc with the health of some of the people in their path. In addition, quarries attract energy leys from a very wide area, due to their earth energy image, as I explained earlier, and the unhealthy waves crossing them will be very close together, transmitting an unusually concentrated unhealthy energy ley of positive ions across country.

The health effect, as far as dust is concerned, is well documented. The Sharav, for instance, the desert wind which is the despair of the Israelis, is caused by masses of dust carried by the wind. Such disturbance ensures that negative ions are eliminated and only positive ions remain. It is responsible for asthma, unbearable tension, suicides, depression, and mindless violence, among other problems. In an experiment, rabbits, the gentlest of creatures, breathing in positive ions, became highly aggressive, and one can hardly be surprised that humans tend to lose control in a massively charged positive-ion environment. Other 'witches' winds' throughout the world are the Föhn from the Alps, the Santa Ana in California and the Chinook in western Canada and the USA.

Encouraged by finding what could prove to be one one of the fundamental causes in healthy energy ley streams changing to unhealthy streams, I decided to do a little more work on railway lines, when I realised that this could solve a problem I had some months before.

RAILWAY LINES

In yet another case of C.F.S. (M.E.) in Edinburgh, a lady was so ill and tired that she could hardly get out of her bed in the afternoon in time to greet me. This at first seemed a puzzling case, as I could find very few unhealthy energy waves as I walked up to her front door. In the front rooms of the house the atmosphere seemed to be perfectly good, but as we went to the back bedroom where she slept, I found spirals increasing in number the further back into the house we went. In her bed, this woman had something like six little unhealthy spirals, but of a different type from those initiated either by underground water, geological faults, or energy leys. Her cats, as usual, found the energies to their taste. They preferred to sleep on her bed!

She asked me if I would like to check her back garden. There we found more spirals. Here, they were lying closer and closer to each other, until at the boundary wall, they were overlapping, in the usual alternating pattern. Peering over the garden wall gave me a possible clue to the origin of the energies — the main railway line. It was not electrified, unfortunately, as this would have furthered my suspicions that this was the culprit. I had to do some more research on railway lines before I could be certain.

The nearest non-electrified railway to me is the Highland line to Inverness, which warranted a visit to find if there was any ion effect there. In the grassy fields on the upstream side of an energy ley, there were the (by now) familiar healthy waves every 4ins.(10 cms) apart, with occasional unhealthy ones, about seven yards apart (7½m). After they had crossed the rails, there was an additional unhealthy wave, with its companion unhealthy spiral.

One of the healthy waves had somehow become unhealthy. I used my little Kombi meter (it measures electric fields from 0-100 volts per metre and magnetic fields from 0-100nT [nano-tesla] to find out why. At a nearby level crossing I held the meter just above the rails, to find that there was no electric field, as I expected, but there was a definite magnetic field. A little while later, two diesel trains rumbled past and I took the opportunity to test the rails again. The magnetic field above the rails had doubled in strength to 25nT. I found that there was yet another unhealthy wave on the downstream side. One healthy wave of telluric energy had apparently captured the ferrous ions emitted by the friction of the wheels and had then altered its polarity to an unhealthy one. The spirals formed as a natural consequence of this.

I have since checked a number of non-electrified railway tracks. Roughly speaking, the more the track is used, the higher the incidence of unhealthy waves and induced spirals on the 'down' side of the railways.

ELECTRIFIED RAILWAYS OR SUBWAYS

Electrified railways are much worse. In a suburb of Glasgow, for instance, I found on one occasion, unhealthy waves every 2ft.(61cms.), apart. After crossing two well-used tracks, they were 2in.(5cms.) apart. I followed them for some few hundred metres, but they still retained their unhealthy content.

Subways are worst of all. One disused railway tunnel I had already investigated for earth energies showed that it acted as a wave guide for telluric energy, which followed the curve of the tunnel. The telluric waves were suddenly magnified inside the entrance, the wavelength being decreased and the amplitude heightened.

It is not surprising that buildings above such enhanced telluric energies have problems. One house built on an old battlefield over a subway on the Great Western Road, Glasgow, has given some of its residents an insight into the way earth energies are enhanced or combine with our more 'modern' electric fields. The mother and two daughters there had Chronic Fatigue Syndrome (M.E.), candida, loss of energy, and the girls were not 'blooming' as they would have liked. One daughter occasionally felt that she was being strangled by invisible hands early in the morning and sometimes awoke paralysed. All felt the presence of what they termed earthbound spirits around them from time to time. The previous occupant may have reacted to the unhealthy fields in his own way, as he had a gross overeating disorder. Eventually he ended his days in an asylum.

Although the house was spacious, they had, apparently, unerringly placed their beds on unhealthy spirals. One night the bed of one of the girls had collapsed, the wooden frame splintered as if it had been hit by a sledgehammer. During the conversation I discovered that they could feel the house vibrating from the electrified subway trains running underneath. This, plus the energies from young adults at the puberty stage, added, perhaps, to the distant echoes of the souls of the dead from the nearby battlefield site beneath their feet, may have been responsible for their problems.

The electric and magnetic fields in tunnels must be very powerful. Professor Yoshi-Hiko has investigated numerous marks found imprinted on the walls and around the tunnels of the subway system in Tokyo. They are little circles, with from one to five shells imprinted on the grimy patina of the concrete.

SCHAUBERGER, WATER FLUMES AND PLOUGHING

Reverting for a moment to the change of polarity of telluric energies crossing railway lines. There is a curiously similar discovery by Viktor

Schauberger (1885-1958), an Austrian, who confounded experts by constructing log flumes to carry timber prodigious distances. Using his knowledge and perception of nature, he achieved the apparently impossible. He transported some types of timber which sink in normal circumstances, by mimicking the spiral vortex of water in nature, and feeding cold water into the system at intervals.

Viktor Schauberger insisted that nearly all modern technology is based on a complete denial of Nature, and has the seeds of its own self-annihilation. Today he is recognised as a pioneer of free energy based on natural systems, and the inventor of a home power generator[3].

He had also noticed that iron-rich ground quickly dispelled water and became dry, and later, that fields, originally ploughed with wooden implements, seemed to lose their growing capability when ploughed by more modern iron ploughs. He came to the conclusion that minute particles of iron were chipped off the plough's tines, covering the damp earth with a fine dust of particles which quickly rusted. Later, as technology advanced and machines became faster, he noted:

"The iron plough's rapid passage through the soil cuts through the field's magnetic lines of energy, causing an electric current to occur in the same way that a coil in an electric generator rotates in an electric field. This in turn leads to an electrolysis in the soil which separates the water into oxygen and hydrogen."

There is a similarity between the charged iron particles sloughed off a railway line and the iron dust particles in a ploughed field. The healthy waves of an energy ley or stream crossing a recently ploughed field in my area has the occasional wave changed to unhealthy, but they are some three metres apart. In this case, these changed waves do not even extend past the fields, but are warped back on themselves.

HIGH TENSION CABLES

If railway tracks can ionize some of the waves of a crossing energy ley, then it seems probable that the national grid high tension cables strung across the country may also constitute a very powerful hazard. I checked local pylons, to find that at their bases there were some local abberations of healthy waves, possibly from the ionization around the glass insulators high above. The effect did not 'travel' any distance, however, and the cables themselves made no impression on the crossing healthy energy ley stream, even in wet weather.

It has recently been suggested by Professor Denis Henshaw of Bristol University that the decay products of radon gas can be attracted to electromagnetic fields and may prove to be the link between power sources and some childhood and adult cancers. If this is proved to be correct, then it may also be possible that they can be transmitted down energy leys like negative and positive ions.

NOTES

1. Wotherspoon, J., Personal Communication from; Glenrothes, Scotland.

2. I have recently discovered that open-cast coalmines are the worst sources of unhealthy telluric energy. Overgrounds emitted from one mine, focusing into powerful spirals above an underground stream are associated with severe illnesses like necrotising fasciitis. Bonnybridge, central Scotland, has a number of mines of both types, plus quarries, and is known as the U.F.O. capital of the U.K.. Presumably, at least some of the visible phenomena are caused by the telluric energies coming into the visible part of the spectrum as they traverse the country, attempting to earth themselves.

3. Alexandersson, O., *Living Water*, Gateway Books, 1990.
    See also *Living Energies* by Callum Coats: Gateway Books, 1996.

CHAPTER 17

NATURAL AND MAN-MADE SOURCES

LEAD MINES AT TYNDRUM

Tyndrum is a scattered little highland village, deep in a beautiful glen, at a road junction. Its main claim to fame is the lead mine on the hill on the opposite side of the glen. I received a call from a nearby hotelier to test his building for earth energies. Here I found such a high incidence of unhealthy energies and spirals that I felt obliged to find the source which was not in doubt, as the scarred landscape above the houses bore mute testimony to the toxic waste dumps from old mines.

A few days later I revisited the site, this time with the intention of climbing up the steep hill face to the mines to test for the telluric energies which it must surely emit. Before I did that, I tested the mounds of sandy soil, the tailings, close to the road, at the east end of the village. I could find nothing unusual here, perhaps because the sand had moderated the unhealthy waves. I had driven along that road for many years and these bare, sandy patches had refused to become vegetated over that time, which, I had assumed, was because of their lead content.

I climbed up toward an old mine shaft. Strewn about, there were hundreds of tonnes of broken rock: galena, snow quartz, barytes, zincblende, chalcopyrite, calcite, pyrites, and a few pieces of rhodochrosite — a geologist's paradise. The lead deposits had been discovered in 1741, and within a few years yielded 1700 tonnes of lead, which was later exceeded by another mining company, which, from 1768 to 1788, also smelted the lead on this location. Over a century later it was reopened to provide lead for ammunition during the First World War.

In the mine I found a small gallery a few hundred feet above the floor of the glen. Here I tried to find radiation with my geiger counter which showed a mere 3 counts per minute, just the same as the background in the surrounding area. When I tried my 'unhealthy energy' divining rod, however, I found energy coming from the tunnel in a tightly packed series of vertical waves of unhealthy energy. They seemed to be about 1mm. or less apart, and came from the mine workings. The average distance between unhealthy waves in the UK being roughly about 1 metre, I realised immediately just how powerful this location was. There were no healthy waves here at all, just the metre-wide vertical wall of solid unhealthy energy streaming down to the village, with some outer waves, all gradually fanning out. The wavelength in this case was 5ft.2in.(158 cms.) and amplitude 9ins (24 cms), very similar to the energy emitted from standing stones.

It has been known for a long time that at the intersections above crossing underground streams, caves, and tunnels that there is a high incidence of lightning strikes. Could it be these positively charged unhealthy waves which lightning is attracted to? One unfortunate potholer in France, for instance, was struck by lightning when he was 200 feet underground![1].

There is a fault in the rock at Tyndrum which contains this seam of different mineral ores, 20ft.(6.1m.) wide at its maximum, and originally horizontal galleries about every hundred feet, with some vertical shafts dug into it. Much of the mine is now in a collapsed and water-logged state. Before the seam was mined, it must have appeared as a snow-white gash, with the quartz moderating the effects of the galena and other minerals locked inside it. Now the disturbed minerals in the fissure radiate out unhealthy waves in a wide stream with a powerful central core.

In the village, which is only a kilometre away from the mine, this powerful energy stream can easily be detected. The whole west end of the village is affected; the waves, very close together there, also form spirals, the result of combining with an unhealthy energy ley or stream travelling up the glen, roughly at right angles to it. It would be interesting to find out how the hard core of unhealthy waves from the mine fissure dissipates with distance. I suspect, like other energy streams I have followed from standing stones, and quarries, that it will be a circuit. These can be sometimes quite large, and return to their sources sooner or later. Some of the main megalithic leys I have followed traverse mainland Scotland and the islands before returning to complete their circuit. Unfortunately, my days of hard walking are now over, and I must leave this to someone else.

At the time of writing, I read that another attempt is about to be made to extract an estimated £62,000,000 worth of gold from another area near Tyndrum. This will help the prosperity of the area, but what will this further disturbance do to the earth energies? I read that the person who invited me to visit the village to search for unhealthy earth energies has asked the mining company to include in their contract, landscaping the area when they have finished, to help restore the telluric wounds. The mining company, fortunately, have agreed.

QUARRIES AND H.T. CABLES

Following information from Geoffrey Allen, whom we met earlier in Chapter 11, I decided to locate and follow the energy waves which, he believes, are emitted from quarries, and attach themselves to H.T. cables.

Outside Crieff is the beautiful Sma' Glen, with the Highland Boundary Fault at its entrance. Associated with this major displacement is a band of slate which has been quarried along its length in the recent past to provide roofing materials. The largest quarry there is rather awkward to get to, and consequently, undisturbed. Heaps of slate and mica schist gleam in the sun, and, unlike most quarries in the lowlands, it has not been used as a rubbish dump. Such dumps can only exacerbate the unhealthy waves. A short distance away from the quarry was a line of H.T. pylons; ideal for my research.

From this quarry I detected unhealthy waves, about ¼in (6mm) apart emitted from the centre, which in this particular case was a deep hole flooded with clear rain water. Instead of radiating outwards in all directions, as I expected, the whole energy stream travelled in a southerly direction, towards the H.T. cables. As they approached the cables at an acute angle, they turned, and ran in parallel waves, about ½in (12 mm) apart, for several kilometres. Then they turned back to the quarry to complete the circuit. It was some months later that I discovered that Dr.Schneck of Bideford, Devon, had done some similar work, and had come to similar conclusions.

I have yet to discover if it is the electric and magnetic fields in the cables which cause the energy stream to be repelled, or simply the physical presence of the steel towers and cables. At the moment I suspect the latter. During my work on the telluric energy network across Scotland, I encountered one roughly circular energy stream which focused accurately between the legs of some ten miles' length of H.T. suspension towers before abruptly veering off back to its original prehistoric course. Assuming that the energy stream was attracted to the electric and magnetic fields, I was later surprised to find that the same energy stream deviated from its route to focus into a windmill derrick. The reason for this is that each leg of a suspension tower or derrick has a narrow ellipse of telluric energy radiating out from it. This captures the wandering energy ley stream, focusing it down the line of pylons of the national grid, one after another.

Another local quarry, in Glen Devon, well away from any H.T. cables and located in layers of the lower old red sandstone period, gives a slightly different energy pattern. With nothing either to deflect or attract the telluric energies, the focal point is in the centre of the floor of the quarry. Unhealthy waves are emitted from it like a giant parabolic reflector. After a few hundred metres, they gradually turn, radiating back to the perimeter, and then into the centre, to complete the circuit. Like the Tyndrum mines, there are no healthy waves to be found.

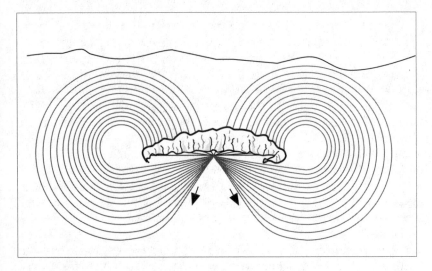

Fig. 28: The energies emitted from a focal point in front of the quarry extend outwards before turning back. A spiral of healthy or unhealthy energy is found also at the focal point, and the polarities vary with the type of rock.

Conversely, at another quarry I found a similar pattern, but this time, practically all of the emitted energies were healthy. Here, it was a sand and gravel quarry, and furthermore, the quarrying was done without blasting the rock. Other than these two factors, it was impossible to explain the difference. It follows, of course, that anyone excavating bedrock on a hillside, to build a house, perhaps, may have problems if he uses explosives, and, possibly, heavy machinery.

BREAKING THE DRAGON'S BONES

There are a number of mines and quarries throughout the country, and one cannot help but wonder just how much damage they do, fanning out unhealthy waves across the country. Until recently, the Chinese would never allow such mines, saying that they "break the dragons' (telluric energies') bones", and archaeologists have wondered why some of the most ancient mines in the world, excavated by Neanderthal man 100,000 years ago, were carefully backfilled.

In South Africa, in the distant past, men dug out a million kilos of

red ochre, then returned the ground to its former condition "to ap-
pease the Plumed Serpent", adding offerings as they did so, seemingly
aware of possible damage to the telluric environment[2].

RADON GAS

Fissures, mines, quarries, wells and underground streams also can emit
one of the deadliest natural gases: radon, which percolates to the surface, and is suspected of causing a number of cancer related deaths in
dwellings above such sites. Granite is the most frequently linked rock
type as far as this gas is concerned. It was at one time thought to be a
problem mainly in certain areas of the country, but recently scientists
have discovered that the gas is much more widespread than originally
thought and may be linked with HT electric transmission lines, to some
forms of cancer.

Tom Williamson believes that it is bands of gas rising from the earth
which dowsers detect as 'black streams'. He points out that many
people can avoid illness simply by ensuring that the basement of dwellings is made impermeable to such gases. Tom is, however, rather
sceptical of the relationship between earth energies and illness[3].

Perhaps decaying radon gas can be picked up and transmitted by
telluric energy acting as a carrier wave, in a similar manner to the ions
at quarries and railway lines, as previously discussed. I will leave this
topic for physicists to argue about, and further investigation by dedicated and competent dowsers.

WELLS AND RADIAL LEYS

One house I visited gave a rather disturbing variation to the usual
alternating pattern of spirals — this one had unhealthy spirals only.
This case provided me with another clue to telluric energies — some
of them have a point source. The husband and wife who owned the
house had moved into it a few years before. Both were unaware of the
effects of telluric energy. They fell ill shortly thereafter, and eventually
called me to investigate. When I arrived at the house, I found that it
had unhealthy spirals spaced about 3 metres apart. There was no
compensating healthy spiral system, any individual healthy waves passing straight through the house.

A well in front of the house was one instigator, radiating energy
waves (both polarities in alternating sequence), in all directions. When
the unhealthy energies entered the house they formed a neat pattern
of unhealthy spirals. Worse still, a healthy energy ley from the east
side of the house passed through a modern cemetery, next to their
garden. This changed all the healthy energy waves entering the cem-

etery into an unhealthy form.

Things were so bad after they moved into the house that the husband walked several kilometres to a nearby river with the intention of committing suicide — he felt acutely unwell. Fortunately, he changed his mind and returned home. A friend, a specialist in another aspect of geopathic stress helped him through his bad patch. The husband later became aware of earth energies and their possible deadly qualities, and asked me to help him. I am pleased to say that since I was able to work with them, both he and his wife have partially regained their health and have become interested in earth energies.

APPARITIONS ON SPIRALS

There are other forms of spirals induced by wells, and they can give rise to other phenomena beside illness. At Balgonie Castle, in Fife, the laird asked me to survey the 15th century tower for telluric energy. His family could hear whisperings round the ancient baronial hall, even when there was no-one else around. His son had seen an apparition, a green lady, walking across the floor of the destroyed grand hall. Apparitions are commonly seen as green, white, or grey and a theory which could explain at least some of these events has been proposed by Tom Lethbridge, archaeologist, psychic researcher and explorer. He believed that they were originally in full colour, but fade over the centuries[4].

The telluric energy system of the castle was healthy. This surprised me, since I expected ghosts (if that is what they were) to be initiated by unhealthy spirals. There was a spiral of healthy energy where the green lady had been seen and also another spiral in the baronial hall where the whisperings had been heard, with another in the old keep. These took the form of part of a semi-curve. With an unusual flash of inspiration, I could see it as a circle of spirals!

When I turned to where the theoretical centre should be, I could see a mound of boulders, which had, apparently, been taken out of the old well in the courtyard. The castle had been designed and built taking in to account the telluric energy produced by this well. This must have been to give a healthy living environment to the occupants. This, I later discovered, was not the first time a building had been constructed to blend with telluric energies. Other examples are the cathedrals at Peterborough, Winchester and Glasgow. They have all been built over holy wells to make use of, and transmit the healthy emissions from the water over a wide area. The well acts as a focal point for a star shaped network of telluric energies. This is the view of Ludovic McLellan Mann, who investigated this phenomenon in the 1930s[5].

The laird and his family were obviously responding to the healthy energies in their castle. Despite the inadequate heating facilities they were hale and hearty, and had never felt so healthy in their lives.

ARTESIAN WELLS

Artesian wells also produce healthy energies in great quantities. A business woman near where I live has her house built over one of a line of wells, of which the local lemonade works have made good use for many years. They sank a well 120ft. deep into this source of pure water. The woman's house is swamped with healthy energy waves, radiating out from the capped well in her kitchen. There is only the occasional unhealthy energy (not from this source) entering her house. Despite a very stressful business, and possibly because of her telluric environment, she has remarkably good health.

Very often I meet people who are in good health, not through their own natural or genetic ability, but because the telluric energies to which they are subjected where they live, work and sleep are the foundations of their health or illness. People are mirrors of their earth energy environment. If that environment is hostile, they can fall prey to any one of a number of serious illnesses in a surprisingly short time.

MODERN SOURCES: ELECTRICITY GENERATING STATIONS

The turbines and transformers in hydro-electric dams which convert power from water to electricity, ionize the air around them (see Chapter 16) and emit energy waves of both polarities in a precise pattern (radial leys). Radiating out like the spokes of a bicycle wheel, the waves travel extremely close together, generally around 2ins (5cms) apart when about three miles (4¾ km) from the source.

Cruachan dam in Argyll, a powerful showpiece 250,000 volt hydro-electric station, emits energy waves of 76ins (193 cms), amplitude 8ins (20 cms). Other major dams in the region, Pitlochry and Loch Tummel, have similar wavelengths. How far these waves travel I have no idea as yet, but they may cover some considerable distance, I suspect, before becoming 'earthed' by derelict quarries and suchlike, and returning to their source. Despite their intensity, it is surprising that the electric and magnetic fields die away within metres of their sources, according to my sensitive Kombi meter.

The means of fuelling a power station, whether it is coal, oil or gas is not likely to make any difference to the energies from the generators, but there is the added disadvantage of chemical pollution in varying degrees. This is the price we choose to pay for our comfort and health, even though there are more conducive ways to achieve a more natural and less energy-intensive way of living. (I refer later to the effects from nuclear power stations.)

TELLURIC SHADOWS

There is also the synergistic or combining qualities of these energies to be taken into consideration. Some ten miles (16km) east of Pitlochry, in Strathardle, a number of families invited me to check their homes, as there seemed to be such a high incidence of illness in that area. The unhealthy energies there, apparently, were coming from the direction of Pitlochry dam, but the healthy/unhealthy sequence had changed. Now they were all bad, indicating either that something had changed the polarity of the good ones, or that the healthy waves had somehow been eliminated. When I returned to Pitlochry to follow the waves from source to destination, I believed that it was the geology of the region which may be responsible. The predominant rock was mica schist, which could, conceivably, alter the waves of healthy negative ions to unhealthy positive ones as they traversed the country.

As I climbed from the dam at Pitlochry into the hills, towards the area with the problem, I had to change my theory. The healthy waves, even after some 3½ miles (5½km) had not changed their polarity at all, but in front of me loomed the possible culprit — the massive television repeater station on the summit of a hill, overlooking both Pitlochry and Strathardle. Nothing varied in the healthy waves as I dowsed them up to the station, but just a short distance past the perimeter fence, they became distorted. Eventually they earthed themselves into the ground in spirals, leaving only the unhealthy waves to pass unhindered.

This radial ley gradually fanned out over a distance with the result that several kilometres of Strathardle became affected by unhealthy radiations. In addition, Faskally and Loch Tummel, another two hydroelectric schemes 2 miles (3kms) and 11 miles (18km) distant respectively, had the same synergistic effect, giving another two shadows of unhealthy waves further down Strathardle.

To exacerbate matters, there is also what I call the 'tandem effect'. If you have two sources radiating energies which overlap each other, you will get a more powerful line extending in both directions from the sources.

TV repeater station near Crieff, Scotland

NUCLEAR POWER STATIONS

Unhealthy waves fan out from the radioactive decay in nuclear power stations in a similar pattern to those from transformers in hydro-electric schemes. At Dounreay, near Thurso, I found unhealthy waves of 96ins (244cms) and amplitude of 23ins (58cms). These came from both the old fast breeder reactor, then containing 960 tonnes of low level waste, and the newer operational reactor. The unhealthy waves were radiating out from both sites. In all probability there is the same healthy form as well, but I did not know about the unhealthy/healthy alternating pattern at the time. The plant may not have been producing electricity when I was there, as I could not find the wavelength which I have come to associate with electric transformers and turbines.

Around this reactor, in common with some other reactors, clusters of childhood leukemia have occurred, although it has since been discovered that power stations of various types (like those driven by coal and oil) also seem to have clusters. It may be that it is the subtle energies from the transformers and turbines which are causing the problem, and not from the reactors themselves.

NUCLEAR SUBMARINE BASES

At Garelochead, north of Glasgow, I discovered one of the most prolific sources of artificial radiation that I had encountered until then. A lady in a house overlooking the loch suffered six miscarriages, usually at mid-term, and not unreasonably, wanted to find out why. In her bed she had one unhealthy spiral at her head level, one at her abdomen level, and one at her feet. Both she and her husband had the impression that their house was extremely unhealthy for them and their children, and were considering moving. They asked me repeatedly if a nearby television repeater mast, this time a rather small one, had anything to do with their problem. In my ignorance, I dismissed it at the time.

After my visit I decided to check the Faslane nuclear submarine base a short distance away, as this seemed the most obvious source. Outside the perimeter fence, about 150 metres from the maintenance sheds, were waves very close together, inducing spirals about 4ins (10 cms) apart, which seemed very bad, as each one spiralled out about 20ft., or so, in an overlapping pattern.

These particular spirals took me by surprise. Earlier, I mentioned that spirals are induced between waves, and appear to feed off the surrounding waves. Here, close to the source, the waves were packed tightly together, yet the spirals overlapped — possibly in their thousands. In addition, these spirals had wide coils, about 10½ins (27cms) apart, unlike the more powerful water spirals, which are about 1ins (2½cms.) apart.

Later, I found that the sheds housed one, possibly two, nuclear powered submarines. As I drove home I stopped every few kilometres to check the background of spirals from that site, but it was about 20km or so before they settled down from their dramatic state.

On reflection, this woman's house, high in the hills, had the television repeater mast between it and the nuclear base, and may have been in the 'shadow' area of that site, similar to the Pitlochry case mentioned earlier. This knowledge was to come years later. I was completely unaware of the synergistic qualities of this form of energy at the time.

The following year I again checked the area, to find the energies had increased dramatically. It was the end of the cold war, and now five nuclear submarines were tied up bow-to-stern at the quayside. Across the sea loch, about ½ mile from the quay and at right angles to it, the waves were of alternating polarities, about ¼in. (6 mm) apart between similar signs, and now about 79in. (200 cms) wavelength, 10in. (25 cms) amplitude.

Here were five sources of radiating energy contributing to the tandem effect. When I projected a line southwards from the submarines, it could be picked up further down the shore of the loch, 2 miles (3¼km) away, as waves so close together that I could not measure them - perhaps 1mm apart, or less.

There is a complication, however, as one ex-submariner pointed out to me. The modern submarine is so powerful that each has to generate a great deal of electricity, enough to supply a small town. It may be that this was the source of the radiating waves, perhaps even modified by the radioactive material on board. The wavelength from these submarines appeared to be rather different — longer than from conventional turbines, etc., but shorter than missiles which we now turn to.

NUCLEAR MISSILE SITES

The storage facility for the Trident missiles is located nearby, and, close to the perimeter fence the waves are about 93ins (236 cms) amplitude 8½ins (22 cms). As I would expect, the waves from such powerful weapons were packed so tightly that I could not determine any distance between them at all, but at least they were slightly longer than the height of a human, and therefore would not resonate to the same extent with anyone lying in bed.

NUCLEAR SUBMARINE GRAVEYARD

At Rosyth Naval base, within sight of the Forth road and rail bridges, and just a short distance from Edinburgh, is the last resting place of several nuclear submarines. From the perimeter fence I could see the sinister black hulks of three submarines, floating in the dockyard. Fur-

Nuclear submarine at the Faslane base in the West of Scotland

ther along, another more modern submarine was tied to the quayside, possibly being repaired at the time, as the base had only just lost its refitting programme.

About a kilometre away the waves were of an alternating pattern, and about 2ins (5cms) apart. The wavelength in this case was 82ins (208 cms), amplitude 8½ins (20cms.), and may have been from the electric generators of the boat still in service. Whether or not the emitted energy will decline once they are permanently dry docked and the electric generators removed remains to be seen.

In the 1990s, there are 12 nuclear submarines patrolling Britain's waters, or being refitted or berthed around the country. Each one is designed to carry approximately 225kg of nuclear fuel on board and each will be contributing subtle radiations to their immediate environment. Russia and its allied states have about 225 submarines, many of which are nuclear powered, while the U.S.A. has many more. What effect they may have on the health of the inhabitants of an area they visit is unknown at present, and, likewise, to the crews manning and maintaining them, but we must at least be thankful that the waves are alternately positive and negative, and may help to balance each other. Also, a submarine only usually stays in one place for a relatively short time.

RADAR AND MICROWAVE TOWERS

Unlike the radial leys from electric generators, sub-stations, missile sites, the two radar stations I have measured seem to emit nothing but unhealthy energies, and in vast quantities. A radar station at Kinross has energy waves of 69in.(175 cms.) wavelength, 7½ins(19 cms.) amplitude, and the local R.A.F. fighter station is very similar. Microwave towers have much the same effect, although the wavelength has not yet been measured.

AN ANCIENT SOURCE: VOLCANIC PLUGS

So far, we have seen how man-made structures have affected or seemingly produced effects in existing energy waves, but there are rather similar and completely natural sources of energies, especially in Scotland. These are the volcanic plugs: ancient volcanoes which have been eroded away to leave sheer lava cliffs, upon which have sometimes been built castles; Edinburgh and Stirling castles being notable examples. These plugs act like 'holes in the landscape', and fan out natural telluric waves of about 7ft.(214 cms) wavelength, once again in the usual healthy/unhealthy/healthy sequence. The 'volcanic' island of Staffa on the West coast has even longer waves at 9ft.(274 cms), particularly concentrated at the caves, like Boat Cave and Fingal's Cave.

There is, however, a curious similarity to the lines of energy waves from nuclear submarines and the tandem and synergistic effects which we have already encountered. Lines from ancient burial grounds radiate outwards from major volcanic plugs, and each burial ground also seems to be situated where at least two of these lines cross. It took me much difficult walking to trace these strange radial leys back to their sources, as very few of the older burial grounds are marked on the government maps, and the lines may not always have the accuracy beloved of some armchair enthusiasts. But follow them I did, through one burial ground after another, for almost one thousand miles, until eventually the picture became clearer.

Since I discovered these strange radial leys, Paul Devereux (who we met earlier) has been researching very similar straight lines of cemeteries, and other forms of straight paths around the world. Cultures, totally unconnected with each other, have evolved straight spirit, faery, coffin and ghost paths, where the dead have been carried on specially built 'dead straight' roads. On these, their spirits could easily leave their bodies and fly in straight lines. Feng shui, he points out, would never allow houses to be built on such lines, as the occupants would be troubled with wandering spirits.

There is something deeply mystifying here which I cannot quite grasp.

Perhaps telluric energies are much more important than I have hitherto believed, and are responsible not only for the health or disease of
the population, but for our very souls. If this is correct, we have ignored it, with, possibly, unfortunate consequences.

The reason for these peculiar alignments is at present speculation,
but another strange feature appeared when I drew a line from the
volcanic plug of Ailsa Craig, an island to the south-west of the mainland, to the Edinburgh Castle volcanic plug. This passes through 'The
Electric Brae' or Croy Brae in Ayrshire, where the laws of gravity appear to be suspended. Driving along this stretch of road, you have to
change to a lower gear to go 'downhill' and you can even coast 'up-

Boat Cave, Isle of Staffa, in the Hebrides

hill' with the engine switched off. Careful surveying has shown that it
is an optical illusion, but there may be more to it than this, as I find that
the telluric wavelengths down this section of road are different from
any I have encountered elsewhere.

When any track or road is cut through virgin ground it forms its own
telluric energy, consisting of a series of parallel waves which follow the
curves and bends of the road. The background energy waves in this
area are 1 metre apart with a wavelength of 16ft.8in., (508cms), a
wave amplitude of 23in.(58cms). On this road I found that the wave
energy was very much more amplified, with a wavelength of 1ft.(30
cms), amplitude 18in.(46 cms). While puzzling over this anomaly, I
decided to do another simple experiment: I picked one wave at random half way down the road and followed it. It weaved sharply from

side to side, all the way down the road, until, a few metres from the sign showing the end of the 'Electric Brae', where the wave suddenly eased out into the normal slow, easy pattern. The same occurred at the sign at the top end of the Brae.

Then I made another attempt in a small parking area. This had the same effect. A highly amplified series of waves on the tarmac, easing out to the normal pattern above and below, on the grass verge. When I tried the fields on both sides of the road, these showed nothing but the same easy sinuous waves. It was only on the metalled surface of the road between the two signs that there was this amplification. I seem to recall reading that this road was perfectly normal many years ago, and the strange effects only occurred after it was first tarmaced.

My little folding bicycle was then pressed into use on the Electric Brae, and I freewheeled eerily uphill and struggled back down. This is the best way to get the 'feel' of this peculiar road. A spirit level placed on my tripod as the simplest of theodolites revealed, alas, that it does appear to be an optical illusion, a 'fortuitous marriage' of the lines of the road and the hills, but that doesn't explain the strange amplification of the energy wave on that short stretch.

There is a similar effect on the island of Mull which was once a highly active volcanic area. It is also found on a new motorway in Cairo, where the granite road surface is taken from the site from which was extracted the granite for the construction of the pyramids.

ELECTRICAL INSTALLATIONS AS EARTH ANOMALIES

Throughout this research it has struck me as very peculiar that standing stones, wells, volcanic plugs, electrical generators, television repeater stations and some others should emit such similar wavelengths of energies. Several authorities on electro-engineering have stated categorically that it is impossible for modern units like radar stations to emit energy waves at these frequencies. However, I am convinced that the wavelengths and amplitudes I have quoted throughout this book are accurate.

The reason may well be that utilities like radar stations, for instance, are telluric anomalies, or 'holes in the landscape', similar to volcanic plugs (or stone circles, for that matter). Natural subterranean earth energies may be attracted up to them, then radiate away in all directions as radial leys — natural earth energies modified by the siting of modern electrical units. Perhaps the wavelengths might be slightly altered by the utility in question, but they are all, certainly, very close together. This theory may also explain why the radial leys from these sources can be captured and earthed by quarries — they are returning to source.

NOTES

1. Devereux, P., Letter in *Cereologist* Magazine, No.6.
2. Boshier, A. and Beaumont, P., "Mining in Southern Africa and the Emergence of Modern Man"; *Optima* Magazine. Johannesburg (1972).
3. Williamson, T. et al, *Ley Lines in Question*: World's Work/Heinemann (1983).
4. Lethbridge, T., writer of 7 titles in 1960s and '70s beginning with *Ghost and Ghoul*, 1961, all published by Routledge Kegan and Paul.
5. McLellan Mann, L., "A Forgotten Researcher", Inst. Geomantic Res., Occas. Paper No.7.

CHAPTER 18

IMPRINTING

It is possible for people to make a lasting impression on the telluric energy of a place. Also, we can transmit our own energy into the fabric of, for example, a castle; as the following story shows.

Garth castle, near Fortingall, Perthshire, is close to the geographical centre of Scotland. This is where 'the Wolf of Badenoch' exterminated many a clansman, binding them hand and foot and kicking them from the top of the battlements into the deep ravine below. Niall Stewart, a later owner of the castle and a descendant of the Wolf, also used the ravine to rid himself of two of his wives. As a punishment he was imprisoned in his own dungeons for over seven years, in a tiny walled-off cell, neither high enough to stand in, nor wide enough to lie down in. Eventually, he died a miserable death. Is it coincidence that in this tiny prison, now a cupboard, an unhealthy spiral could be found?

A recent owner was a Dutch lady, Maryse Vogelaar, who has stamped her own character indelibly into the ancient fortress. She felt, when she and her husband first saw the castle, that it 'rocked them in its arms', 'absorbed them'. When I surveyed the magnificent dining room, into which Maryse had projected her own energy, there were numer-ous small eddies of healthy spirals, with any unhealthy waves passing straight through, without staying to create any difficulty. Maryse ex-plained that, from time to time, she felt the presence of entities, but being an unusually strong minded woman, and more aware than most of any strange presences in the castle, persuaded them to depart, one by one. For me, it was a salutary lesson that we all produce our own energies, which can be imprinted into our surroundings in either a negative or positive manner.

A POWERFUL AND BENEFICIAL SHRINE

This was further impressed upon me in a house belonging to a Paki-stani couple which had a number of unhealthy spirals through it, from subterranean water in this case. As I was about to survey one of its rooms, the owner politely asked me to remove my shoes, since it was a very special sanctuary for them both. The room was a beautiful shrine to the Indian mystic Sri Satya Sai Baba. I was intrigued to find that there was no unhealthy energy in it at all, unlike the rest of the house, which was full of unhealthy spirals. My divining rod for 'unhealthy energies' showed that there was a healthy spiral, centred on the shrine. Whether this was an input from the occupants or emitted from the shrine, or a little of both, I have no idea at present. What did intrigue me was that there was an unhealthy spiral immediately below the room. This should in theory have been radiating vertically and equally unpleasantly into the shrine room above. Some aspect of the shrine room was apparently keeping the unhealthy spiral at bay.

Another house had a very similar pattern, including a powerful spiral on one side of the bed, at the level of the husband's throat. He suffered from sleeplessness and panic attacks, as well as a painful throat. Only one room was devoid of unhealthy earth energies, and this was the room in which he used his radionic machine. Radionics is a means of 'tuning in' to people at a distance, using a sample of hair, blood, sputum, etc., and broadcasting remedies to the patient. I have some difficulty in coming to terms with this method, but it does work, and even helps to keep its immediate environment free of unpleasant telluric energy.

So, even badly irradiated houses can be 'cleaned' by some aspect of the occupants themselves, without resorting to any of the practices suggested in Chapter 19. Perhaps buildings, or the fabric of which they are composed, are capable of picking up and absorbing some subtle emanations of the occupants, or it may be that it is the ever present telluric energies which may contain past information. After friends and I have a meditation group, for instance, there is always a healthy spiral to be found in the room, but not in the exact centre of either the room or the group, as one would expect. Even when I meditate alone with a little visualization, there is also a little spiral to be found, although it will disappear after an indeterminate period. This may be the origins of the 'housewarming party,' to give the new house and its owners the best possible start.

Similarly, in a church, with its different energy system, it is taboo to laugh or clap. Singing hymns, chanting or praying may enhance its special energies. It may be that vibrations of these types may 'inject' their special energies into the fabric of their surroundings. In an old monastery I visited recently, at Meigle, Perthshire (built from hand-cut sandstone) healthy waves radiated all around it, excluding all unhealthy ones.

HOUSE BUILT ON THE SITE OF A STONE CIRCLE

An area with a rock structure which contains a high number of subterranean fissures and underground water courses can initiate energy fields which may be imprinted by sufficiently powerful and emotional events, according to the late T.C.Lethbridge[1].

A lady who had recently moved from a house which had been built on the site of a stone circle told me of her experiences. The atmosphere in her house was incredibly bad. Her teenage son woke one morning with scratch marks down his face, a cross scratched on his chest and a trident symbol: a 'U' shape with a vertical shaft through it on his abdomen. She later discovered that a witch had been burned to death there some centuries earlier! They moved from that house shortly after, leaving the problem with the incoming family.

Another worried person asked me my opinion of his new house, which he had just moved into. Until then, he had a perfectly good job. He and his wife enjoyed good health and got on well together, but now everything seemed to be going wrong. Their health had deteriorated, and he was having a run of 'bad luck'. After only a little questioning he volunteered the information that his house had been built on top of a bubonic plague pit!.

Other locations in the country though, have similar problems. The cathedral in Perth, Scotland, for instance, has been built on the site of an abattoir!

DESCENDING ORDER OF UNHEALTHY EARTH ENERGIES

Various sites can feel the effects of naturally occurring and man-made, unhealthy energies. In descending order of magnitude, I list below the different types of location where I have recorded noticeable effects. This list will no doubt have to be changed.

1. Directly above an underground 'unhealthy' river or stream.
2. On the energy ley between an open-cast coal mine and a quarry.
3. Downstream of two graveyards.
4. Downstream of a quarry. (In a working quarry, this depends on the type of rock being quarried, whether dynamite is or has been used, and the amount of dust emitted. In disused quarries it depends on the type of rock present and whether or not it is used as a rubbish dump).
5. On the site of an old graveyard or battlefield.
6. Downstream of a graveyard.
7. Wells radiating into an energy ley passing through a cemetery, refuse or chemical dump, etc. (Remember that wells are usually sited on crossing underground streams). In addition, some-times

disused wells are pressed into service as septic tanks.
8. Above and around deep coalmines, especially if they are disused and flooded.
9. Other old mine workings.
10. The area close to power cables near quarries and geological faults.
11. The area near busy railway lines. This only extends to about 40 metres on unelectrified tracks, but very much further downstream of electrified lines.
12. In the 'shadow' of a television repeater mast.
13. Around transformers and turbines at power stations.
14. Around nuclear reactors and dumps, missile storage sites.
15. Above underground train systems.
16. Crossing energy leys from standing stones and circles.
17. On the downstream side of banks of polluted rivers, canals.

CHANGES IN STRENGTH

The telluric energies we have been discussing change position or intensity quite dramatically over the years. I find this quite usual. Early in 1992 I became aware that they seemed to be increasing in intensity to such an extent that I was becoming a little alarmed. When I gave talks throughout the country I found that spirals seemed much more common in the halls and houses I visited. An unhealthy spiral had the affrontery to place itself within one metre of my armchair, and another in my spare bed! Fortunately because I was aware of them and was able to work on them to change their polarity, I had no problems with my health.

Also to be considered is the possibility that I may be altering the energies myself, which, if true, would complicate this type of research dramatically. I have seen so many people apparently altering the energy fields around them simply by visualizing them, that I have the uneasy feeling that they may be capable of being altered at will (or subconsciously). Throughout the research for this book I have tried to go with what I find without knowingly or subconsciously influencing the result. I wonder if I have been successful!

NOTE
1. Lethbridge, T., see note on p.178 (chap.17).

CHAPTER 19

ELIMINATING UNHEALTHY EARTH ENERGY

Clearing a house of unhealthy energies can be done in a number of ways. If there is only a simple grid pattern of unhealthy waves present, with intersections in a bed for instance — if it is not practicable to move the bed to a safer place — then quartz crystals can be put down on the incoming waves to change them from unhealthy to healthy.

Since unhealthy waves will not pass (as previously stated), through windows, but instead enter indirectly, at the side of the glass, these are the best locations to place crystals. Using your 'unhealthy' divining rod, find, as accurately as you can, the places where the unhealthy waves enter the window frame. If you have a cluster or geode of crystals, such as amethyst or clear quartz, place one on the window ledge where you find the incoming wave. This can be done on any floor of a house or building, and will effectively clear both upper and lower storeys as well. Do this wherever you find the unhealthy waves entering key points in the house, where you sleep, sit, or stay for extended periods. Remember that window frames often have vertical wooden or metal parts where unhealthy waves will easily penetrate. If you have single crystals, the larger the crystal the better, use these to give you more leeway.

Crystals may be purchased at lapidary shops, and can sometimes even be bought in book or souvenir shops. The crystals must be the naturally occurring variety. The artificial types of crystal used in the old-fashioned chandeliers will not work. Another form of semi-precious stone, the massive lumps of quartz which may be found in shapeless masses, like quartzite, rose quartz, or massive amethyst will not work in quite the same manner. It is preferable to use semi-precious crystals, at least until you are more proficient in finding and eliminating unhealthy telluric energy.

For those more experienced with divining rods, it is preferable to place the crystals on the centre line of each incoming wave. However, detection has to be absolutely exact, or the unhealthy wave will simply divert a short distance, to pass round the crystal. If the crystal is left at the correct point, the incoming wave will pass through and around the amethyst in a 'shape wave' of clean energy. Wing Commander Beadon, an energetic researcher into earth radiation, favours two amethyst crystals in tandem, upstream of the area to be protected, although, of course, the placing of these must be even more exact.

However, we are all individuals. What may be good for some may be thoroughly unpleasant for others. Some very sensitive people, like those suffering from electro-stress, for example, may find that the use of copper coils or certain crystals will magnify their symptoms, so it is a matter for experimentation. Remember, also, that mirrors can warp the unhealthy waves around their edges. A large mirror on a dressing table, suitably placed near the head or foot (or side) of the bed, can be used to deflect them. You will recall from earlier that this may be why, in Feng-shui, pictures and mirrors are hung on walls at an angle, to help disrupt what the Chinese call the 'bad breath'.

Dowsers have known for some years that a large clump of crystals can also be used with advantage to clean the energies from VDUs, televisions, microwaves, etc. The crystal, the larger the better, is simply left on top of the appliance, roughly at the front, above the screen, where it will automatically clean up some of the electromagnetic waves issuing from the appliance. According to some people who are sensitive to crystals, they should never be picked up with the naked hand when they are used for clearing, and must have a cloth placed over them when being removed. The crystals themselves should be cleansed periodically under a running tap, or left for some time immersed in sea salt.

Why crystals like amethyst, clear quartz, etc., clean an unhealthy wave is not yet known, but it is of interest to note that bishops' mitres have a large amethyst in them, and that bishops often wear a large amethyst ring on the hand. Some say, cynically, that they wore these to offset the unpleasant effects of too much wine and women! The Romans, too, used amethysts encrusted on their drinking cups to 'purify' the water.

KILLING 'VAMPIRES' — ENERGY LEYS

Another method (see Chapter 15), if you can locate accurately the overground unhealthy waves from an energy ley stream entering a house, is to use stakes inserted in the garden on the upstream side of each wave. They can be made of perforated angle iron (as used to support shelves). Stake them about 1ft.(30 cms) into the ground, with the same length above the surface. The 'V' shape should warp the incoming wave away from your residence. You must use your divining rod for unhealthy energies to check that it has been done correctly. Be careful you don't give your neighbours your own problem. Also be careful not to sever any telephone cables, etc. This form of killing 'vampires' is included here for interest, as personally I find it loses its effectiveness after a short time. Overground energy waves seem to change position over a period, eventually missing the stakes entirely and passing through the house as before. Nowadays there are so many unhealthy overgrounds that this method is likely to be ineffective.

— AND SUBTERRANEAN STREAMS

If the problem is an underground stream of water, then staking it can be effective. Find the centre wave of the stream and hammer a copper or iron rod (some people favour a wide metal sheet) about 1ft. (30cms.) long into the ground, and, if possible, another on the downstream side of the house. This is the old established method of clearing harmful radiation from a dwelling, and can be used in addition to the much simpler method I use, which is discussed in the next chapter. Again, be careful that no other houses are affected. With a little positioning you may be able to deflect it in another direction, into an area clear of habitation, if there is one.

A length of iron pipe can also be used, placed horizontally on the ground, although it is cumbersome and unsightly. I include this also, simply for interest. The incoming unhealthy waves bounce off the pipe and travel around the sides, but only if the pipe is lying on the ground. The pipe must be about 4ins.(10cms.) diameter or more.

Early one morning, stumbling around in the darkness outside a derelict haunted house, I noticed that the waves, instead of passing into the house, seemed to be warped back on themselves. When I returned in daylight, the reason became obvious. The house was being renovated and the builders had left an old iron down pipe on the ground. Hot water radiators and their plumbing make no impact on the telluric energies in a building, possibly because they are filled with liquid, and scaffolding around a building seems to have no effect as well, perhaps because the tube diameter is not wide enough.

Another technique which can be effective in 'de-raying' dwellings, but again rather clumsy, is to surround a house (or a bed), with a copper wire, leaving a 6ins.(15cms.) 'spark gap.' This, in a miniature form was used by the late Bruce MacManaway, the noted healer from Fife. He used a small copper coil, perhaps 6ins.(15cms.) in diameter, to alter the polarity of individual waves. This, like the amethyst or quartz crystals, can be placed on the inside of the window ledge.

Clearing a larger area has its own problems, as I found at a farm where the owner had a high death rate in his stock. One young foal even killed itself by trying to jump out of the enclosure, impaling itself on the fence. The field had two streams of water beneath it, which initiated two lines of unhealthy spirals down its length. The unhealthy waves from these two underground streams were negated by angle irons placed directly above them. In this case, the irons were put under a wire fence, where they would not be disturbed.

This produced an unpredicted result — the incoming waves bounced back on themselves, then followed the wire fence for some distance, before turning at right angles and following another boundary fence away from the area.

ELIMINATING SPIRALS

Where you find an unhealthy spiral, you must tackle it in a different manner. Putting down a Lakhovsky coil accurately in the centre of a spiral can change the character of its waves from unhealthy to healthy. This is approximately ten turns of fence wire, or copper, wound anticlockwise from the centre, the end at the top of the coil acting like a small aerial. The coil acts like a condenser or capacitor in a radio circuit[1]. The larger the spiral the better, since these spirals can subtly change their position over a period. A little more research is needed, but the centre of one spiral I checked, itself spirals around in a complicated pattern, about 1ft.(30cms.) diameter.

These coils are equally effective wound either clockwise or anticlockwise from the centre, or without the aerial, placed in the attic, under the floor, or carpet. Once the spiral has been dealt with, the normally unhealthy waves, instead of focusing into the centre of the spiral, will now cross the house in the normal grid pattern, but will still have to be dealt with by placing crystals, etc., as already mentioned.

A number of devices are available which are helpful in de-raying a house or area. One, the 'Beadon Cube' is a small perspex cube with a copper coil surrounded by chips of semi-precious stones. I have used only one of these on an unhealthy spiral. Although it easily negated the unhealthy spiral, it had to be placed exactly in the centre of the spiral and this can wander. There are other devices of a similar nature, and a few electrical circuits which rely on plugging into the mains supply to give a protected area. Although they do not eliminate unhealthy spirals, it helps in some cases, possibly by negating unhealthy earth energies which enter a house through the electric wiring system. These may be the same as those from quarries and the ends of geological faults, discussed earlier.

SINGING CRYSTALS

Harry Oldfield, who has been working with crystals for many years, markets an electro-crystal therapy unit. This unit pulses low voltage DC electricity into a tube of crystals immersed in a saline solution. The pulses can be tuned to different frequencies and intensities. This unit can be used initially in a diagnostic mode. If a person holds such a tube of crystals in his hand, his whole body will resonate at that frequency. A simple sound meter is zeroed at a healthy part of the body, and the rest of the body is scanned with the meter to find any anomalous reading which may indicate a past, present or future area of illness. The unit may then be used therapeutically to give safe stimuli of energies at set frequencies.

It is interesting to note that this unit can warp unhealthy waves away from an area. The tube of crystals, left in the centre of the unhealthy spiral in my own home, warped the unhealthy waves away, starving the spiral and changing it to a healthy one. The higher the frequency and rate of the pulsed crystals, the more effective it is in an unhealthy spiral, but it is not powerful enough if the waves are close to a large electric power generating station.

I have mentioned before that mirrors and glass as very good insulators for earth energies. They can also warp the unhealthy waves from electric sub-stations as well as the powerful turbines at generating stations. Emissions from nuclear submarines and quarries can also be deflected in this way. It is possible that placing a protective shield of poor quality glass around such sources may, effectively and cheaply, shield the environment from such subtle energies.

OBSERVE CAUTION

The de-raying techniques in this chapter all have problems. Some only work for a short time, some de-raying devices are expensive, and most need the help of a skilled dowser. Anyone using dowsing, or any similar techniques to those described, on another person's property would open themselves to civil liability if the owner can claim that some harmful effect has been caused to them by the 'treatment'.

I stumbled upon a simple way of clearing a house or building at the end of my research. It has few disadvantages, and, in any case, can be 'switched off,' at any time, within seconds. This also must be used prudently and with sensitivity, as I have not yet investigated it sufficiently to guarantee total protection to every individual. The story of petroglyphs, or cup-marked stones, which have mystified archaeologist and layperson alike for centuries is related in the next chapter.

NOTE

1.   Moody, F., *British Society of Dowers* Magazine, No.188.

CHAPTER 20

CUP-MARKED STONES

Yet another part of my research into earth energies was to investigate the purpose of cup-marks. Recounting the full story of the adventure is outside the scope of this book, but it is sufficient to say at present that creating cup-marks in stone is a very good way of eliminating unhealthy energies, particularly spirals.

Cup-marks are hollows carved into stone. Sometimes called rock art or petroglyphs, their existence has puzzled scientists and archaeologists around the world. Since there is little or no dateable evidence associated with them, experts can only guess their age. In 1979, one eminent archaeologist, Ronald W.B.Morrison, who spent much of his working life investigating them, suggested a date of approximately 3,200BC to AD100. This has been challenged little by more recent researchers.

Cup-marks range from simple little hollows (about ½in.(12mm) across, generally round, but occasionally oval-shaped), to much larger 'basins', 6in.(15cm) wide. Some are surrounded by an additional ring or rings, which may have a gap, or have a groove running through them. Others are joined together by a groove. The grooves usually run down from the cup, suggesting to some that the stones have been used for sacrificial purposes, letting the blood from the victims flow down, although there is no archaeological evidence of this[1].

Cup-marks are to be found usually in clusters in parts of the world. In Britain there are few south of Yorkshire. Some can be found in Derbyshire. They may be discovered above ground on standing stones, earth-fast boulders in fields, small moveable boulders, horizontal rock faces or hidden in caves, like Wemyss Cave, Fife. They are also to be found in souterrains (sometimes called weems, fogues, or earth houses), or cists, stone-age coffins, or in chambered mounds.

The beautifully sculpted marks in the rock at Ormaig, near Kilmartin, Argyll, are good examples. Since childhood, I have been fascinated by these mysterious legacies from the distant past and, having completed most of my research into the energy leys across Scotland, I determined to try and find out what our ancestors may have done

Bronze Age petroglyphs - cup-marked rocks at Kilmartin, West of Scotland

with these strange sculpted stones.

I tuned into a local, rather unimpressive cup-marked stone. From eight cup-marks on this stone there was given off a stream of individual waves which traversed the country for many kilometres, until they came to a major geological fault, where the ground had been displaced vertically. Now a waterfall tumbled over it. I followed the energy waves as they turned upstream, close to the tumbling water. Eventually, they led me almost to the source of the river, then, unexpectedly, turned at right angles to the water, forming a little circle of energy. Inside that little pool of energy were the remains of a shieling, a rough shelter for a shepherd.

What was happening was that the energy from this stone, using the 'carrier wave' emitted by an underground stream directly beneath it, crossed the country until it came to a river running over a major fault. It followed this almost to its source, presumably picking up negative ions on its way. At this point were large circular patterns scattered around the glen, similar in shape to those on the original stone. The patterns on the stone initiated small pools of energy, inside of which were the remains of small habitations.

Rather nonplussed at this strange effect, yet realising that there was something very important and powerful to be discovered, I determined to find the reason our apparently highly skilled and intuitive ancestors had used and manipulated such a curious system of natural energies. I used my divining rod to find how any unhealthy energy waves reacted to such an energy field. All unhealthy waves were diverted around the shielings. The eight cup-marks on that stone, many kilometres away, were protecting the eight ancient homes from unhealthy energies.

This led me to try and make my own cup-marked stones. I discovered that when you hammer such a mark into a stone, you create a magnified image of that mark some ten metres from the stone. The size of the image is about seventy times the size of the cup-mark. This is projected towards the Sun. Carving a ring around the cup-mark magnifies the size of the pool of energy, and carving a line towards the Sun shows the direction of the projected energy.

If you can imagine a lollipop on a stick, you will get an idea of the shape of energy from the stone. The wavelength is about 33in.(84 cms.), and amplitude 5½in.(14 cms.)

The extraordinary thing about this ancient technology is that the magnified image or pool of energy from the stone is further magnified when placed outside a building. Such a marked stone can be left outside a house to protect it and deflect the unhealthy waves around the building.

CARRIER WAVES

As time passed, however, it became obvious that this was not the complete picture. As stated, some badly affected houses had 100 per cent invasion of unhealthy waves, with no healthy waves at all. When I cleared these unhealthy waves from such a house, there should have been no waves of either type inside at all. Yet this was not the case, there were waves, many of them, and they were, apparently, healthy.

One explanation for this anomaly may be that the waves are in two parts: a carrier wave of healthy energy, which has a wave of unhealthy positive ions attached to it. Using a cup-marked stone as an energy shield around a house may deflect the unhealthy waves of ions around the house, leaving the healthy carrier waves to pass into the house.

We have already seen something similar to this splitting of energy waves: Fig.11 (p.115) shows how elements of the vertical energy waves above an underground stream are warped to either side at 45 degrees. In fig.21 (p.136) the overgrounds of an energy ley tune into two spirals above an underground stream. A spiral boxed in by two sets of crossing waves, pirates its energy from them in what is probably a complicated circuit (fig.27, p.150). None of these incidents included the existence of cup-marked stones.

Another unexpected finding was that unhealthy spirals in a house protected by a cup-marked stone were changed to healthy ones. This may be because the single wave directly above the centre of a subterranean stream may have a polarity depending on the type of geological strata it passes through on its way to the surface. Clay, for example, would give an unhealthy quality to that line, and any unhealthy component of the surface energy ley would tune into it, to be reflected back as an unhealthy spiral.

If there is no unhealthy energy ley stream available to focus into the wave above the stream, then the spiral will be starved, and cannot reflect upwards to give the normal double unhealthy spiral as in fig.19.

MAKING YOUR OWN CUP-MARKED STONE

Here are step-by-step instructions on how to make your own cup-marked stone. It is easier if the selected stone is carefully kept in the same position throughout the exercise.

1. Find a stone with a diameter of about 1ft.(30 cms). It must be of a size which you can pick up without too much difficulty, but sufficiently heavy that it will not be disturbed easily when in place. You will need a type of rock that is not too hard. The rocks I have used contain some quartz, which may help to create the effect we want.

2. With a heavy hammer and cold chisel, make a depression about 1ins.(2½cms) deep and 2ins.(5 cms) across. Use goggles when cutting the stone, and gloves, as stone chips can easily damage eyes and hands.

3. Accurately chalk a line from the centre of the cup-shaped depression towards the Sun and hammer this until you have carved a deep groove. It is best to wait until the Sun is fairly low in the sky, and not overhead, unless you wish to experiment. Since it is the Sun which literally attracts the energy from the stone towards itself, the lines of waves into the Sun will fan out slightly during the 20 minutes or so that the stone is being carved. This will allow for easier orientation when you come to place it in position — accuracy here is essential.

4. Chalk a ring about 5ins.(13cms) diameter around the depression, and carve this out as well.

5. Check, if possible, with your dowsing rod that the waves are, in fact, flowing in the direction marked.

6. Carve your initials prominently on the stone, to avoid the possibility of the local amateur archaeologist removing it to the much safer premises of a museum!

7. The energy waves from the stone will have become 'fixed' after a few hammer blows and, after completion, the stone can be turned in

any direction, the Sun now having no effect. It can now be placed in an area of the garden where it will not be disturbed, within one metre of your house, with the line from the centre of the cup pointing directly forward to the house wall. In other words, the line and the wall of the house should take the form of a 'T', the line on the stone the vertical component of the 'T', and the wall of the house the top part of the 'T'. Any side of the   house will do, although I prefer the sunny south side. The stone should be aimed preferably at a middle line of the house rather than near a corner.

If this has been done correctly, energy waves projected from the stone should travel towards the building, split into two, then follow the walls in both directions, forming a complete 'shield ring' around it. Any size of house or building can be protected by this simple and inexpensive device, even an entire street, providing all the buildings are connected and have no alleyways for the energy to return to source. Any incoming unhealthy waves will be diverted around the building, down the streets or lanes at either side. You can check this with your dowsing rod for unhealthy energies, although anyone without this ability can protect their own house perfectly easily by simply following the instructions.

Check any unhealthy spiral that entered the dwelling before the cup-marked stone was placed, to make sure that it has changed polarity. This can be verified if the incoming healthy energy now passes through glass windows and mirrors into the centre of that same spiral.

I have found that over a period, the pool of energy created by the stone tends to contract back towards the stone a little. It may eventually fall short of the building itself, if it is placed too far away, therefore setting the stone as close to the building as possible is a wise precaution.

If the exercise does not work, it may be that the stone is directly above an underground stream which may be causing your problem. The energy wave above the stream serves as a carrier wave, sending the energy from the cup-marked stone downstream and negating the exercise. Shift the stone to another part of the house, if necessary, until any incoming unhealthy waves are diverted around the house.

Another common problem is when the energy waves from the stone are not projected towards the wall at $90°$, and, instead of splitting and running around the house, are diverted to one side or another for only a few metres. If this happens, try turning the stone just a few degrees at a time until any unpleasant effect in the house is removed.

There should now be no incoming unhealthy waves except, perhaps, from one line directly above any water vein[2]. Even this line can be diverted by inserting a metal stake, or better still, a wider sheet of metal in the upstream side of the underground stream in the garden as described in a previous chapter. A carefully placed crystal of amethyst or other semi-precious stone can also be beneficial, providing it doesn't cause its own problems to any sensitive person.

CURRY AND HARTMANN GRIDS

There should now be very few unhealthy energy waves in the house. There will still be some from internal microwave ovens, VDUs, televisions, etc., but now they will not be able to earth their energy into any unhealthy spiral, since these have their polarity automatically changed by this remedial action. The only remaining problem may possibly be from the Hartmann and Curry grids, which, as far as I know, are not diverted by this form of protection. (See Chapter 14 for a fuller explanation of these Grids.) Unfortunately, since this form of protection requires a garden, or at least an area where such a stone can be sited, many buildings in built up areas will not be able to use such a device.

It is imperative that you understand that it is not beneficial to use this method if neighbouring property will be affected. This form of energy shield is perfect around a bungalow or semi-detached house (if the neighbours are agreeable), but has obvious disadvantages in a larger building with a number of families, some of whom might be sensitive to such changes. Apart from this, in a large building, the unhealthy energy is warped in close waves around it, perhaps giving neighbouring buildings a slightly higher dose of the deflected energy waves.

One notable advantage this form of clearing a building has over others, is that if anyone feels that his/her health is deteriorating as a result of using this method, then the stone can easily be turned to point away from the dwelling, in other words, 'switched off,' within moments.

OBSERVE CAUTION WITH HEART PROBLEMS

Since I have started using this technique to clear buildings, I have had a great deal of success in helping people back to health. It works best with those who have recently moved into a geopathically stressed zone, if they are aware enough to seek help quickly. Also, it seems to give some relief to people suffering from long-term illness. Occasionally, the results can be very pronounced, although I suggest that for some illnesses like heart problems, for example, the stone should be left in the working position for a few hours during the day at first, gradually building up to a round-the-clock protection.

To date, I have had no negative feedback from anyone whose house has been protected in this way. In three cases of illness and associated attacks from demonic spirits and poltergeists, the cup-marked stone appeared to have made these paranormal phenomena worse. In spite of this, the health of the occupants improved. So, be very careful with this ancient technology; use it only for yourself and your family, and then with great care, because what benefits one person may cause discomfort to another.

Every year or so, it is advisable to strike the cup-marked depression on the stone a few blows to further amplify the energy. Do not forget to turn the stone so that the grooved line faces into the sun when you hammer it, and also, please remember to protect your eyes with good quality goggles.

Cup-marked stones have a variety of uses, and in their original form, may have been used in protecting houses from apparitions and evil spirits. Given the variety of types of prehistoric cup-marked stones still seen around the country there must be other uses yet to be discovered. There is an old Welsh saying that when cup-marked stones are finally decoded, then all of the ancient arts and sciences will be revealed!

HAMMERING STONES

J.Havelock Fidler also wrote some years ago of hammering stones, and the peculiar qualities of stones thus worked. Following T.C.Lethbridge's discovery that stones could be imprinted with a female energy simply by asking a woman to handle one for a short time, or conversely, a male energy by a man, he found that the energy 'rate' could be fixed, simply by heating the stone in a fire, leaving it near an electromagnet, or by hitting the stone with a hammer, being careful not to touch it himself in the process. (See earlier references to the work of J.Havelock Fidler and T.C.Lethbridge).

I had not read J.Havelock Fidler's book for some ten years, and had forgotten much about his discoveries. This was important to me, since I did not wish to be prejudiced in my own research. When I re-read his book, I found interesting parallels. Three stones he hammered and set up in a row projected a line of energy fore and aft, which immediately reminded me of the tandem effect from nuclear submarines and power stations, etc. Hammering a stone in my hand gave a slightly shorter wavelength than his — 41ins.(104 cms) against his 45½ins.(116 cms). A 'female charged' stone, which I presume was handled by his wife, gave an even longer wavelength of 55ins. (140cms). We must remember that the shorter the wavelength, the greater the energy imprinted in the stone, although this has nothing to do with how hard or how often the stone is hit, as it can reach a 'saturation point'.

It may be, therefore, that some people are unable to work cup-marks into stones and gain the full effect, because of the wavelength of their own energy. If you cannot get a stone to work, try gettting someone else to do it for you.

Dr.Fidler believed, as I had come to, that by painstakingly hammering and sculpting standing stones and circles, pyramids and statues, and later monasteries and cathedrals, men imparted their energy into the fabric of the stone. This is still discernible, even many years later, if you seek to find this energy by using the tools our ancestors used.

NOTE

1. Morrison, R.W.B., *The Prehistoric Rock Art of Argyll*; and *The Prehistoric Rock Art of Galloway and the Isle of Man*: Dolphin Press (1979).

2. This remaining line is much more important than I originally suspected. The worst cases of C.F.S., for instance, have had this line running the length of the victim's body. As the line tends to wander around at random, it is difficult to locate with divining rods, and the best advice is simply to shift your sleeping place until the symptoms disappear. Since this line travels vertically upwards, glass windows and mirrors have no effect on it, as it 'sees' them as an obstacle only a few millimetres thick.

CHAPTER 21

HUMAN DISEASE AND MOTHER EARTH

A useful tip for the prospective owner of a new house is to enquire after the health of the previous occupants. If there has been serious illness, if the house has been termed an 'unlucky' house, there is the possibility that the occupants have been affected by unhealthy earth energy. In particular, if there are paranormal events, this may indicate a highly stressed area. A house may have had several owners in a short time, and occupiers may be only too glad to sell and move away.

On some occasions, clients complain that even the plants taken from their old home begin to wilt in their new surroundings, in a similar manner to the occupants. Often, I visit people who are so tired and listless that it is obvious to me that the unhealthy energy in the house, is literally sucking the vitality out of their bodies. They tell me that they are also electro-sensitive, and have trouble with household electrical appliances, sometimes short circuiting them or suffering shocks. This form of 'vampirism' can end in only one way, unless the symptoms are understood and steps are taken to eliminate them. The body will fall prey to some disease, possibly a hereditary weakness.

Many people discover for themselves that it is their own home or working environment which causes the illness. So often I have heard people say that they feel so ill in their house. They recover only when they spend some time at another location or on vacation. These feelings should be regarded as a timely warning, and action taken before it is too late.

SOME DISEASES ASSOCIATED WITH TELLURIC ENERGIES

Modern man, in his ignorance, has long forgotten how to be aware of and live with Mother Earth and her powerful energies. Quarries and mines now appear like giant open sores in her flesh. Modern utilites like electric generators and sub-stations, radar stations and microwave towers, now flood their energies into natural earthing points, like the spirals above aquifers and underground streams. The more dependent we become on technology, the more electricity we use, and the problem gets worse. Many people, unfortunately, may pay with their health for our inability to realise that these energies even exist.

It is appreciated that illness has many causes and the sufferer must give the broadest attention to his/her symptoms. Nevertheless, the following are a few of the major illnesses which I have found to be associated repeatedly with the presence of unhealthy energies from telluric energy anomalies.

Alzheimer's Disease is a degenerative disease of the brain tissues, probably caused by abnormal protein deposits, or a toxic substance.

Cancers - According to the World Health Organisation, it is estimated that 75% of all cancers are caused by environmental factors. Some other researchers state as much as 90%[1].

Chronic Fatigue Syndrome (Myalgic Encephalomylitis) - In the 70 plus cases I have investigated, I have almost inevitably found an unhealthy spiral, sometimes centred as much as two metres from the subject's bed, but always close enough to sap the vitality of the occupant and lower his or her resistance. In the one case where there has been no spiral present, the sufferer told me that she must have contacted the disease in her previous house, or at work, which she had to leave. Now relieved of her personal 'vampire' she progressed with the help of medical aid.

In the course of my own work as a geopathic stress consultant, I always make a point of asking my clients if their own particular illness coincided with a change of house, or employment. I find that many women have a refined intuitive sense of the feeling, the 'atmosphere' of a house. Men, often traditionally brought up to be scientific, hard-headed, logical and sceptical, have the ability to a much lesser degree. Many women sense something 'not quite right' about the house, feeling uncomfortable, sometimes changing beds and furniture around. Since it is common for the woman in a partnership to spend more of her time in the home, it is she who may be the first to react and most powerfully, especially, if there is more than one spiral in the house.

Multiple Sclerosis and, more recently, the 'flesh-eating bug', Necrotising Fasciitis are diseases that have started to feature more heavily in the subjects that I visit. The latter is deemed to be linked with a type of streptococcus. Current theory believes that a virus attaches itself to the bacterium and injects itself into it to make the bacterium release its flesh destroying toxins.

USING YOUR INSTINCT

For anyone suffering from illness, or who feels instinctively that there is a problem arising from, for example underground water, or crossing energy leys, it is important not to dismiss such impressions. These feelings may be telling you something. Taking simple steps can be effective, such as changing the position of your bed or moving to another bedroom.

It will be obvious that to try and recover from an illness when still living or especially sleeping over a geopathically stressed area is like attempting to lift oneself up by the bootstraps. Even when the area has been identified and possibly eliminated the body is still diseased, and has to be treated.

The primary aim of this book has been to show the reader how to find geopathic or electro-stress and either eliminate it or choose a safer place in which to work and sleep, even though some scientists and members of the medical profession may still insist that scientific proof is needed first.

CHECKLIST

For anyone suffering an illness, ask yourself these questions:
— Did my illness begin shortly after moving into this house (or place of work)?
— Do I feel better when I am away from the house?
— Do any of my family feel uneasy about the 'atmosphere' in the house?
— Does my cat have its favourite sleeping place near or on the bed/ favourite chair or in the room vertically above or below?
— Did the previous occupant/s suffer from any serious illness?
— Does the illness seem to be worse during autumn or spring? (when underground water may be flowing at a higher velocity).
— Were there any nearby disturbances which may have caused underground water veins to flow into different channels under my house prior my illness? (Working quarries, dynamiting, building work, etc.).
— Is there any unpleasant paranormal phenomenon in the house, such as an apparition or poltergeist?
— Have I ever felt that I have been physically pushed into bed, awakened in a paralysed state, or felt strangled by invisible hands?
— Does the house or any part of it, feel unnaturally cold or damp? If the answer to any of these questions is 'yes', then it is possible that the house and the inhabitants could be experiencing the effects of unhealthy telluric energies.

NOTE
1.   Chaitow, L., *The Radiation Protection Programme*, Thorsons.

CONCLUSION

We have come a long way from energy leys emitted from standing stones, unhealthy spirals from underground streams and faults, and we have even managed to include several archaeological mysteries and the paranormal as well.

We have also seen the subtle, but sometimes harmful energies emitted from such widespread sources as power stations, quarries, nuclear submarines and missiles, and how even benevolent energy leys can interact with burial-grounds, refuse dumps and other sources of decaying material, to change their character, irradiating whole swathes of countryside with insidious energies. As their wavelength is generally about our own height, we are at risk of resonating with these waves when we are in bed, when our bodies ought to be recovering and repairing themselves.

Our present standard of living owes much to the far-sightedness and inventiveness of the construction designers, engineers and builders of, for example, power stations, and hydro-electric schemes. The siting of railway lines, quarries, refuse dumps or burial-grounds assume that nature will adapt to our needs. Similarly we take for granted fast transport on metalled roads provided by quarries. We place cemeteries, refuse dumps, sewage farms and transformers in convenient locations. However, what we have not taken into account is that our decisions can result in making people ill.

The origin of our distress is our own glamourised view of a science that will only believe in physical phenomena. Had we taken the advice of Baron von Pohl some sixty years ago when he found the link between the subterranean streams of Vilsbiburg and its cancer victims, we would all be aware of such hidden dangers, and would have taken steps to avoid them long ago.

FENG-SHUI

Many ancient cultures knew of these highly stressed and dangerous areas, especially the Chinese who placed burial-grounds, houses and palaces in harmony with their surroundings. This was the form of geomancy called Feng-shui (wind-water), and many international corporations still use Feng-shui practitioners in their choice of sites, like the Citibank and Chase Manhattan Bank in Singapore, for example.

Hong Kong residents, 95% of whom are Chinese, would never dream of building a skyscraper, without consulting a Feng-shui expert, and many Westerners have been amazed at the apparent incongruity of some of their architecture. One apartment block at Repulse Bay has been built with a 'window' seven storeys high, to ensure that the "mountain dragon's view of the sea was not spoiled" (see photo). Part of the mountain can be seen through the gap in the picture. The loss in revenue to keep the 'beast' happy is estimated at about £1,000,000 per annum, as an average rent for a two-bedroomed flat is about £7000 per month.

Apartment block at Repulse Bay, Hong Kong

Considering their undoubted financial success in marrying science with ancient magic, perhaps we in the West should learn a few lessons from these ancient religions, and investigate the nature of 'black streams'. Many dowsers and water diviners have been impressed by the link of the earth energies to illness, and irritated at not being able to interpret their work scientifically. Until very recently, no type of meter had been developed which was able to measure these energy fields. A number of dowsers may go to a house and disagree on the type of energy present, giving them less credibility in the eyes of any observer. The difference of opinion may be because of the number of different energies present: beneficial or unhealthy grid, spirals of both polarities, and energies from wells, electrical sub-stations, and power generators, which may be involved.

Earth energies seem to touch a raw nerve in our civilization, perhaps because most of us can sense that they exist, and our ancestors, thousands of years ago, worked with and manipulated them, as evidenced by the remains of the megalithic culture dotted around the world. Stonehenge, the pyramids of Egypt, the Easter Island statues, ancient cathedrals, and many others have left a distant echo in all our minds, just waiting for the proper time to re-surface.

This book might encourage more scientists themselves to try dowsing, as some already have, to investigate energies which cause disease and effects like apparitions and poltergeists.

When the energies are better understood, we will have a much better chance to develop methods of protecting our homes and ourselves from black streams and spirals of all types. Take, for example, the intriguing discovery that the television relay station near Pitlochry filters the surrounding beneficial energies to earth, and leaves only the unhealthy energies to pass unhindered. Armed with this knowledge, it should not be too difficult, or costly, to reverse the process, and earth the unhealthy energies, perhaps even at the transformers and generators themselves, and this must also be possible with nuclear reactors and missiles.

Each country has its local geological structure and differences in its electric supply utilities which will affect the wavelengths of the energies. Nevertheless people all over the world have to become more aware of how these energies are affecting their lives.

SURVIVAL HANDBOOK

This book is also intended to be a survival handbook, to help the reader understand, or at least be aware of, the dangers of his hidden environment, and more importantly, to educate the homemaker into taking steps to ensure that his/her family live and sleep in as healthy a place as possible, since it is he or she who is responsible for the health of the family and is naturally more aware of the subtle energies which surround them. It is much better to avoid such traps to begin with, than have expensive, high-tech patch-up work done to a sick body, years, or perhaps even months later.

You do not appreciate good health until you lose it, and the reader is invited to think of his circle of friends and relations. How many of them enjoy good health? For all the benefits of our brilliant science, I suspect you will find very few.

It is wise to remember the words of the un-named doctor in the television programme "Randi, The Psychic Investigator": "If geopathic stress can be scientifically verified, it will be the greatest breakthrough in medical history." The reader, we hope, now has an advantage over his fellows to be aware of the problems in our incredibly hostile environment and use it to his own advantage, and anyone else who is interested.

On the Continent, in Russia and the Far East, the effects of earth energies are known in practically every household, and scientists there are at work trying to understand them and build devices to help eliminate this scourge. In the United Kingdom very few people have even heard of the problem, let alone investigated what promises to be a major breakthrough in our understanding of disease and other doctrines which are just beyond science. Some scientists are even almost hysterically denouncing the very existence of earth energies, and one wonders what the reaction of the general public will be if they listen to them and eventually discover that at least some of their illnesses is caused or aggravated by energies they ought to be aware of, at least intuitively, if not scientifically. Perhaps we have gone off on the wrong track, and instead of peering down electron microscopes to study the molecular structure of viruses and bacteria which attack a weak and sick body, we should peer down at our feet and wonder what kind of energies our living planet presents us with as she breathes.

CHEMICAL SWAMP

Another potentially expensive and disastrous health scare in the U.K. - B.S.E., or bovine spongiform encephalopathy in cattle, passed into their food chain by contaminated food. There is as yet no scientific connection with its - human equivalent, C.J.C (Creutzfeldt-Jakob disease), although they are both thought to be associated with prion, a protein in the brain of the affected cattle and humans *in the form of a spiral and beginning to unwind.* If so, then earth energies in the stall of the affected cattle and/or the beds of the human victims, as well as electrostress may be contributing factors.

The medical profession is under pressure, handing out drugs, some of which have little benefit, and some which have unpleasant side-effects. The doctors are under great stress in this sick society, and, I am quite sure, once the general public takes steps to avoid the unnecessary use of chemicals of all kinds, and understand both electrostress and geopathic stress, the standard of health and quality of living will improve dramatically.

The chemical swamp also includes the land, and the rivers, poisoned by insecticides and fertilisers. As a keen salmon, sea-trout and brown trout fisherman I have been dismayed at the decline in these fish. It distresses me that future generations will not have the pleasure of sleeping under the stars, fishing the remote hill lochs for the wild brown trout, or spending the night in the middle of a river, waiting for the thrilling tug and mighty splash as a large sea trout falls to his home-made fly. In such a short space of time, these pleasures are being denied to us and our children.

Let us face this fact also: there are more people on the planet than she can sustain, feed, clothe and house, without being destroyed by chemical, electromagnetic, sewage, and radio-active pollution in the process. It is a rather silly parasite which suffocates and poisons its host as homo sapiens is doing to mother Earth.

MORE FUNDING NEEDED

In electrostress as well as geopathic stress, it is certain that we need more research and funding, especially into the possibly serious, even fatal, effects of chronic exposure to different types of field. There is an urgent need for the results of exposure to microwave radiation, for instance, from ovens, computers, radar and communications to be investigated and for clear and responsible exposure to be set.

You may, however, now be convinced that a case has already been made for the existence of the possibly less serious, but still distressing, effects of ELF exposure in electrostress. In that case, in the short term the measures we have discussed are open to you. In the long term, as far as electrostress is concerned, the responsibility must lie with equipment manufacturers to build adequate shielding into mains apparatus, and that effectively means that every government will need to legislate, for little voluntary action seems likely. Equally, the setting of adequate rights-of-way surrounding power lines is long overdue and serious consideration needs to be given to the possibility of limiting electromagnetic pollution in the same way that other environmental pollution is, or should be, controlled.

Truly, the discovery of the means of production and movement of electricity and our ingenuity in exploiting it has led to undreamed of complications. We must wake up to the perils of our hidden environment before we have done terrible injury to ourselves and future generations.

GLOSSARY

AQUIFER. A rock layer containing water which may be released in appreciable amounts. The rock contains water-filled pore spaces (e.g chalk or limetone). When the spaces are connected, the water is able to flow through the matrix of the rock.

BLACK STREAMS. A term used originally by earlier generations of water diviners to indicate that an underground stream of water was unsafe to drink. It is also believed that they give off energies which are unhealthy to anyone living above.

CANCER VERTICAL. Energy which rises vertically and which has been linked with incidences of cancer in persons living above such a phenomenon. It can be measured with an electroscope and other instruments.

EARTH ENERGIES. It is thought that these originate within the planet, but they have not yet been identified with magnetism and electricity. One theory is that they are simply the electric field between the charged earth and the ionosphere. They naturally form the Curry Grid, the Hartmann net, the St. Michael line, the Chinese dragon and tiger lines, and can be emitted from quarries and open-cast coal mines, etc. They have been intentionally modified by our ancestors into energy leys and streams for their own specific, and as yet unresolved purpose, using standing stone and stone circles.

ELECTROMAGNETIC FIELDS. Radiating energy fields produced by conductors and equipment connected to an electrical source. They have two parts: the electrical component which is produced all the time a voltage is present (whether the circuit is closed or not); and the magnetic component which is produced only when current flows.

ENERGY LEY. A straight line of ancient sites with earth energy flowing between them. Originally believed to be anything from a few centimetres to several metres wide, they are wide streams or corridors of individual waves (overgrounds). Simplistically, they are artificially constructed and manipulated earth energies.

ENERGY STREAM. To differentiate from a straight energy ley, an energy stream is curved, or even be roughly circular. They are vertical lines of closely spaced sinuous waves (overgrounds) of energy flowing across country for considerable distances, from some specially constructed cup-marked standing stones. They may also be emitted from quarries, open-cast coal mines, geological faults, etc. The greatest width of any found during the research for this book was over two kilometres.

GAUSS. A unit of magnetic field strength (see also *Tesla*). 1 gauss = 10000 tesla.

HARMONIC. A harmonic of a frequency (or a note) is a whole number of times greater than the original. So each 'C' in a musical scale has twice the frequency of the 'C' below it and they are harmonics of each other. Harmonics tend to resonate (*q.v.*) readily.

IONISATION. An electrically charged particle formed by loss or gain by an electron.

IONS. Negatively or positively charged particles which may have resulted from being knocked off their original atoms or molecules. They are unstable and will attach themselves to any other particles of opposite polarity.

OVERGROUNDS. The vertical sinuous waves of energy which are emitted as energy leys from standing stones, energy streams from quarries and radial leys from radar stations etc. At source they may be healthy or unhealthy, as far as humans are concerned. They have been likened to invisible magnetic curtains. The waves can be very close together, sometimes too close to be measured. All of the waves can easily be identified as they run in regimental, parallel streams, unlike subterranean fissures, for example, which wander around in a haphazard way.

PIEZO-ELECTRICITY. The appearance of a positive electric charge on one side of certain non-conductive crystals and negative charge on the opposite side when the crystals are subjected to mechanical pressure.

RADIAL LINES. Individual waves radiating out from a source such as an electrical turbine or sub-station. These are of opposite polarities in sequence (i.e. positive/negative/positive/negative), or they may all be of one polarity, such as those from radar stations which seem to be composed of entirely unhealthy energy waves. At a distance these waves appear to be an energy ley (lines of parallel waves), but actually diverge from a point source.

RATE. In the sense used by Tom Lethbridge. Using a 'long pendulum', he measured various objects by gradually lengthening the thread of the pendulum as it oscillated above that object. When the pendulum gyrated, that was the rate. Silver, for example, gyrated at 22 inches, as did lead, calcium and sodium. At 29 inches gold can be found, and also the concepts of yellow and female. Mental constructs can be accessed in this way, like the cardinal points of the compass: east, south west and north, which are 10, 20, 30 and 40 inches respectively. Shortly after discovering these rates, he also found that the number of gyrations an object or a concept gave differed widely, making his method much more sensitive; e.g. silver gyrates at 22 inches with 22 gyrations, while sodium which also gyrates at 22 inches, has 36 gyrations.

RESONANCE. The way in which a sound at one frequency can cause a substance to vibrate even though the substance vibrates at a higher or lower frequency, which is called a harmonic (qv) of the frequency in question.

RORSHACH TEST. Psychological test where subjects are asked to describe what they see in 10 inkblots. The test operator may then attempt to describe the personality of the person taking the test.

SIDEBANDS. An underground stream emits earth energy vertically to the surface and also at 45° to each side, giving three parallel lines on the surface. The outside lines are the sidebands, warped to each side by the geological strata present. In water divining, there are seven sidebands on each side of an underground stream, but for the sake of simplicity, in this book we only look at the outer bands.

STANDING WAVE. Sometimes called a stationary wave. Produced by the combination of two waves moving in opposite directions, each having the same amplitude and frequency.

TELLURIC ENERGY. See *Earth energy.*

TESLA. (See also *Gauss*) A unit of magnetic field strength. 1 Gauss = 10000 Tesla.

VOLCANIC DYKE. A steeply inclined layer of igneous rock located in other strata.

BIBLIOGRAPHY

Are You Sleeping in a Safe Place? by Rolf Gordon: Dulwich Health Society. The author discovered that his son who died of cancer had been sleeping over an underground stream. Gordon produced this book on the illnesses encountered over these noxious zones, how to find them and how to eliminate them.

Body Electric, The, by Dr.Robert O.Becker and Gary Seldon: Wm Morrow. Becker researched regeneration and its relationship to electric currents. He found clues to the healing process in the long discarded theory of the 18th century vitalists that electricity is vital to the life process. The book explores new understanding of evolution, acupuncture, psychic phenomena and cancer.

British Society of Dowsers Magazine, Sec and Treasurer: M.D.Rust, Sycamore Cottage, Tamley Lane, Hastingleigh, Ashford, Kent. TN25 5HW. The Society has a list of members who are experienced in their various fields from healing to water divining. Members have access to a postal library and there is a very interesting book list. Their magazine is quarterly.

Circles of Silence by Don Robins: Souvenir Press. Using geiger counters and ultrasonic detectors, a group of people have been monitoring the Rollright Stones in Oxfordshire, giving the first scientific proof that the megaliths transmit energy. The author recalls how his first lonely dawn vigils with a simple meter showed a strange pulsing ultrasonic effect.

Cross Currents by Dr.Robert O.Becker: Jeremy P.Tarcher. The startling effects of electromagnetic radiation on your health. This book breaks new ground, exploring how many healing techniques rely on the body's electrical system for their effect; also how electrical energies attack our bodies and cause many illnesses.

Diviner's Handbook, The, by Tom Graves: Turnstone and Thorsons. Invaluable book on how to use divining rods to search for a wide variety of objects and earth energy. Essential reading for anyone interested in man's hidden senses.

Dowsing, by Tom Williamson: Robert Hale. A scientist's view of a wide variety of earth energies, from water divining to crop circles and ball lightning. The author is, unfortunately, highly critical and dismissive of geopathic stress and its relationship to illness.

Dowsing for Health, by Arthur Bailey: Quantum. Covers a range of holistic healing.

Dowsing for You, by Bruce Copen: Academic Publications. This teaches the basic rudiments of water divining and dowsing to find minerals, missing objects etc. There is nothing, however, about earth energies, since the book was published in 1975. This was before the concept of using divining techniques to find telluric energies became widely known.

Earth Currents, Causative Factor of Cancer and Other Diseases, by Gustav Baron von Pohl. Revived book showing how negative energy fields from underground streams affect individuals.

Earth Radiation, by Kathe Bächler: Wordmaster. Investigates 3000 irradiated homes. This work by an Austrian researcher is a must for any researcher.

Earthlights, by Paul Devereux: Turnstone Press.   An inexplicable event caused the author to delve deeply into the mysterious. Studies UFOs as pockets of naturally produced energy.

Electric Shock Book, The, by Michael Shallis: Souvenir Press.   Looks at various types of electromagnetic radiation and their effects on the human body.   Hypersensitive people have much to teach us about our electrically polluted environment.

Harmful Radiations and their Elimination, by Bruce Copen: Academic Publications. A scientific study of the harmful effects of earth rays which can cause severe illness.

Ion Effect, The, by Fred Soyka & Alan Edmunds: Bantam Books.   A wealth of information on our environment and the effects of both positive and negative ions on our health and behaviour.

Ley Lines, their Nature and Properties, by Dr.J.Havelock Fidler: Turnstone Press. Fidler shows how stones may be charged with energy and measured. Included are experiments of germinating seeds on lines of different energy strengths.

Living Earth Manual of Feng-Shui, The, by Stephen Skinner: Routledge & Kegan Paul.   The ancient Chinese art of living in harmony with the planet and using Ch'i in the siting of cities, houses and tombs.

Living Energies, by Callum Coats: Gateway Books.   This is the first really in-depth study of Viktor Schauberger's practical methods of working with nature. He was an impeccable observer of natural processes and developed many devices which harnessed nature's energies. Themes include river and flood management, soil fertility, water purification, free energy devices, home power generation and water-fuelled devices for transportation. A mine of fascinating insights.

Living Water, by Olof Alexandersson: Gateway.   An introductory book about the extraordinary life and work of the Austrian, Viktor Schauberger whose theories have staggering implications for whether humanity can have a future on this planet.

Needles of Stone Revisited, by Tom Graves: Gothic Image.   Theorises that the standing stones and circles are a form of acupuncture of a living planet, working on the Feng-shui system. This author is a pioneer of earth energy research.

Old Straight Track, The, by Alfred Watkins: Abacus.   First published in 1925, this is Watkin's vision of the ancient tracks across the country, linking churches, beacon hills, mounds, earthworks and moats.

Points of Cosmic Energy, by Blanche Merz: C.W.Daniel.   Very interesting book on telluric energies translated into English from French.

Power of the Pendulum, The, by T.C. Lethbridge: Arkana.   Telepathy, dreams, bio-electronics, other realms beyond the present.

Spiritual Dowsing, by Sig Lonegren: Gothic Image.   Useful for earth energy work.

Terminal Shock, by Bob de Matteo: N.C. Press.   Rather dated now, but interesting as the first book which sounded the alarm about the health hazards of computer video display terminals.

SUPPLIERS

Listed below are a few companies and organisations which provide some of the equipment and services referred to in this book. While not an exhaustive directory, we hope that it may be of some assistance. The information believed to be correct at the time of going to print.

Main areas of interest are indicated after contact details as follows:
E - Electromagnetic fields   T - Electromagnetic therapies
G - Geopathic fields
X - others, including biologically friendly architecture

U.K.

The British Society of Dowsers
Sycamore Barn, Tamley Lane, Hastingleigh, Ashford, Kent TN25 5HW
Tel: 01233 750 253

Coghill Research Assoc.
Lower Race, Pontypool, Gwent, NP4 5UH
Tel: 01495 763389. Fax: 01495 769882. E-mail 0071.1170 Compu Serve.com
Main Area: E. Books; Courses; On-site Surveys; Field Eliminators (Electropollution); Field Meters.

Dulwich Health Society
130 Gipsy Hill Road, London SE19 1PL
Tel: 0181 6705883 Fax: 0181 7666616
Main Areas: G T. Books; Food Supplements; Magnetic Therapy; Neutralising devices (geopathic stress); Pendulums; Surveys (by remote dowsing).

Feng Shui Society
75 Bathurst Gardens, London, NW10 5JH Tel: 0181-969 4194

Hartwin Busch
'Tara', Rectory Lane, Ashdon, Saffron Walden, Essex, CB10 2HN
Tel: 01787 584727
Main Area: X. Advice on Hazardous chemicals in buildings; biologically friendly architecture; On-site surveys; Wiring design (low-stress).

International Feng Shui Network
2 Thayer Street, London W1M 5LG
Tel: 0171- 935 8935

MDI Ltd.
17 Owen Road, Diss, Norfolk, IP22 3ER
Tel: 01379 644234 Fax: 01379 652973
Main Area: T. Makers of Empulse; Information including contact details of your nearest practitioner.

Michael Schimmelschmidt
66 Whitehall Park, London, N19 3TN
Tel: 0171 2632718/7226311 Fax: 0171 7228124
Main Area: X. Biologically friendly architecture; Psychotherapy/counselling.

People's Research Centre
Town Hall, Front Street, Alston, Cumbria CA9 3RF
Tel/Fax: 01434 381842
Main Area: G. Books; Research into Geopathic stress

Powerwatch UK,
Orchard House, High Common, Barsham, Beccles, Suffolk, NR34 8HW
Tel: 01502 715637

Natural Therapeutics
25 New Road, Spalding, Lincs, PE11 1DQ
Tel: 01775 761927 Fax: 01775 761104
Email 100045.2307@CompuServe.com
Main Areas: E G T. Advisory services; Books; Demand switches; Protective undersheets; Field meters; Protective devices (geopathic and electro-stress).

U.S.A.

American Society of Dowsers,
Box 24, Danville, VT 05828-0024
Tel: 802.684.3417

Natural Energy Works,
PO Box 1148, Ashland, OR 97520
Tel: 541.552.0118

AUSTRALIA

Australian Kinesiology Association
PO Box 155, Ormond 3204
Tel: 03.578.1229

Australian Water Diviners Association
122 Goodwin Drive, Bribie Is., Qld 4507
Tel: 07.408.1726

Environment Surveys
14 Farm St, Speers Point, N.S.W. 2284
Tel: 049 58 4000

Feng Shui Society of Australia,
PO Box 597, Epping, N.S.W. 2121

CANADA

Canadian Society of Dowsers,
RR4, Havelock, OB K0L 1Z0
Tel: 0705.778.7243

ABOUT THE AUTHORS

DAVID COWAN was born in Glasgow before the Second World War, and was educated there before moving to Crieff, Perthshire at the edge of the Scottish Highlands, where he entered the printing trade. He did National Service in the R.A.F. (Signals) and, on demobilization returned to the printing trade as a foreman linotype operator and finally as a computer/Nyloprint operator.

During this time he discovered his own latent abilities as a dowser, sensitive to the energies from standing stones and circles. He spent a gruelling eight years walking the energy leys of highland Perthshire, on a series of weekend walks which covered a crippling 3,000 miles, but which yielded many secrets of energies which most scientists and archaeologists deny even exist.

Eventually, he concentrated on particularly fascinating aspects of earth energies — unhealthy streams and spirals — which he is firmly convinced are one of the basic causes of many illnesses. Now he helps people with problems related to geopathic stress.

He is currently vice-chairman of the Scottish Dowsing Association and teaches students the art of eliminating unhealthy earth energies. He is now writing a book on energy leys and their connection to folklore, petroglyphs, apparitions, 'demons' and poltergeists.

RODNEY GIRDLESTONE graduated as a chemical engineer and teacher. He subsequently worked as a teacher, then as a chemical engineer and later as an industrial training consultant before moving into the field of natural medicine, he and his wife opening a health food shop.

Through business contacts in Germany he was introduced first to the health benefits of some magnetic fields (he dealt in magnetic therapy equipment for some time) and later to the hazards of electro-magnetic radiation. It was this latter which became a major interest. He has lectured and written on the subject and also helped people with problems in their houses and offices. He is also a director of a company supplying food supplements, homeopathic remedies and other products to practitioners of complementary medicine.

Now things have gone full cycle and he has again become involved with the beneficial side of electricity with new electro-diagnostic instruments, such as 'Eclosion' which he describes in Part I. He and his wife live in Lincolnshire, England.

INDEX

ff means 'pages following' and usually indicates the most important entry for subject.